CANADIAN WRITERS

ÉCRIVAINS CANADIENS

CANADIAN WRITERS

ÉCRIVAINS CANADIENS

A Biographical Dictionary Edited by
Un dictionnaire biographique rédigé par

GUY SYLVESTRE

BRANDON CONRON

CARL F. KLINCK

New edition revised and enlarged
Nouvelle édition revue et augmentee

The Ryerson Press, Toronto

ISBN 0-7700-0039-8

© THE RYERSON PRESS 1964

FIRST EDITION 1964
REVISED AND ENLARGED 1966
REVISED 1967
REPRINTED 1970

Printed and bound in Canada by The Ryerson Press, Toronto.

INTRODUCTION/AVANT-PROPOS

During the last years of his life, Dr. Lorne Pierce laid plans for the revision of his *An Outline of Canadian Literature (French and English)*, first published in 1927. This new revised dictionary of *Canadian Writers/Ecrivains canadiens*, dedicated to his memory and his purposes, brings that *Outline* up-to-date for readers more than a third of a century later.

The growth of Canadian literature and scholarship has led to modifications in this work, but Dr. Pierce's basic principles are so valid as to demand repeated emphasis. "This *Outline*," he wrote, "is the first attempt at a history of our literature, placing both French and English writers side by side. Hereafter they must share equally in any attempt to trace the evolution of our national spirit."

Because historical research and criticism of literature in Canada now happily recognize the extent and complexity of our dual culture, the demand for summary outlines of the general subject is not as great as the need for reliable biographical and bibliographical data. *Canadian Writers/ Ecrivains canadiens* has become mainly an alphabetically arranged handbook of information concerning more than three hundred and fifty authors and their works. Thus it has been possible to preserve some of the features of Dr. Pierce's *Outline*: brevity, accessibility of information and a consequent "radical sifting of our authors through a coarse screen." The writers included have for the most part produced a notable first or second book and have thereafter embarked upon a literary career with repeated publications of generally acknowledged merit. A chronological table and a list of basic reference works have been included. *Canadian Writers/Ecrivains canadiens* is designed to be a valuable reference book, giving biographical and bibliographical information not otherwise readily available to the reader.

Si on compare l'histoire des deux littératures nationales du Canada, on a vite fait de remarquer que l'une et l'autre ont suivi une évolution parallèle et qu'elles ont plus de caractères communs qu'on ne le croit habituellement. Le tableau chronologique qu'on trouvera au début de cet ouvrage le souligne nettement et on pourra s'en rendre compte encore plus clairement en comparant les oeuvres des écrivains des deux groupes linguistiques à une époque donnée. On a tenu compte du caractère biculturel du Canada en rédigeant cet ouvrage et on espère qu'il rendra de précieux services à ceux qui étudieront l'une ou l'autre de nos littératures nationales, ou les deux. Il a fallu évidemment opérer un choix et on a toujours accordé la préférence aux écrivains proprement dits, quoique les auteurs d'ouvrages relevant de diverses disciplines ont aussi trouvé place dans ce répertoire pourvu que leurs écrits manifestent une rare distinction intellectuelle en même temps que des qualités d'écriture réelles.

"Placing both French and English writers side by side" needs no explanation and no defence in a country which is growing ever more conscious of its bicultural nature. A logical development of this principle is the use of both English and French in the accounts of writers given in this book. Readers who can understand titles, which are of necessity in one of the original languages, will have little or no difficulty in mastering the whole of an article written in the French or English which has been employed in *Canadian Writers/Ecrivains canadiens*. What this book has lost in historical discussion is more than compensated by the lively reflection of two national literatures conveyed by the two original tongues.

The authors have sought their material in the best sources, which are too numerous to mention in the short bibliographies. The reader's attention is always directed to the longer general list at the back of this volume, especially to the *Literary History of Canada* and Pacey's *Creative Writing in Canada*. Current information may be found in the annual issues of "Letters in Canada" of *The University of Toronto Quarterly* and in the quarterly journal, *Canadian Literature,* which publishes an annual check list. On pourra aussi consulter chaque année *Livres et Auteurs canadiens* pour se renseigner sur la production courante.

Acknowledgments for personal assistance are gratefully made to the late Lorne Pierce. Very special thanks are due to the Canada Council and to the University of Western Ontario for grants-in-aid. The authors wish to express their gratitude also to Mr. Carl Ballstadt, to Mr. Donald Walimaki and to Mme Charlotte Bastien who collected valuable information for the first edition. Finally, the authors would appreciate having any errors brought to their attention.

CONTENTS/TABLE

CHRONOLOGICAL TABLE/
TABLEAU CHRONOLOGIQUE
(1606-1965)

For the period after 1961 this list of literary and historical events omits the creative writings of individual authors. Pour les années qui suivent 1961 les oeuvres d'imagination ont été omises.

1606 Lescarbot à Port-Royal
1608 Fondation de Québec
1749 Founding of Halifax
1752 Halifax *Gazette* established
1760 British military rule established
1763 Traité de Paris
Pontiac's Conspiracy (1763-1764)
1764 *Gazette de Québec* founded
1769 Frances Brooke's *History of Emily Montague*
1774 The Quebec Act
1776 The American Declaration of Independence
1778 Fondation de la *Gazette littéraire de Montréal*
1783 The coming of the Loyalists
1789 La Révolution française
1791 The Constitutional Act; Separation of Upper and Lower Canada
1793 The *Upper Canada Gazette* (Niagara) founded
1806 Pierre Bédard fonde *Le Canadien* (Québec)
1812 American-Canadian War (1812-1814), Death of Brock and Tecumseh
1816 The first of Adam Hood Burwell's Port Talbot poems
1821 Thomas McCulloch's *Stepsure Letters* (1821-1823) in the *Acadian Recorder*
The Scribbler (Montreal, 1821-1827)
1822 Etienne Parent débute au *Canadien*
1823 *The Canadian Magazine* (Montreal, 1823-1824)
1824 William Lyon Mackenzie's *Colonial Advocate* (1824-1834)
Fondation de la Sociéte littéraire et historique de Québec (Literary and Historical Society of Quebec)
The Canadian Review (Montreal, 1824-1825)
1825 Goldsmith's *The Rising Village*
Michel Bibaud fonde la *Bibliothèque canadienne* (1825-1830)
1826 Fondation de *La Minerve* (Montréal, 1826-1899)
John Galt in Canada (1826-1829)
1827 Joseph Howe's purchase of the *Nova Scotian*

[ix]

1901	Bucke's *Cosmic Consciousness*
1902	Société du Bon Parler français
1903	Asselin et Bourassa fondent le parti nationaliste *Emile Nelligan et son oeuvre*
1904	*Les Gouttelettes* de Lemay *Les Aspirations* de Chapman Asselin fonde *Le Nationaliste* (1904-1922)
1906	*Poésies* d'Alfred Garneau
1907	Service's *Songs of a Sourdough* *L'Ame solitaire* de Lozeau *Essais sur la littérature canadienne* de Camille Roy
1908	Peter McArthur's articles began in the Toronto *Globe* L. M. Montgomery's *Anne of Green Gables*
1909	MacInnes' *Lonesome Bar*
1910	Leacock's *Literary Lapses* Bourassa fonde *Le Devoir* *Les Phases* de Guy Delahaye
1911	*Le Paon d'émail* de Paul Morin
1912	Premier congrès de la langue française à Québec *Les Blessures* de Jean Charbonneau
1913	Marjorie Pickthall's *The Drift of Pinions* *Le Coeur en exil* de René Chopin
1914	The First World War began *Maria Chapdelaine* de Louis Hémon *Chez nous* d'Adjutor Rivard
1915	*La Revue Dominicaine* (1915-1961) Stringer's prairie trilogy (1915-1922) Fournier fonde *L'Action*
1917	*L'Action canadienne française* (Montréal, 1917-1928)
1918	Wilson MacDonald's *Song of the Prairie Land* *Le Nigog* (Montréal) *La Scouine* d'Albert Laberge
1919	John McCrae's *In Flanders Fields* *The Canadian Bookman* established *Le Cap Eternité* de Gill *Au service de la tradition française* de Montpetit Group of Seven
1920	R. P. Baker's *A History of English-Canadian Literature* *The Canadian Forum* established *Le Mauvais Passant* d'Albert Dreux *Les Atmosphères* de Loranger
1921	Canadian Authors Association established *Dalhousie Review* established Victor Barbeau publie les *Cahiers de Turc* (1921-1927)

1922 Grove's *Over Prairie Trails*
      Poèmes de cendre et d'or de Paul Morin
      L'Appel de la race de Groulx
      Mon encrier de Jules Fournier

1923 Pratt's *Newfoundland Verse*
      Salverson's *The Viking Heart*
      Merrill Denison's *Brothers in Arms*
      Prix littéraires et scientifiques de la province de Québec

1924 Mabel Dunham's *The Trail of the Conestoga*
      J. D. Logan and D. G. French, *Highways of Canadian Literature*
      Notre maître le passé de Groulx

1925 Martha Ostenso's *Wild Geese*
      A travers les vents de Choquette
      The McGill Fortnightly Review (1925-1927)

1926 Lionel Stevenson's *Appraisals of Canadian Literature*
      Vincent Massey's *Canadian Plays from Hart House Theatre*
      The Dictionary of Canadian Biography (revised, 1945)

1927 De la Roche's *Jalna*
      Pierce's *Outline of Canadian Literature*

1928 Callaghan's *Strange Fugitive*
      The Canadian Mercury (1928-1929)
      Patrie intime de Beauchemin
      L'Offrande aux vierges folles de Desrochers
      Poètes de l'Amérique française de Louis Dantin

1929 Knister's *White Narcissus*
      Callaghan's *A Native Argosy*
      A l'ombre de l'Orford de Desrochers
      L'Immortel adolescent de Simone Routier
      Littérature canadienne de Marcel Dugas

1930 Innis' *The Fur Trade in Canada*
      Les Bois qui chantent de Desaulniers

1931 *University of Toronto Quarterly* established
      Avec ma vie de Lucien Rainier
      Carquois d'Albert Pelletier
      Nord-Sud de Desrosiers

1932 *Le coffret de Crusoë* de Dantin
      Dolorès de Harry Bernard

1933 Philip Child's *The Village of Souls*
      Leo Kennedy's *The Shrouding*
      Né à Québec de Grandbois

1934 *Les demi-civilisés* de Harvey
      La rivière solitaire de Marie LeFranc
      Chaque heure a son visage de Medjé Vézina
      Asselin fonde *l'Ordre* (Montréal, 1934-1935)
      La Relève (Montréal, 1934-1941)

1935   Fondation de la Société des Ecrivains canadiens
Un homme et son péché de Grignon
La Forêt de Bugnet
Albert Pelletier fonde *Les Idées* (1935-39)
Pratt's *The Titanic*
Initiation of annual "Letters in Canada" in the
University of Toronto Quarterly
Social Planning for Canada
Dorothy Livesay's *The Outrider*

1936   W. E. Collin's *The White Savannahs*
New Provinces
Les Pamphlets de Valdombre (1936-1941)
Les Carnets viatoriens (Joliette)

1937   *Regards et Jeux dans l'Espace* de Saint-Denys-Garneau
Menaud, maître-draveur de Savard
Pour nous grandir de Victor Barbeau
Governor General's Literary Awards established
Creighton's *The Commercial Empire of the St. Lawrence*

1938   *30 arpents* de Ringuet
Les Engagés du Grand Portage de Desrosiers

1939   The Second World War began
McDowell's *The Champlain Road*
Anne Marriott's *The Wind Our Enemy*
Raddall's *Pied Piper of Dipper Creek*
Vitrail de Cécile Chabot

1940   Klein's *Hath Not a Jew . . .*
Mondes chimériques de François Hertel
Culture (Québec)
Regards (Québec, 1940-1942)

1941   *Contemporary Verse* (British Columbia, 1941-1951)
MacLennan's *Barometer Rising*
Ross' *As for Me and My House*
Alan Sullivan's *Three Came to Ville Marie*
Ils posséderont la terre de Charbonneau
Les Opiniâtres de Desrosiers
Amérique française (Montréal, 1941-1955)
Relations (Montréal)
La Nouvelle Relève (Montréal, 1941-1948)

1942   Birney's *David and Other Poems*
Les Songes en équilibre d'Anne Hébert
La Chesnaie de Desmarchais
First Statement founded by John Sutherland (1942-1945)
Hutchison's *The Unknown Country*
Preview (Montreal) founded by Patrick Anderson and others (1942-1945)

1943   Smith's *The Book of Canadian Poetry* and *News of the Phoenix*
E. K. Brown's *On Canadian Poetry*

1943   *Gants du Ciel* (Ottawa, 1943-1946)
        Anthologie de la poésie canadienne française de
        Sylvestre

1944   *Les îles de la nuit* de Grandbois
        Au pied de la pente douce de Lemelin
        Connaissance du personnage de Charbonneau
        La civilisation de la Nouvelle-France de Frégault
        Fondation du prix Duvernay
        Unit of Five

1945   *Bonheur d'occasion* de Gabrielle Roy
        Le Survenant de Germaine Guèvremont
        Victor Barbeau fonde l'Académie canadienne-française
        F. R. Scott's *Overture*
        Layton's *Here and Now*
        The Fiddlehead founded
        End of the Second World War
        Miriam Waddington's *Green World*
        La Fin de la joie de Jacqueline Mabit
        Les médisances de Claude Perrin de Baillargeon
        Northern Review (1945-1956) founded by Suther-
        land's merger of *First Statement* and *Preview*

1946   Finch's *Poems*
        P. K. Page's *As Ten as Twenty*
        Souster's *When We Are Young*
        Institut d'histoire de l'Amérique française

1947   Davies' *The Diary of Samuel Marchbanks*
        Liaison (Montréal, 1947-1950)
        Le chant de la montée de Rina Lasnier
        Les Soirs rouges de Clément Marchand
        John Sutherland's *Other Canadians*
        Frye's *Fearful Symmetry*
        Ethel Wilson's *Hetty Dorval*
        Hiebert's *Sarah Binks*
        Lowry's *Under the Volcano*
        McCourt's *The Flaming Hour*
        W. O. Mitchell's *Who Has Seen the Wind*
        Gabrielle Roy reçoit le prix Femina

1948   Lister Sinclair's *A Play on Words and Other Radio
        Plays*
        Kreisel's *The Rich Man*
        Le Pan's *The Wounded Prince*
        Rivages de l'homme de Grandbois
        Refus global
        Les Plouffe de Lemelin
        Neuf jours de haine de Richard
        Au delà des visages de Giroux

1949   *Le poids du jour* de Ringuet
        Prix du Cercle du Livre de France
        Reaney's *The Red Heart*

1950   *La Fin des songes* de Robert Elie

[xv]

1950   *La Fille laide* de Thériault
       Le Torrent d'Anne Hébert
       Tit-Coq de Gélinas
       Cité libre (Montréal)

1951   Callaghan's *The Loved and the Lost*
       Rapport de la Commission Massey
       Fondation du Théâtre du Nouveau Monde
       Klein's *The Second Scroll*
       McLuhan's *The Mechanical Bride: Folklore of
       Mechanical Man*
       Buckler's *The Mountain and the Valley*
       L'Ampoule d'or de Desrosiers
       Objets trouvés de Sylvain Garneau
       Fondation de la *Nouvelle Revue canadienne*
       Testament de mon enfance de Roquebrune

1952   Pratt's *The Last Spike*
       Cerberus, Dudek, Layton, Souster
       Pacey's *Creative Writing in Canada* (revised, 1961)
       Television introduced in Canada
       Le Combat contre Tristan de Pierre Trottier
       Pierre le magnifique de Roger Lemelin
       L'homme d'ici d'Ernest Gagnon
       Le Grand Marquis de Guy Frégault

1953   *Explorations* (1953-1959), established by Marshall
       McLuhan and E. S. Carpenter
       Stratford Festival initiated
       L'Inquiétude humaine de Jacques Lavigne
       Le Pan's *The Net and the Sword*
       Le Tombeau des Rois d'Anne Hébert
       Poussière sur la ville d'André Langevin
       Les Témoins d'Eugène Cloutier
       Suite marine de Robert Choquette
       Zone de Marcel Dubé

1954   *Histoire littéraire de l'Amérique française* de Viatte
       Journal de Saint-Denys-Garneau
       P. K. Page's *The Metal and the Flower*
       Alexandre Chenevert de Gabrielle Roy
       Aaron d'Yves Thériault
       Les Canadiens errants de Jean Vaillancourt
       Totems de Gilles Hénault
       Les Armes blanches de Roland Giguère
       L'Etrangère de Robert Elie
       Le fédéralisme canadien de Maurice Lamontagne
       Fondation des Editions de l'Hexagone
       Fondation des *Ecrits du Canada français*

1955   Klinck and Watters' *Canadian Anthology*
       (revised, 1966)
       Wilfred Watson's *Friday's Child*
       Rue Deschambault de Gabrielle Roy

[xvii]

1960   *Alphabet* established
       Les insolences du Frère Untel
       Histoire de la littérature canadienne française de Tougas
       Avison's *Winter Sun*
       Callaghan's *The Many Coloured Coat*
       Margaret Laurence's *This Side Jordan*
       Mandel's *Fuseli Poems*
       Moore's *The Luck of Ginger Coffey*
       A. J. M. Smith's *The Oxford Book of Canadian Verse*
       Doux-Amer de Claire Martin
       Choix de poèmes: Arbres de Paul-Marie Lapointe
       Mémoire sans jours de Rina Lasnier
       Souvenirs pour demain de Paul Toupin
       Le Libraire de Gérard Bessette
       La Corde au cou de Claude Jasmin
       Emille Nelligan de Paul Wyczynski
       Canadian Dualism: la Dualité canadienne

1961   Callaghan's *A Passion in Rome*
       Lowry's *Hear Us O Lord*
       Un amour maladroit de Monique Bosco
       Le Temps des jeux de Diane Giguère
       Laure Clouet d'Adrienne Choquette
       Convergences de Jean Le Moyne
       Fondation des *Archives des Lettres canadiennes*
       Théâtre de Paul Toupin

1962   *Livres et Auteurs canadiens*
       Une littérature qui se fait de Gilles Marcotte
       La poésie canadienne d'Alain Bosquet
       Etablissement du ministère des Affaires culturelles de
       Québec

1963   Establishment of the Royal Commission on
       Bilingualism and Biculturalism
       Mon Babel de Pierre Trottier
       La ligne du risque de Pierre Vadeboncoeur
       Anthologie d'Albert Laberge
       Fondation de *Parti pris*

1964   *Pour la conversion de la pensée chrétienne* de Fernand
       Dumont
       Littérature et société canadiennes françaises (colloque
       de l'Université Laval)
       Rapport Bouchard sur le commerce du livre

1965   *Literary History of Canada*
       Canadian Flag adopted
       Fondation du Grand Prix littéraire de la Ville de
       Montréal
       Fondation d'*Etudes françaises*
       Fonctionnement de l'Etat de Gérard Bergeron
       Dans un gant de fer de Claire Martin

MILTON ACORN (1925-   ). Born in Charlottetown, Prince Edward Island, Milton Acorn attended primary and secondary school there. He worked part time as a carpenter and a stevedore in the Maritimes before going to Toronto, where he married poet Gwendolyn MacEwen. He later moved to Vancouver.

He has published several small collections of poetry: *In Love and Anger* (1956); *Against a League of Liars* (1958); *The Brain's The Target* (1958); and *Jawbreakers* (1963); In his verse Acorn, who describes himself as "an industrial, proletarian poet," often treats civilization as a force destructive of a vanishing rural beauty. His commentaries on society, which he feels exercises an undesirable pressure on the individual to conform, are made concrete by the inclusion of current events, and express the ironic discrepancy between human aspiration and actual achievement.

GRANT ALLEN (1848-1899). Born near Kingston, Ontario, Charles Grant Blair-findie Allen was educated at Oxford University 1867-1871. He developed a great interest in biology and philosophy and was a friend of Herbert Spencer and Charles Darwin. For four years after graduation he taught in Jamaica, but he returned to England after being encouraged by the reception of his first book *Physiological Aesthetics* (1877) to seek a literary career. He wrote on science, philosophy and religion in such volumes as *The Evolutionist at Large* (1881) and *The Evolution of the Idea of God* (1897). Some thirty of his seventy-five books were novels, of which *The Woman Who Did* (1895) startled the public with its frank treatment of sex. Allen also published occasional short stories, articles and poetry.

RALPH ALLEN (1913-1966). Born in Winnipeg and educated in Ontario and Saskatchewan, Allen worked as a reporter for the Winnipeg *Tribune*. In 1938 he joined the news staff of the Toronto *Globe and Mail*. During World War II he served first in the Royal Canadian Artillery; then as a war correspondent he covered the Allied landings in Sicily, Italy and Normandy and was awarded the O.B.E. He was on the editorial staff of *Maclean's* from 1946 until 1964, when he became managing editor of the *Toronto Star*.

Allen's first novel *Home Made Banners* (1946) reflected his war experiences. *The Chartered Libertine* (1954) is a sharply pointed and urbane satire of the struggle between private broadcasting interests and the publicly owned CBC. *Peace River Country* (1958) is an entertaining parable of a mother and her son and daughter travelling from Saskatchewan to the Peace River Country. In 1961, Allen produced *Ordeal by Fire: 1910-1945* as part of the Doubleday "Canadian History Series." His novel *Ask the Name of the Lion* (1962), portraying the diverse forces and conflicts in the adolescent Congo, points out the slow recognition by the Western Hemisphere of the actual problems of this emerging continent. In *The High White Forest* (1964) Allen returns to the central theme of *Home Made Banners* and considers again the problems of conscience of the conscripts, the so-called "Zombies," of World War II.

ALLID. *See* Lanigan, George Thomas.

PATRICK ANDERSON (1915-   ). Born in England, Anderson received his education at Oxford and later at Columbia University where he studied under a Commonwealth Fellowship. He took up residence in Montreal in 1940 and subsequently taught in a private school for six years. In 1945 he became a Canadian citizen and published his first book of poetry *A Tent for April*. Following a year's visit to England, he returned to Canada to teach English in Montreal. *The White Centre*, his second and somewhat larger collection, appeared in 1946.

Influenced by the ideas of Marxist socialism, and by the rich phrases and rhythms of Dylan Thomas, he was the centre of a quickening poetic activity in the forties. With his contemporaries P. K. Page and F. R. Scott, he established *Preview*, which in 1945 merged with John Sutherland's *First Statement* to form *Northern Review*. His poems, depicting self-alienation in a mechanical society and prophesying a future of self-determination, are more successful than those by others of his group. His belief in poetry as a vital

force both in the war and in social struggle seems idealistic.

In 1950 he travelled to Singapore to act as lecturer at the University of Malaya, an experience which supplied material for much of his subsequent work. Three years later he returned to London, where he has since remained.

The Colour as Naked appeared in 1953 and included some of Anderson's best work. His poems have an intensity and evocative power which belies the quiet, conversational tone in which they are often presented. "Song of Intense Cold," "A Monkey in Malaya" and "The Strange Bird" are among the outstanding poems of this last collection.

Since his return to England, Anderson has also published *Snake Wine, A Singapore Episode* (1955), *Search Me* (1957), *The Character Ball* (1963), and *Dolphin Days* (1964), autobiographical travel books. Northrop Frye, "Letters in Canada: 1953," *UTQ*, XXIII (April, 1954); Wynne Francis, "Montreal Poets of the Forties," *Can. Lit.*, 14 (Autumn, 1962); John Sutherland, "The Poetry of Patrick Anderson," *Northern Review*, 2 (April-May, 1949).

FELICITE ANGERS. *Voir* Conan, Laure.

HUBERT AQUIN (1929-   ). Né à Montréal, il a étudié au Collège Sainte-Marie, à l'Université de Montréal dont il est licencié en philosophie, à l'Institut d'Etudes politiques de Paris dont il est diplômé et à l'Université de Paris. Il a été réalisateur à Radio-Canada, scénariste et réalisateur à l'Office national du Film. Il a été directeur de la revue *Liberté* (1961-1962) et a écrit de nombreux essais et des textes pour la radio et la télévision. Séparatiste et terroriste, il a été arrêté, interné et libéré. Il a aussi été comédien. Après une sorte de conte philosophique paru dans les *Ecrits du Canada français* en 1959: *Les Rédempteurs*, il a publié *Prochain épisode* (1965), roman qui semble bien avoir des parties autobiographiques et qui est l'histoire d'un intellectuel anarchiste poursuivi et arrêté—il y a ici un roman policier—qui se poursuit également lui-même pour chercher à se comprendre et à juger du sens de son action. Le passage constant et rapide de la réalité au rêve et du rêve à la réalité en rend la lecture aussi difficile que l'explication.

HENRI D'ARLES (1870-1930). Né à Arthabaskaville, Henri Beaudet a étudié au Séminaire de Québec et est entré chez les Dominicains. Ordonné prêtre en 1895, il fit du ministère paroissial en Nouvelle-Angleterre pendant quinze ans, puis sortit de l'Ordre des Frères Prêcheurs et continua son ministère comme prêtre séculier. Il séjourna aux Etats-Unis, en France, visita la Terre Sainte et devint secrétaire du cardinal Vanutelli à Rome où il mourut.

Il a publié sous le pseudonyme de Henri d'Arles de nombreux ouvrages, d'un style précieux et raffiné, dont une partie est faite d'impressions de voyages, d'effusions mystiques ou de méditations sur diverses formes de la beauté, *Pastels* (1905), *Laudes* (1925), etc., et dont l'autre partie est faite de critiques d'art et de littérature. Dans *Essais et conférences* (1910), *Eaux-fortes et tailles-douces* (1913), *Estampes* (1926) il a réuni des essais qui sont parmi les premiers au Canada français à insister sur l'aspect esthétique des oeuvres. Il a aussi écrit un ouvrage sur *Nos historiens* (1921). On peut consulter à son sujet l'essai d'Adolphe Robert paru dans *Le Canada français* (1942).

JOSEPH FRANCOIS OLIVAR ASSELIN (1874-1937). Né à Saint-Hilarion, Asselin a étudié au Séminaire de Rimouski et fut d'abord journaliste aux Etats-Unis, puis secrétaire de Sir Lomer Gouin. Venu à Montréal en 1903, il fut un des chefs du parti nationaliste, participa à la Fondation du *Nationaliste* et du *Devoir*. Il s'engagea dans l'armée canadienne en 1915 et servit outre-mer jusqu'en 1917 avec le rang de major. If fut ensuite secrétaire de la Mission militaire canadienne et délégué à la conférence de la paix. Il travailla ensuite pour un courtier en valeurs, mais en 1930 revint au journalisme comme rédacteur en chef du *Canada*. En 1934, il fonda *L'Ordre* et, l'année suivante, *La Renaissance*.

Il fut un des journalistes les plus vigoureux de sa génération, maniant l'ironie avec une cruauté sans égale et s'attaquant aux travers des hommes avec une logique implacable. Les articles réunis après sa mort dans *Pensée française* (1938) donnent une idée incomplète de son oeuvre et de son talent d'écrivain. Il avait publié *L'oeuvre de l'abbé Groulx* (1923) et quelques autres brochures. Sa biographie a été écrite par Marcel Gagnon (1962). La revue *Regards* lui a rendu hommage (avril 1941).

AUBERT DE GASPE (1786-1871). Né à Québec, Philippe Aubert de Gaspé était le fils d'un membre du Conseil législatif du Bas-Canada à qui il succéda comme seigneur de Saint-Jean Port-Joli. Il étudia au Séminaire de Québec et devint avocat après avoir fait sa cléricature chez Jonathan Sewell. Il mena un grand train de vie et, endetté et insolvable, fut emprisonné. Il se retira ensuite dans son manoir de Saint-Jean Port-Joli, où il vécut jusqu'à l'âge de quatre-vingt-quatre ans.

A soixante-quinze ans, il entreprit d'évoquer les moeurs canadiennes du temps de son enfance et il le fit dans un long roman qui est un classique du dix-neuvième siècle et le livre le plus charmant de cette époque, *Les Anciens Canadiens* (1863). L'affabulation est élémentaire et la psychologie des personnages est sommaire; ce qui fait la valeur et l'intérêt du récit, ce sont les descriptions de moeurs et les légendes qui y sont insérées. Par là, le livre a une valeur documentaire très grande sur ce que fut la vie des anciens Canadiens sous le régime seigneurial.

Les souvenirs qu'il n'avait pu faire entrer dans son récit, Aubert de Gaspé les a réunis dans ses *Mémoires* (1866) qui sont une chronique de première main sur cette lointaine époque. Il se dégage de tout ce qu'il a écrit une nostalgie du passé et une bonhommie qui allaient disparaître bientôt des lettres canadiennes. *Les Anciens Canadiens* marquent, en même temps que la véritable naissance du roman canadien français, la fin d'une époque. Le fils de l'auteur, Philippe (1814-1841) avait publié dès 1837 le premier roman canadien français, *Le Chercheur de trésors* ou *l'Influence d'un livre*. *Les Anciens Canadiens* a été traduit par Sir Charles Roberts (1890). Il existe plusieurs études sur Aubert de Gaspé dont celles de Casgrain (1871) et de Pierre-Georges Roy (1943).

MARGARET AVISON (1918-   ). Born in Galt, Ontario, Margaret Kirkland Avison was educated at the University of Toronto and won a Guggenheim Fellowship in Poetry 1956/57. She lives in Toronto and has published the greater portion of her work in literary journals and anthologies in Canada and abroad. Her first book of poems, *Winter Sun,* appeared in 1960.

In her second book, *The Dumbfounding* (1966), she had produced what A. J. M. Smith calls "the most significant book of poetry published by a Canadian since the modern movement got under way more than a score of years ago." Particularly moving in this collection is a series of devotional poems.

Although she has been variously called "metaphysical" or "mythopoeic," a northern Wallace Stevens or a Cana-

dian Marianne Moore, her works are individual enough to escape anything other than superficial classification. Her vision of reality is intensely personal, intensely realized. For Miss Avison, as Ronald Bates remarks, poems may be "imaginary gardens with real toads in them," but she presents "gardenless gardens," "a territory without a name," a house "made of newspapers," full of objects like eggshells, lilacs, old scores for hautboy, Rouault hoops, a moustache-cup or a pair of gym shoes. The effect is both startling and beautiful, obscure but visually and emotionally clear, even simple.

From these conjunctions of things within an oppressively cluttered space, there arises a structure of life, ordered by an intellectual, almost mathematical clarity, which finally fuses the private and public. It is often said that a poet who is rooted in a home locale attains universality by this very concentration on the particularities of the region. Miss Avison has gone one step further and has reached the universal through a microscopic and even blinkered view of the subjective and personal. What we see through her microscope, however, is a true poetic universe. Ronald Bates, Review of *Winter Sun, Alphabet,* 3 (December 1961); Eli Mandel, Review of *Winter Sun, Queen's Quarterly,* LXVII (Winter, 1961); A. J. M. Smith, "Critical Improvisations on Margaret Avison's *Winter Sun," Tamarack Review,* 18 (Winter, 1961); A. J. M. Smith, "Margaret Avison's New Book," *The Canadian Forum,* 46 (September, 1966); Milton Wilson, "The Poetry of Margaret Avison," *Can. Lit.,* 2 Autumn, 1959).

ALFRED BAILEY (1905-   ). Born in Quebec, Alfred Goldsworthy Bailey was educated at the University of New Brunswick and the University of Toronto. He continued postgraduate study at the London School of Economics and is now a noted historian,

Dean of Arts and Head of the Department of History and Anthropology at the University of New Brunswick.

His early poems were published in *Songs of the Saguenay and Other Poems* (1927), and some of them were revised and reprinted in Taô (1930). In 1937, Bailey produced the *Conflict of European and Eastern Algonkian Culture, 1500-1700,* a study in Canadian civilization. In his *Border River* (1952), a book of 35 poems, he displays great metrical variety and skill. Their metaphysical quality reflects his sense of history with its clash of cultures as well as his interest in philosophical concepts as diverse as those of Toynbee and Laô-tse. Bailey was elected F.R.S.C. in 1951. He was one of the editors of the *Literary History of Canada* (1965).

PIERRE BAILLARGEON (1916-1967). Né à Montréal, Baillargeon étudia au Collège Jean de Brébeuf et il avait entrepris des études de médecine à Poitiers lorsque la guerre le ramena au Canada. En 1941, il fonda la revue littéraire *Amérique française* qu'il dirigea jusqu'en 1943. Après la guerre, il retourna en France—il a épousé l'écrivain français Jacqueline Mabit, auteur d'un excellent roman, *La fin de la joie* (1945) —où il a occupé divers petits postes et il est rentré au pays en 1960 et est redevenu journaliste. Elu à la Société royale du Canada en 1962.

Baillargeon est un satiriste et un moraliste qui s'est appliqué à peindre nos travers et à souligner les faiblesses de notre système d'enseignement dans des livres qui sont à peine des romans et où le personnage principal n'est que le porte-parole de l'auteur. Il reprend toujours les mêmes idées et refait le même livre, avec un art toujours égal à lui-même: pureté de la langue, sens du raccourci et du paradoxe, art de frapper des formules heureuses. Ses oeuvres sont *Hasard et Moi* (1940), *Les Médisances de Claude Perrin* (1945),

Commerce (1947), *La Neige et le feu* (1948), *Le scandale est nécessaire* (1962) et une fantaisie dramatique d'une cruauté délicieuse, *Madame Homère* (1963). Il a aussi publié dans *Amérique française* des poèmes de style valéryen.

MARIUS BARBEAU (1883-). Né à Sainte-Marie de Beauce, il a étudié au Collège Sainte-Anne de la Pocatière, le droit à l'Université Laval et, boursier Rhodes, à Oxford. Avocat, il a consacré toute sa vie à l'anthropologie et au folklore, s'intéressant surtout aux moeurs et aux légendes des Indiens et aux contes et chansons des Canadiens français. Il a recueilli dans ces domaines une immense documentation au Musée National du Canada dont il était l'archiviste, et il a publié plus de cinquante ouvrages tant en anglais qu'en français, en plus de collaborer à maintes revues savantes. Il a aussi écrit sur toutes les formes d'art populaire et sur quelques peintres; en 1948, il a publié un roman d'inspiration indienne, *Le Rêve de Kamalmuk.* Il a été membre de la Société royale du Canada et est membre de l'Académie canadienne française. On trouvera au tome II des *Archives de folklore* (1947) un important *Hommage à Marius Barbeau.*

VICTOR BARBEAU (1896-). Né à Montréal, Barbeau a étudié au Collège Sainte-Marie, à l'Université de Montréal et à la Sorbonne. Lieutenant d'aviation pendant la première grande guerre, il fut journaliste au *Devoir,* au *Nationaliste* et à *La Presse,* et professeur de littérature française à l'Ecole des Hautes Etudes commerciales. Il fut président de la Société des Ecrivains canadiens de 1937 à 1944 et fonda l'Académie canadienne-française en 1944. En 1946, il fonda la revue *Liaison* qu'il dirigea. De 1921 à 1927, il avait publié *Les Cahiers de Turc,* pamphlets qui étonnèrent par la fermeté du ton et la pureté de la langue.

Toujours préoccupé par la question linguistique au Canada, il a publié *Le ramage de mon pays* (1939). Un des apôtres de la coopération économique, il a fondé en 1937 la coopérative *La Familiale* et exposé ses vues à ce sujet dans *Initiation à l'humain* (1944). Il avait fait un relevé retentissant de la pauvreté des Canadiens français, *Mesure de notre taille* (1936) et son meilleur livre, *Pour nous grandir* (1937) démontre comment l'éducation et la politique sont les deux moyens les plus efficaces pour améliorer cette situation. Il dirige les *Cahiers de l'Académie canadienne-française* où il a publié un essai remarquable sur le régionalisme littéraire canadien *La danse autour de l'érable*. En 1962, à l'occasion de sa retraite comme professeur, ses collègues ont publié un volume sur son oeuvre et son action.

LESLIE GORDON BARNARD (1890-1961). Born in Montreal, Barnard was educated at Westmount Academy. After service with the YMCA during World War I, he returned to Montreal to become a full-time writer. His short stories have appeared in leading periodicals in Canada, the United States and abroad. *One Generation Away* (1931) and *So Near Is Grandeur* (1945) are collections of these stories in which Barnard expresses his preference for wholesome and unsophisticated characters. He has also published two light romantic novels: *Jancis* (1935), set in the lower St. Lawrence region, and *Winter Road* (1939), as well as a short essay in the form of a Christmas letter to an unknown friend, *The Immortal Child* (1941). Barnard was President of the Canadian Authors Association from 1937 to 1939.

RONALD BATES (1924-). Born in Regina, Saskatchewan, Ronald Gordon Bates was educated at the University of Toronto where he obtained his Ph.D. in English with a doctoral thesis on Joyce's *Finnegans Wake*. His volume of verse *The Wandering World* (1959), much of which was written during a three-year stay in Sweden, reflects his interest in the language of poetry and in the metaphysical and mythopoeic traditions. A second volume of poems, *The Unimaginable Circus, Theatre and Zoo*, was privately printed in 1965. Bates teaches English at the University of Western Ontario.

NEREE BEAUCHEMIN (1850-1931). Né à Yamachiche, Beauchemin a étudié au Séminaire de Nicolet et à la faculté de l'Université Laval. Toute sa vie, il a pratiqué la médecine à Yamachiche où il est mort octogénaire. Il a publié *Les Floraisons matutinales* (1897) et *Patrie intime* (1928), deux des meilleurs recueils de poèmes parus au Canada. En 1950, un *Choix de poésies* a paru avec une préface de Clément Marchand. Beauchemin fut le plus parfait des poètes canadiens du terroir. Il a repris plusieurs des thèmes de Lemay— sentiments religieux, vie familiale, contemplation de la nature—mais les a traités sur un ton intime d'une grande sincérité et avec une perfection de forme rarement atteinte au Canada français avant lui. Beauchemin ne fut en rien un novateur, il était traditionaliste à tous points de vue; mais il avait un goût sûr, une fine sensibilité et le respect de la perfection technique. C'est pourquoi il a pu porter la poésie à un niveau de perfection jamais atteint avant lui au Canada français. Il fut néanmoins un poète mineur. Gonzalve Poulin lui a consacré un petit livre (1935). Il existe de bonnes études sur lui dans Camille Roy, *Regards sur les lettres,* et Carmel Brouillard, *Sous le signe des muses.*

HENRI BEAUDET. *Voir* d'Arles, Henri.

ARCHIBALD STANFELD BELANEY (1888-1938). Although his own versions have led to confusion as to his place of birth, Belaney was probably born in England of Anglo-Saxon stock. In his youth he emigrated to Toronto and later moved to the Cobalt area. He joined the Canadian army in 1914 and served overseas until 1917 when he was wounded and returned to Canada. Settling down in the woods as a trapper and conservationist officer, he became interested in the preservation of the beaver from extinction. In 1920, Belaney was adopted as a blood-brother by the Ojibwa tribe: thereafter he called himself "Grey Owl," and in 1925 he married an Indian girl. His books—*Men of the Last Frontier* (1932), *Pilgrims of the Wild* (1934), *Adventures of Sajo and Her Beaver People* (1935), *Tales of an Empty Cabin* (1936) and *The Tree* (1937)—reflect his knowledge of Canadian wildlife and his devotion to its conservation. These works created a literary sensation in London.

REAL BENOIT (1916-   ). Né à Sainte-Thérèse de Blainville, il a été journaliste, critique de cinéma et cinéaste. Il est maintenant attaché au service des films de Radio-Canada. Il a séjourné en France, aux Antilles et au Brésil. Il a débuté en 1945 par un recueil de nouvelles fantaisistes, *Nézon,* et après un long silence, a publié dans les *Ecrits du Canada français* en 1961 un récit inspiré par l'enchantement de son séjour sous les tropiques, *Rhum soda* et, en 1964, *Quelqu'un pour m'écouter,* roman qui lui valut le Grand Prix littéraire de la ville de Montréal. C'est le long monologue intérieur d'un homme qui, anéanti par la mort de son fils, revit, au moment où il va quitter le foyer conjugal, toute sa vie qui surgit du fond de la mémoire. Ce rêve éveillé, composé avec un art accompli, est plein de poésie et de tendresse.

CONSTANCE BERESFORD-HOWE (1922-   ). Born in Montreal, Constance Elizabeth Beresford-Howe graduated with distinction from McGill University and took her doctorate at Brown University. She teaches in the English Department at McGill and writes book and music reviews for *The Montrealer* and *The Montreal Star.* Her numerous short stories have appeared in *Saturday Night, Canadian Home Journal* and *Maclean's.* She has published several historical romances, *The Unreasoning Heart* (1946), *Of This Day's Journey,* (1947), *The Invisible Gate* (1949) and *My Lady Greensleeves* (1955).

HARRY BERNARD (1896-   ). Né à Londres, Bernard a étudié au Séminaire de Saint-Hyacinthe et, après un court séjour au *Droit* d'Ottawa (1919-1923), il devint directeur du *Courrier de Saint-Hyacinthe* en 1923 et l'est toujours. De 1924 à 1932, il publia six romans qui sont tous des études de conflits conjugaux dus à la différence de classe, de race ou de religion ou simplement de goûts: *L'homme tombé, La maison vide, La dame blanche, La ferme des pins, Juana, mon aimée* et *Dolorès.* Vingt ans plus tard, il publia un autre roman, *Les jours sont longs* (1951) d'une psychologie aussi superficielle et d'un style sans couleurs. En 1929, il avait publié des *Essais critiques* et, en 1949, il publia une longue thèse de doctorat sur *Le roman régionaliste aux Etats-Unis.* Membre de la Société royale du Canada, il a obtenu un grand nombre de prix littéraires pour ses romans. Il a publié d'innombrables chroniques littéraires dans plusieurs journaux de province sous le pseudonyme de l'Illettré. On peu lire sur son oeuvre romanesque des essais d'Albert Pelletier dans *Egrappages.*

JOVETTE BERNIER (1900-   ). Née à Saint-Fabien, Alice Bernier a étudié au couvent des Ursulines de Rimouski et a été institutrice en Gaspésie (1917-1924) avant de devenir journaliste, d'abord à Québec et à Sherbrooke, puis à Montréal. Elle a aussi écrit de nombreux sketches pour la radio et une continuité pour la télévision.

Elle a publié quelques recueils de poésies, d'une fantaisie souvent charmante et, par moments, d'une gravité touchante. Après *Roulades* (1924) et *Comme l'oiseau* (1926), elle a publié des recueils d'une plus grand densité, *Tout n'est pas dit* (1929) et surtout *Les masques déchirés* (1932). Son dernier recueil, *Mon deuil en rouge* (1945), est plus faible, la virtuosité nuisant souvent à la sincérité. Elle a aussi publié le roman d'une fille-mère, *La chair décevante* (1931). Son oeuvre exprime surtout l'angoisse d'une femme qui souffre d'être mal aimée et qui s'interroge au sujet du sens de la vie; elle est d'un humour désinvolte qui ne parvient pas à guérir la douleur dont elle se rit souvent. Avec Simone Routier, Jovette Bernier fut la plus romantique des poétesses canadiennes de sa génération. On peut lire à son sujet des pages de Gilles Marcotte dans *Une Littérature qui se fait*.

PIERRE BERTON (1920-   ). Born in Whitehorse in the Yukon, Berton was educated at Victoria College, British Columbia, and the University of British Columbia (B.A. 1941). He was city editor of the Vancouver *News Herald* in 1942 when he joined the Canadian Army, in which he served with the infantry. He returned to the Vancouver *Sun* as a feature writer (1946/47) before joining the staff of *Maclean's*. He is the author of a number of volumes ranging from journalistic reporting to a children's book, *The Secret World of Og* (1961). Among these the most notable are *The Mysterious North* (1956) and *Klondike* (1958), both of which won Governor General's Award for creative non-fiction, and *Just Add Water and Stir* (1959), which won the Leacock Medal for Humour. Berton was associate editor and controversial columnist for the Toronto *Daily Star* from 1958 to 1962, when he returned for a year to *Maclean's*. Collections of his articles have been made under the titles of *Adventures of a Columnist* (1961), *The New City* (1962), *Fast, Fast, Fast Relief* (1962) and *My War with the Twentieth Century* (1965). *The Big Sell* (1963) was an exposé of hucksterism, and *The Comfortable Pew* (1965), a best seller, was a critical examination of the major Protestant churches. Berton is well known as an interviewer on television, and as a member of the panel of "Front Page Challenge." He is editor-in-chief of the Canadian Centennial Publishing series of books, commemorating the 100th anniversary (1967) of Confederation.

GERARD BESSETTE (1920-   ). Né à Sainte Anne de Sabrevois, Bessette a étudié à l'Externat classique Ste-Croix à Montréal, à l'Ecole Normale et à l'Université de Montréal dont il est docteur ès lettres. Il a enseigné la littérature française à la University of Saskatchewan, à Duquesne University (Pittsburgh), au Royal Military College de Kingston, à l'Université Laval et il est maintenant à Queen's University. Il a voyagé au Mexique et en Europe. Après avoir publié des *Poèmes temporels* (1954), il a publié sa thèse de doctorat sur *Les images en poésie canadienne française* (1960), puis quatre romans: *La Bagarre* (1959), *Le Libraire* (1960, *Not For Every Eye*, 1962), *Les Pédagogues* (1961), et *L'Incubation* (1965). Il est membre de la Société Royale du Canada.

En plus de son travail de bénédictin sur le rôle des images dans la poésie française et chez quelques-uns des meilleurs poètes canadiens, Bessette a lui-même publié des *Poèmes temporels*, i.e. des poèmes de facture classique sur le thème du temps, et surtout trois romans qui sont des récits pleins d'idées, presque des romans à thèse: *La Bagarre* évoque un milieu d'intellectuels mal équilibrés, *Les Pédagogues* est une satire de l'enseignement au Québec et, le meilleur des trois, *Le Libraire,* est le récit bref et ironique des mésaventures d'un libraire libertin dans un petit village aux moeurs conservatrices.

Son quatrième roman, *l'Incubation* est un long monologue intérieur—technique héritée du "nouveau roman" qui a le désordre des divagations d'un alcoolique qui vit—et revit—dans une sorte de rêve éveillé ses malheurs présents et passés. Le roman est noir—il est plein de guerre, de mort, de stupre, de déchéances—et nous livre sans doute le fond de la pensée et des hantises de l'auteur à qui nous devons justement une *Anthologie d'Albert Laberge.* C'est une réussite technique dans le goût du jour qui lui a valu le Prix du Gouverneur général pour le roman, en 1965. Glen Shortcliffe lui a consacré une conférence qui a été publiée par l'Université de Montréal.

MICHEL BIBAUD (1782-1857). Né à Montréal, Bibaud étudia au Collège Saint-Raphael et vécut longtemps d'enseignement et de journalisme avant de devenir traducteur à la Commission géologique du Canada. Il fut le premier polygraphe du Canada français et il a fondé plusieurs journaux éphémères, dont *L'Aurore des deux Canadas* (1816), la *Bibliothèque canadienne* (1825) et *l'Encyclopédie canadienne* (1842). Il publia le premier volume de vers au Canada français, *Epîtres, Satires, Chansons, Epigrammes et Autres pièces de vers* (1830), poèmes didactiques lourds et gauches ou pièces de circonstances d'un style officiel. Il est aussi l'auteur d'une *Histoire du Canada* en 3 volumes (1837, 1844, 1878: ce dernier écrit par son fils Maximilien), qui suit servilement la chronique de Charlevoix. Mauvais écrivain, il fut un éveilleur à une époque où presque personne ne s'occupait ni de littérature ni d'histoire. On peut lire sur lui une étude de Gérard Malchelosse dans le volume du *Centenaire de l'Histoire du Canada de Garneau.*

SARAH BINKS. *See* Hiebert, Paul Gerhard

WILL R. BIRD (1891-). Born in Nova Scotia of Yorkshire stock and educated at Amherst Academy, William Richard Bird served with the Canadian Army during World War I in which he won the Military Medal. On returning from overseas, he settled in Halifax and joined the staff of the Nova Scotia Bureau of Information and Publicity. He had been writing for years and had published *A Century of Chignecto* (1928) and *Maid of the Marshes* (1936), both set like many of his tales in Nova Scotia, before he achieved success with his novels *Here Stays Good Yorkshire* (1945) and *Judgment Glen* (1947).

Will R. Bird has been a prolific writer of novels, stories and articles which have been published in leading magazines here and abroad. *Here Stays Good Yorkshire* is considered his best work. A historical romance, overcrowded with people and episodes and replete with colloquialisms and clichés, it moves quickly and combines regional atmosphere with a refreshing dry humour. His characters are for the most part simple people depicted under particular stress in the setting of the Maritimes or against the background of the World War. His recent books include *The Passionate Pilgrim* (1949), *Tristram's Salvation* (1957), *Despite The Distance* (1961), and *North Shore (New Brunswick) Regiment* (1963).

EARLE BIRNEY (1904-). Born in Calgary, the son of a western pioneer family, Alfred Earle Birney spent his childhood in the central Alberta bush, and at the age of seven moved with his family to the mountain village of Banff. Upon graduation in 1920 from high school in the Kootenay region of British Columbia, he worked as a manual labourer for two years to earn money to attend the University of British Columbia. He graduated with his B.A. (1926) and a fellowship to the University of Toronto, where he specialized in Chaucer. Among contemporary poets, his chief interests during this period were Hardy, Housman, Eliot, de la Mare and Jeffers—the influence of Hardy and Housman especially is often apparent in his work.

Upon leaving the University of Toronto (M.A. 1927), he spent three years as a teaching fellow at the University of California. He began his formal academic career as an Instructor at the University of Utah (1930/32), and after study at the University of London on a Royal Society of Canada Fellowship (1934/35) returned to Canada and completed his Ph.D. (1936) at the University of Toronto, where he was appointed Lecturer in English. Although he became interested in poetry in high school and produced occasional pieces at university, it was at Toronto that he began seriously to write verse. During this period, influenced by his admiration for Auden, Spencer and Day Lewis, he became involved in the left-wing political theories prevalent at the time.

From 1936-1940 he was editor of *The Canadian Forum* in which many of his own poems appeared. In 1942 he published his first collection of verse *David and Other Poems,* which won a Governor General's Award and set the tone for the work which has followed. The theme of the title poem "David," in Birney's words, is "the duality of human experience as symbolized . . . by mountain-climbing—the hair's breadth between, on the one hand, beauty, and the exhilaration of being alive, and, on the other, fear and nightmare and death and the static dumb hostility of the non-human world." In this dilemma man can only cling to the humanistic value of personal emotion and the opportunity for positive individual response to life's challenges. In this, as in all his poems, Birney is skilful in making his images and prosody reinforce his theme.

In 1942 he enlisted and served overseas with the Infantry Personnel Selection Service from 1943 to 1945. Returning to Canada, he published his second collection of poems *Now is Time* (1945), which also received a Governor General's award. Inspired by the new optimism of the post-war period, he comments in this volume on the immediate past of war, the present of rehabilitation and the place of love and reason in planning the society of tomorrow. The central theme is much the same as that expressed in *David.* A strong sense of optimism pervades the book in which, with Chaucerian attention to the detail of contemporary life, Birney resumes his role as Canadian chronicler.

He became Supervisor of Foreign Language Broadcasts for the International Service of the CBC in Montreal in 1945. One year later, however, he returned as Professor of English to the University of British Columbia, and at the same time became editor of *The Canadian Poetry Magazine,* a position which he held for two years. *The Strait of Anian* (1948) continued the theme of the first two volumes, but with a note of increasing skepticism that men would ever co-operate to build a better world. Despairing contemplation of the future, however, is tempered by some good pieces of satire and humour. This sense of the comic is applied to prose in *Turvey* (1949), republished in 1960 under the title of *The Kootenay Highlander,* a picaresque novel which received the Stephen Leacock medal for humour, and presents a realistic and hilarious account of the experiences of Private Thomas Leadbeater Turvey during World War II.

Returning to poetry, Birney published his fourth volume *Trial of a City* in 1952. The title piece is a verse play, and the volume also contains thirteen new poems. In "Trial of a City" an oddly assorted group of people discuss the fate of Vancouver and, allegorically, the fate of mankind, with humour, satire, simple wisdom and pervading humanism. Birney's gifts for penetrating social commentary and for natural description are combined to present his central thoughts with convincing artistry. In 1952 he was awarded the Lorne Pierce Medal for his contributions to Canadian literature.

In 1953, Birney edited an anthology *Twentieth Century Canadian Poetry*. The following year he was elected F.R.S.C. and spent several months in Brittany working on his second novel *Down the Long Table* (1955). This fictional treatment of life in the grim thirties has some vividly realistic passages of description, and employs in a striking way the Dos Passos technique of displaying old newspaper headlines.

In *Ice Cod Bell or Stone* (1962), collected from a decade's writing, Birney ranges in space from the Arctic seas to the Far East. In the best of the poems there are present the same humour, forceful imagery and evocative power which have placed him among Canada's foremost poets. A distinguished critic, he presented the lecture on "E. J. Pratt and His Critics" in *Our Living Tradition* (1959). After a year of travel in the West Indies and Latin America, he published a new book of poems, *Near False Creek Mouth* (1964), named for a part of Vancouver Harbour, but emphasizing the precarious existence shared by people thousands of miles apart, whether at home or in South America. In 1965 and 1966 he was on leave from the University of British Columbia to be Writer-in-Residence at the University of Toronto. *Selected Poems, 1940-1966* was published in 1966; it includes his radio play "The Damnation of Vancouver." E. K. Brown, *On Canadian Poetry* (1943); Roy Daniels, "Earle Birney et Robert Finch," *Gants du Ciel*, 11 (Spring, 1946); Desmond Pacey, *Ten Canadian Poets* (Toronto, 1958); Miriam Waddington, "Poetry of a Frontier World" [*Review of Selected Poems*], *The Globe Magazine*, May 21, 1966; Paul West, "Earle Birney and the Compound Ghost," *Can. Lit.*, 13 (Summer, 1962).

CLAUDE T. BISSELL (1916-   ). **Born in** Meaford, Ontario, Claude Thomas Bissell was educated in the Toronto secondary school system and graduated with honours from the University of Toronto. He obtained his doctorate from Cornell University in 1940, where a part of his doctoral thesis *Evolutionary Ethics in Samuel Butler* was later published. After a year on the staff of Cornell, he moved to the University of Toronto in 1941. Following service overseas with the Infantry and later at Khaki College, he returned in 1946 to University College as Assistant Professor of English and Dean in Residence. From 1947 to 1959 he wrote the annual survey of Canadian fiction in "Letters in Canada" for *The University of Toronto Quarterly*.

Appointed Vice-President of the University of Toronto in 1952, Bissell edited and contributed to *University College: A Portrait; 1853-1953*. He spent four months in 1954 in Australia on a Commonwealth exchange plan. In 1956 he was appointed President of Carleton College, Ottawa, just as it attained university status. While there he introduced the *Our Living Tradition* series on leading figures in Canadian life and edited the first volume. He was elected F.R.S.C. in 1957. Returning to the University of Toronto in 1958 to become its youngest president, he has continued to produce literary articles as well as timely studies on the problems in education today. He served a term as Chairman of the Canada Council, was one of the editors of the *Literary History of Canada* (1965), and recently edited *Great Canadian Writing* (1966), an illustrated anthology in the "Canadian Centennial Library" series.

MARIE-CLAIRE BLAIS (1939-   ). Née et éduquée à Québec, elle a suivi des cours de lettres à l'Université Laval. Elle a obtenu une bourse Guggenheim en 1963 et, depuis lors, elle vit sur la péninsule de Cape Cod où, dans la solitude, elle produit une oeuvre dont elle vit: sept livres en sept ans. Toute son oeuvre, depuis *La Belle Bête* (1959) *(Mad Shadows)* jusqu'à *Une saison dans la vie d'Emmanuel* (1965) qui est son meilleur livre à date, est l'évocation hallucinante d'un univers horrible et insensé où toutes les misères physiques et morales d'êtres déchus et souvent sordides font de leur vie un véritable cauchemar. La haine, la maladie, l'idiotie pourrissent cette humanité où les morts violentes et les suicides sont monnaie courante. Les plus malheureux sont ceux qui y survivent. Dans cette oeuvre désordonnée et inégale, on trouve des pages d'une réelle puissance d'évocation et d'écriture. Edmund Wilson lui a consacré quelques pages dans *O Canada* (1965).

W. H. BLAKE (1861-1924). Born in Toronto, Ontario, William Hume Blake graduated from the University of Toronto (B.A. 1882) and in 1885 was called to the bar in Ontario where he practised law.

Because of his interest in Quebec, he produced excellent translations into English from the original French of Hémon's *Marie Chapdelaine* and Rivard's *Chez Nous,* books depicting the life of the French Canadian in

Quebec. *Brown Waters* (1915), *In a Fishing Country* (1922) and *A Fisherman's Creed* (1923) describe his experiences on Laurentian fishing trips. These books of essays, with their unpretentious yet artful style, reflect Blake's quiet intellectual approach to the world of nature and his appreciation of skill in fishing, the courage of the trout and the hospitality and shrewdness of the French guide.

MONIQUE BOSCO (1927-   ). Née en France, elle est venue au Canada en 1948, a obtenu son doctorat ès lettres de l'Université de Montréal en 1951 avec une thèse sur *L'isolement dans le roman canadien-français* (inédite); elle est professeur de littérature française à l'Université de Montréal et critique littéraire du *Magazine Maclean.* Il y a certes beaucoup de sa propre expérience dans son premier roman, *Un amour maladroit* (1961), qui raconte la jeunesse d'une jeune Israëlite, d'abord en France pendant l'occupation allemande, puis à Montréal où le sentiment de sa solitude s'accroît encore parce qu'elle s'adapte mal à ce monde nouveau et qu'elle ne sait pas se faire aimer d'un jeune Canadien qui reste insensible à sa détresse. Son second roman, *Les Infusoires* (1965), est très différent: au cours d'un congrès à Venise, quatre Canadiens, sollicités par l'aventure amoureuse à laquelle le dépaysement invite, s'y découvrent prisonniers de leur enfance, incapables de se libérer de leurs complexes et comprennent qu'ils ont manqué leur vie. L'auteur y peint un triste portrait de notre société.

GEORGES BOUCHER DE BOUCHERVILLE (1814-1894). Né à Québec, Boucherville étudia à Montréal et fut admis à la pratique du droit en 1837; il s'enrôla alors dans les Fils de la liberté et, après la rébellion, il dut s'enfuir aux Etats-Unis et ne rentra au pays que lorsque les patriotes furent amnistiés. Greffier du Conseil législatif de Québec de 1867 à 1889, il avait toujours aimé écrire et on a de lui plusieurs textes dont le plus connu est le roman d'aventures *Une de perdue, deux de trouvées* paru dans la *Revue canadienne* en 1864 et 1865. Ce récit extravagant où les épisodes extraordinaires se succèdent n'a qu'une mince valeur littéraire, mais c'est un des rares romans canadiens du dix-neuvième siècle qui aient retenu la faveur du public et aient été maintes fois réédités.

ERROL BOUCHETTE (1863-1912). Né à Québec, fils de Robert Bouchette et petit-fils du topographe Joseph Bouchette, il a étudié au Séminaire de Québec et à l'Université Laval. Admis au barreau en 1885, il pratiqua le droit, puis devint bibliothécaire à la Bibliothèque du Parlement à Ottawa. Membre de la Société royale du Canada, il fut un des premiers Canadiens français à s'intéresser à l'économie et à prêcher l'émancipation économique du Québec. Il a exposé ses vues dans quelques ouvrages dont le plus important est *L'Indépendance économique du Canada français* (1906). Il avait cherché à vulgariser ses vues dans une nouvelle intitulée *Robert Lozé* (1903).

HENRI BOURASSA (1868-1952). Né à Montréal, fils du peintre Napoléon Bourassa et petit-fils de Louis-Joseph Papineau, Bourassa reçut une éducation privée et fut d'abord journaliste. Il collabora au *Nationaliste* et se fit élire à la Chambre des communes comme libéral indépendant en 1896. Il fit campagne contre la participation du Canada à la guerre sud-africaine et fut très vite reconnu comme le chef du mouvement nationaliste au Canada français et un des meilleurs orateurs de sa génération. Il fonda *Le Devoir* en 1910 et en fut le directeur jusqu'en 1932. Il y donna quantité d'articles vigoureux et bien informés sur les événements politiques et religieux du Canada et du monde. Il fut député aux communes pendant la plus grande partie de sa maturité. Défait aux élections de 1935, il vécut relativement retiré de tout jusqu'à sa mort.

Il a publié plusieurs brochures importantes dont les principales sont *Que devons-nous à l'Angleterre?* (1915), *Hier, Aujourd'hui et Demain* (1916) et *Le pape arbitre de la paix* (1918). Sa biographie a été écrite par Robert Rumilly (1953) et des numéros spéciaux lui ont été consacrés par *L'Action Nationale* (janvier 1954) et *Le Devoir* (25 octobre 1952), tous deux reproduits en volumes.

A. S. BOURINOT (1893-). Born in Ottawa of a distinguished family, Arthur Stanley Bourinot received his degree from the University of Toronto the same year in which he published his first book of verse *Laurentian Lyrics* (1915). After graduating in law from Osgoode Hall, he went overseas with the Canadian Army during the First World War. On his return he practised law in Ottawa and published *Lyrics from the Hills* (1923), *Selected Poems* (1935) and *Rhymes of the French Regime* (1937).

He won a Governor General's Award for a collection of verse *Under the Sun* (1939). He was editor from 1948 to 1954 of *The Canadian Poetry Magazine* and of the *Canadian Author and Bookman* in 1953/54. His *Five Canadian Poets* (1954) and booklets of letters by D. C. Scott, Lampman and E. W. Thomson and of some essays from "At the Mermaid Inn" have provided valuable information on this period. He published his *Collected Poems* in 1947 and selections from his verse of 1947 to 1966 in *Watcher of Men* (1966).

GEORGE SIDNEY BRETT (1879-1944). Born in Briton Ferry, South Wales, of

English parents, George Sidney Brett was educated at Christ Church, Oxford (B.A., 1899; M.A., 1902). After teaching in England he became professor of philosophy at Lahore, India, from 1904 until 1908 when he was appointed to Trinity College, Toronto.

Although Brett's early publications, *Philosophy of Gassendi* (1908) and *The Government of Man* (1913) are important contributions to scholarship, his most outstanding work is the three-volume *History of Psychology* (1912-1921). As Professor John A. Irving has commented, this study is "an exercise in the history of philosophy of science with extensive reference to epistemological and metaphysical problems." Its style is lucid and engagingly straightforward.

Brett was elected F.R.S.C. in 1919. He was the first editor of the *University of Toronto Quarterly*; and he played a significant part in the growth of that university's School of Graduate Studies. John A. Irving (adapted by A. H. Johnson), "The Achievement of G. S. Brett," *Literary History of Canada* (1965).

ELIZABETH BREWSTER (1922-   ). Born in Sussex, New Brunswick, Elizabeth Brewster was educated at the universities of New Brunswick, Toronto and Indiana. She has published three short collections of poems, all of them written against a New Brunswick background of scenery and folklore: *East Coast* (1951); *Lilloet* (1954); *and Roads and Other Poems* (1957). This artful regional verse ranges from descriptions which reflect a close observation of external nature to a nostalgic and even melancholic recollection of village life.

ROGER BRIEN (1910-   ). Né à Nicolet, Brien a étudié au Collège Séraphique de Trois-Rivières, au Collège Sainte-Marie et aux universités de Montréal et Laval; il fut journaliste et il a fondé à Nicolet un Centre marial dont il est le directeur. Poète prolifique, il est membre de l'Académie canadienne française. Son oeuvre est d'inspiration surtout religieuse et son style ampoulé et abondant trahit une exaltation effrénée. Ses principaux recueils sont *Faust aux enfers* (1936), *Les yeux sur nos temps* (1942), *Cythère* (1946), et *Prométhée* (1965), immense épopée en quatre volumes où des personnages célèbres de tous les temps dialoguent sur tout et n'importe quoi.

FRANCES BROOKE (1724-1789). Born in Lincolnshire, England, Mrs. Brooke even in her youth attracted the attention of such a notable friend as Samuel Richardson who did much to encourage her literary ambitions. In 1755 she established and edited, under the pseudonym "Mary Singleton, Spinster," a weekly periodical for women *The Old Maid* which ceased publication after her marriage in 1756. Mrs. Brooke, however, continued writing essays, poetry, drama and a translation of a French romance. Her first novel *The History of Lady Julia Mandeville* (1763) was published before she embarked in 1763 for Canada to join her husband who was the Garrison Chaplain and deputy to the Auditor General in Quebec. There, and in adjacent Sillery, she remained for nearly five years, except for a brief visit to England, and entered with spirit and good humour into the society of the garrison.

On her return to her native England, she published and dedicated to Guy Carleton, Governor of Quebec, *The History of Emily Montague* (1769), not only the first Canadian but also the first American novel. Set in Quebec City in the 1760s, this four-volume tale was similar in construction to Richardson's *Pamela*. Two hundred and twenty-eight letters, mostly dated from

Sillery, follow one another without chapter divisions or narrative links. They trace the fortunes of two pairs of lovers who meet and court in Quebec before leaving to take up residence in England.

The brief progressive epistles, recording interesting and vivid descriptions of the Canadian landscape and the routine of a colonial garrison, contain colourful accounts of social life, scandals and entertainments of the day. This charming love story, in which no one is seduced or harmed and there is no villain, is told in a style that is rapid and lively, whimsical and aphoristic. The reader is captivated by the gaiety and variety of presentation of rather conventional characters and trivial events.

On her return to England in 1768, Mrs. Brooke continued her writing career but none of her other works related, except incidentally, to Canada or life in the colony. Lawrence J. Burpee, Introduction to *The History of Emily Montague* (Ottawa, 1931); Carl F. Klinck, Introduction to *The History of Emily Montague* (Toronto, 1961); Desmond Pacey, "The First Canadian Novel," *Dalhousie Review*, 26 (July, 1946).

E. K. BROWN (1905-1951). Born in Toronto, Ontario, Edward Killoran Brown graduated in 1926 from the University of Toronto with the Governor-General's Medal in modern languages. After postgraduate work at the University of Paris, he served on the faculty of the Universities of Toronto, Manitoba, Cornell and Chicago. From 1932 to 1941, as joint editor of the *University of Toronto Quarterly*, he was largely responsible for starting the annual survey of "Letters in Canada" to which he contributed many discriminating assessments of Canadian literature. His historical survey *On Canadian Poetry* (1943) won a Governor-General's Award.

Brown won an international reputation by his scholarly works. His *Matthew Arnold: A Study in Conflict* (1948) is a penetrating textual study of Victorian poetry and prose. Brown also wrote about contemporary American novelists like Wharton and Cather. In 1949 he gave the Alexander Lectures at the University of Toronto published as *Rhythm in the Novel* (1950). After his death his *Willa Cather: A Critical Biography* (1953) was completed and published by Leon Edel.

AUDREY ALEXANDRA BROWN (1904-   ). Born at Nanaimo, British Columbia, Miss Brown was educated in the public school system and St. Anne's Convent. Her collections of poems include *A Dryad in Nanaimo* (1931), *The Tree of Resurrection and Other Poems* (1937), *Challenge to Time and Death* (1943) and *All Fool's Day* (1948). In the words of E. K. Brown, "Her poetry is essentially a capturing of moments which she values for their intensity." She continues the tradition of the nineteenth century. Her *The Log of a Lame Duck* (1938) is autobiographical.

CHARLES BRUCE (1906-   ). Born in Nova Scotia, Charles Tory Bruce graduated from Mount Allison University, New Brunswick. From 1927, when he became a reporter on a Halifax newspaper, he has devoted the greater part of his career to journalism. The same year brought the publication of *Wild Apples,* the first of six collections of poems written within a farm-and-fishing-village convention.

In 1945 he became General Superintendent of the Canadian Press. *Grey Ship Moving* appeared in 1946. *The Flowing Summer* (1947) is a poetic narrative of a child's visit to a Nova Scotian village. *The Mulgrave*

Road, which won the Governor-General's Award for Poetry in 1951, is distinguished by the aptness of its representation of Maritime life. It was followed by the first of his longer works *The Channel Shore* (1954), a novel, and later by *The Township of Time: A Chronicle* (1959), dealing with Nova Scotian settlers and their descendents. Claude T. Bissell, "Letters in Canada: 1954," *UTQ*, XXIV (April, 1955); Northrop Frye, "Letters in Canada: 1951," *UTQ*, XXI (April, 1952).

___

JEAN BRUCHESI (1901-). Né à Montréal, Bruchési étudia au Collège Sainte-Marie, à l'Université de Montréal dont il est licencié en droit, à l'Ecole libre des Sciences politiques, à la Sorbonne et à l'Ecole des Chartes. Professeur d'histoire et de science politique à l'Université de Montréal de 1927 à 1937, il devient sous-secrétaire de la province de Québec (1937-1959) puis ambassadeur en Espagne, puis en Argentine. Membre de la Société royale du Canada dont il fut président général (1953-1954), il est l'auteur de plusieurs ouvrages d'histoire d'un style clair et facile dont les principaux sont *Histoire du Canada pour tous* (1934-1935), *Canada: Réalités d'hier et d'aujourd'hui* (1948) et *Témoignages d'hier* (1962). Il a écrit un grand nombre d'études plus courtes sur de nombreux personnages et événements de l'histoire canadienne, notamment dans les *Cahiers des Dix.*

___

BERTHELOT BRUNET (1901-1948). Né à Montréal, Brunet étudia au Collège Sainte-Marie et à l'Université de Montréal. Notaire, il exerça de 1922 à 1929 puis vécut dans une demi-solitude, collaborant à plusieurs journaux et revues. Après avoir recueilli dans *Chacun sa vie* (1942) des essais où voisinent des observations originales sur les moeurs du Canada français et des

réflexions sur la religion, il a publié des contes, *Le Mariage blanc d'Armandine* (1943), qui sont des caricatures de personnages dessinés comme ceux de La Bruyère avec un goût du paradoxe, un don de satiriste et une verve intarissable qui en font un des livres les plus drôles du Canada français. Un roman, *Les Hypocrites* (1945) est de la même veine et est une charge contre le chauvinisme et l'hypocrisie religieuse menée avec une cruauté rare. Tout ce qu'a écrit Brunet abonde en formules heureuses, en traits acerbes et en paradoxes amusants, mais il ne s'est jamais imposé de discipline et ses livres ne sont pas composés. Il est délicieux ou exécrable, jamais banal. Paul Toupin a rappelé son souvenir dans un petit livre touchant (1950), repris et augmenté en 1965.

___

MICHEL BRUNET (1917-). Né à Montréal, il a étudié à l'Université de Montréal où il a pris une maîtrise en histoire et une licence en sciences sociales et, boursier Rockefeller, à la Clark University dont il est docteur. Il est professeur d'histoire à l'Université de Montréal et membre de l'Académie canadienne française. Dans *Canadians et Canadiens* (1954) et dans *La Présence anglaise et les Canadiens* (1958), il a surtout étudié les problèmes politiques, sociaux et économiques qu'a posés, et continue de poser, la coexistence des deux races au Canada.

___

RICHARD MAURICE BUCKE (1837-1902). Born in England, Bucke settled with his family on a farm on the outskirts of London, Upper Canada, in 1838. Although his initial formal education was irregular, he was an avid reader and was encouraged by his father, a well-educated clergyman, to read widely in his excellent library. Setting out in 1853 in search of adventure, Bucke spent the next five years roaming the mid-west and western United States as a railhand, bushman, Indian fighter and gold miner. After losing one foot and part of the other as a result of frostbite in the Sierra Nevadas, he entered medicine at McGill University. Bucke's graduation thesis "The Correlation of the Physical and Vital Forces" won first prize and was published. He spent 1862/63 in England and France doing postgraduate work. On his return to Canada in 1864, he set up practice in Sarnia, worked briefly in Hamilton, and from 1877 was superintendent of the London Asylum for the Insane, the largest in Canada.

Influenced by such poets as Shelley, Keats, Browning and Shakespeare, he was profoundly and even mystically affected by Walt Whitman's *Leaves of Grass* and became his enthusiastic disciple and devoted friend. Bucke's early articles written for medical journals had established him as a leader in the treatment of the insane; after coming to know Whitman in 1879, he began to write essays on *Leaves of Grass* and to lecture on the American poet. In the same year Bucke dedicated to Whitman his first major literary effort, *Man's Moral Nature* (1879).

After Whitman visited Bucke in London in 1880, Bucke wrote an authoritative biography of the poet *Walt Whitman* (1883). He published many articles on Whitman and, as one of Whitman's literary executor's, he co-edited *In Re Walt Whitman* (1893), and edited Whitman's letters, *Calamus* (1897), *The Wound Dresser* (1898) and *Notes and Fragments* (1899). *Cosmic Consciousness*, published in 1901 and frequently reprinted, attempted to reconcile science and religion, positivism and mysticism and analyze the evolving "cosmic consciousness" of man. Bucke was elected F.R.S.C. in 1882 and received various other honours for his contribution to psychiatry. Bucke's papers are deposited in the Library of the University of Western Ontario.

[J. R. Colombo], *Richard Maurice Bucke, Catalogue to the Exhibition,* Canadian Medical Association, Annual Meetings, June 10-14, 1963, Toronto; James Henry Coyne, *Richard Maurice Bucke: A Sketch* (Toronto, 1923); G. H. Stevenson, "The Life and Work of Richard Maurice Bucke," *American Journal of Psychiatry,* Vol. 93, No. 5 (1937). H. B. Timothy, "Rediscovering R. M. Bucke," *Western Ontario Historical Notes,* XXI, No. 1 (March, 1965).

ERNEST BUCKLER (1908-). Born at Dalhousie West, Nova Scotia, Buckler received his early education in a one-room school house, and obtained his B.A. from Dalhousie University in 1929. The following year, after completing an M.A. in philosophy at the University of Toronto, he returned because of ill-health to his parents' Nova Scotia farm. Since then, apart from five years as an actuary for a Toronto life insurance company, he has devoted his time exclusively to farming and writing.

In 1938 he published a prize-winning article in *Coronet* magazine. Subsequently, short stories and articles have appeared in other publications like *Esquire, Saturday Night* and *Maclean's. The Mountain and the Valley,* his first novel, appeared in 1952. This study in alienation and frustration presents with psychological symbolism farm and family life in Nova Scotia. Buckler's poetic prose has strength and intensity, but style, as he himself states, is not his major concern.

In 1962, he published a book of short stories, and he completed his second novel, *The Cruelest Month,* a psychological study of seven people, frustrated in their respective wastelands, who find some hope when they deliberately isolate themselves at a small resort called "Endlaw," an anagram of

Walden. Buckler's work is frequently used by CBC radio, and his articles and short stories appear in many Canadian publications. Claude T. Bissell, Introduction to *The Mountain and the Valley* (1961); Warren Tallman, "Wolf in the Snow," *Can. Lit.*, 5 (Summer, 1960).

GEORGES BUGNET (1879-   ). Né à Chalon-sur-Saône, Bugnet étudia à l'Université de Dijon et, à l'âge de vingt-cinq ans, décida d'émigrer au Canada. Il séjourna à Saint-Boniface, puis s'installa avec sa femme sur une ferme du nord de l'Alberta. Bouleversé par la situation faite aux Peaux Rouges par l'invasion continuelle des Blancs, il a analysé les rapports des uns et des autres—et aussi des métis—dans un roman intitulé *Nipsya* (1924) publié sous le pseudonyme de Henri Doutremont. Après une sorte de méditation qui montre combien l'auteur était resté profondément attaché aux anciennes valeurs européennes, *Siraf* (1934), il a évoqué les difficultés pratiquement insurmontables auxquelles doivent faire face un Français et sa femme dont le ménage est menacé par ce dépaysement complet qu'est l'émigration vers des terres aussi lointaines et aussi incultes: *La Forêt* (1935) est aussi un roman où le sentiment de la nature se manifeste avec beaucoup de force et d'originalité. Bugnet a aussi publié des poésies où se retrouvent les mêmes thèmes, *Les Voix de la solitude* (1938). Des essais parus dans diverses revues n'ont pas été réunis en volume.

ARTHUR BUIES (1840-1901). Né à Montréal, Buies fut confié dès l'âge de trois ans à deux tantes de Rimouski par ses parents qui allaient tenter fortune en Guyane anglaise. Elève indiscipliné, il fréquenta successivement le Collège de Sainte-Anne de la Pocatière et les séminaires de Nicolet et de Québec. Son père, qui était d'origine écossaise, l'envoya à Dublin pour terminer ses études, mais il s'enfuit à Paris, s'inscrivit au lycée, puis s'engagea dans l'armée de Garibaldi et fit la campagne de Sicile. Rentré à Paris, il échoua au baccalauréat et décida de revenir au Canada où sa vie se divisa en deux périodes nettement distinctes.

Dès son retour en 1862, il se proclama agnostique et il entreprit d'émanciper le peuple de la domination du clergé. Devenu membre de l'Institut canadien de Montréal, il prononça de nombreuses conférences et il collabora à divers journaux, notamment au *Pays*. Reçu avocat en 1866, il renonça presque aussitôt à la pratique du droit et, au retour d'un autre voyage en France, fonda *La Lanterne* (1868-1869), *L'Indépendant* (1870-1871) et, plus tard, *Le Réveil* (1876). Il écrivait une prose unique au pays alors et s'affirma comme le pamphlétaire le plus vigoureux de sa génération, ainsi que comme le chroniqueur le plus spirituel. Ses meilleurs textes ont été repris dans *Chroniques, Humeurs et Caprices* (1873) et les textes de *La Lanterne* ont été réédités sous ce titre en 1884.

En 1879, il avait rencontré le curé Labelle et cette rencontre le transforma et donna une nouvelle orientation à sa vie. Fasciné par la personnalité du curé et converti à ses idées sur la colonisation des terres vierges, il décida de l'appuyer par la plume et par la parole. C'est ainsi que son goût des voyages put être mis à contribution et qu'il fut amené à publier des monographies vivantes sur diverses régions du Québec, le Saguenay, l'Outaouais, la vallée de la Matapédia, etc. Revenu à la pratique de la religion, il se maria en 1887 et le libertaire des années 60 devint un patriote ardent dévoué au développement du pays et au relèvement économique des Canadiens de langue française.

Il avait aussi travaillé toute sa vie à l'épuration de la langue parlée et écrite et publié *Anglicismes et cana-dianismes* (1888). On lira principale-ment sur lui les livres de Raymond Douville (1932) et de Léopold Lamontagne (1957) et de Marcel Gagnon (1965).

MARTIN BURRELL (1858-1938). Born in England, Burrell came to Canada in 1886 and took up fruit farming in the Niagara Peninsula and British Colum-bia. In 1908 he was elected to the House of Commons, served as Minister of Agriculture (1911-1917), and in several other portfolios until his retire-ment from political life. Appointed parliamentary librarian in 1920, he contributed a weekly column (1924-1938) to the Ottawa *Journal* and wrote two books of distinguished essays *Betwixt Heaven and Charing Cross* (1928) and *Crumbs Are Also Bread* (1934).

DOUGLAS BUSH (1896-). Born in Morrisburg, Ontario, John Nash Douglas Bush graduated with distinc-tion in Classics and English from Victoria College, Toronto, and Harvard University. After teaching for some years at the University of Minnesota, he returned to Harvard in 1936, where he continued as Professor of English until his retirement. In 1940 he became an American citizen.

Along with such critics as E. K. Brown and A. J. M. Smith, Bush con-tributed to *The Canadian Forum* essays on Canadian literature during the early twenties. His scholarly training in the Classics and English produced a genial irreverence for the introspection and moral seriousness of both Canadian literature and the Canadian character. An ability to single out the precisely fitting quotation, a gift for witty phras-ing, humour, apt and often sly allusion, as well as an illuminating mastery of subject, characterize his writings.

Among his important contributions to scholarship are, *Mythology and the Renaissance Tradition in English Poetry* (1932, rev., 1963), *Mythology and the Romantic Tradition in English Poetry* (1937), *The Renaissance and English Humanism* (1939), *Paradise Lost in Our Time* (1945), *English Literature in the Earlier Seventeenth Century* (1945, rev., 1962), *Science and English Poetry* (1950), *English Poetry: The Main Currents from Chaucer to the Present* (1952), *John Milton* (1964), *Prefaces to Renaissance Literature* (1965), and *John Keats* (1966). Winner of a number of fellow-ships and recipient of many awards and honorary degrees for his writings and foundations lectures, Bush has gained international fame as a brilliant scholar and critic of literary history.

ARTHUR DE BUSSIERES (1877-1913). Né à Montréal, peintre de métier, ami de Nelligan, cet artisan aimait écrire des vers et fut un des membres les plus actifs de l'Ecole littéraire de Montréal. Influencé surtout par Hérédia, il a écrit des sonnets exotiques d'une belle facture qui ont été recueillis par Casi-mir Hébert et publiés en volume sous le titre *Les Bengalis* (1931). Il y a une bonne étude sur lui par Odette Condemine dans le vol. 2 des *Archives des lettres canadiennes*.

MORLEY CALLAGHAN (1903-). Born in Toronto, of Irish parentage, Edward Morley Callaghan was educated at St. Michael's College, University of Toron-to (B.A. 1925), and Osgoode Hall Law School. During this academic period he worked as a reporter on the Toronto *Daily Star* and was encouraged by an-other member of its staff, Ernest Hemingway, in his ambition to write. In 1928 he was admitted to the bar and produced his first novel *Strange Fugitive,* the story of a Toronto lumber-yard foreman turned bootlegger, which, like many of his later works, dealt in an artfully casual style with the problem of the individual unable to adjust to society.

For some time before the publication of this first novel, his short stories had appeared in magazines and literary journals on both sides of the Atlantic. Characteristic in their terse style, skilful use of symbolism and irony, and their expression of compassion for the insignificant individual or the outsider, these tales were collected under the title of *A Native Argosy* (1929). The success of this book and *Strange Fugitive* enabled Callaghan to spend several months in Paris during 1929, where he associated with such writers as Ernest Hemingway, Scott Fitzgerald and James Joyce.

A second novel *It's Never Over* appeared in 1930 and is concerned with the impact of past experiences of war, violence and love on human lives. A short novella *No Man's Meat* was privately printed in Paris in 1931. After a brief period working between Pennsylvania and New York, Callaghan returned to live in Toronto. *A Broken Journey* (1932) moves in its setting from that city to the rugged beauty of Northern Ontario where a young couple's dream of happiness is shattered.

There is strong emphasis in Callaghan's work upon Christian love as the answer to the social injustices of the depression era. He has more faith in a liberalized and humanized Christianity than in the church itself, which, although it preserves Christian values, is often portrayed as reactionary. These sentiments are obvious in *Such Is My Beloved* (1934), the story of an unworldly Catholic priest, who attempts to redeem two prostitutes, and his ultimate defeat at the hands of hierarchy and society.

They Shall Inherit the Earth appeared in 1935. Its important characters, who here assume moral responsibility for their failures and find in humility some measure of atonement, are skilfully delineated, the style is confident and the structure well integrated. In 1936 another book of short stories *Now That April's Here, and Other Stories* appeared. *More Joy in Heaven* (1937) has as its theme the unsuccessful attempt of a paroled convict to reestablish a normal existence in society. In 1939, Callaghan turned briefly to theatre, writing two stage plays *Turn Again Home,* purchased by the New York Theatre Guild, and *Just Ask for George.* These plays were presented in Toronto by the New Play Society in 1950 and 1949 respectively under the titles *Going Home* and *To Tell the Truth.*

During the war Callaghan worked for a time with the R.C.N. on an assignment for the National Film Board. He also travelled across Canada as chairman of the program "Citizen's Forum." After the war he produced, in 1948, *The Varsity Story,* a thinly fictionalized and nostalgic portrayal of the complex college federation of the University of Toronto, and a juvenile novel, *Luke Baldwin's Vow.* In 1951, *The Loved and the Lost* won a Governor General's Award. Set against a background of racial discrimination in Montreal, this novel reveals dramatically the tension between the self-assertive temporal world and the self-renouncing spiritual world. Although these two worlds, represented by Jim McAlpine and Peggy Sanderson, fail to come together because of McAlpine's tragic lack of faith at the critical moment in Peggy's life, love somehow triumphs even when all is lost.

In 1959, in a volume entitled *Morley Callaghan's Stories,* Callaghan collected his best short stories. Set primarily in Toronto and its surrounding countryside, these stories, "the ones that touch times and moods and people I like to remember now," like Sherwood Anderson's *Winesburg, Ohio,* are presented with a strong sense of place, a regionalism which is endowed with universality by penetrating and compassionate study of character. The style at times approaches lyricism, and despite portrayals of the grim and sordid aspects of life, the dominant emotion aroused is tenderness.

In *The Many Colored Coat* (1960), the central character, Harry Lane, a public relations representative for a Montreal distillery, betrayed because of his magnanimity, after a suspenseful attempt to assert his innocence finds a belated solution to the dilemma of social rejection. In *A Passion in Rome* (1961), Sam Raymond, a cynical newspaper photographer, realizes his lifelong artistic yearning in the redemption of an alcoholic singer, Anna Connel. These heroic characters through a process of self-discovery triumph over the conflicts which threaten to destroy them. Their final separation, although disappointing to readers who have anticipated a conventionally happy ending, is logical and inevitable. The Italian setting, at the time of the death of Pope Pious XII and the election of John XXIII, is rich in suggestion and vividly depicted.

"One of the most literary of Canadian novelists," as he is described by Milton Wilson, and certainly one of Canada's few world authors, Callaghan in *That Summer in Paris* (1963) recalls with delightful charm his youthful career and his association with other famous literary figures of an earlier period. In 1963 he began working on a novel *Thumbs Down on Julien Jones* with a wartime setting first in New York and then at sea. Margaret Avison, "Callaghan Revisited," *The Canadian Forum*, 39 (March, 1960); Brandon Conron, *Morley Callaghan* (1966); Hugo Macpherson, "The Two Worlds of Morley Callaghan," *Queen's Quarterly*, 64 (Autumn, 1957); Frank Watt, "Morley Callaghan as Thinker," *Dalhousie Review*, 39 (Autumn, 1959);

Edmund Wilson, "Morley Callaghan of Toronto," *The New Yorker*, 36 (November 26, 1960); Milton Wilson, "Callaghan's Caviare," *Tamarack Review*, 22 (Winter, 1962); George Woodcock, "Lost Eurydice: The Novels of Morley Callaghan," *Can. Lit.*, 21 (Summer, 1964).

GEORGE FREDERICK CAMERON (1854-1885). Born in New Glasgow, Nova Scotia, Cameron early devoted his spare time to writing poetry. At fifteen he moved to Boston with his family, and after graduation from Boston University, entered a Boston law office. During this period he contributed to various literary journals. Returning to Canada in 1882, Cameron entered Queen's University where he was the prize poet in 1883. He was editor of Kingston's *Daily News* for this same year until shortly before his death from heart disease at thirty-one.

No volume of his works was published during his lifetime. In 1887 a selection of his poems entitled *Lyrics on Freedom, Love and Death* was published by his brother, Charles, who promised that other volumes would follow if this book were well received. Although Lampman was lavish in praising Cameron as "the poet of most genuine and fervid poetic energy this country has produced," no later collection was undertaken. There is little Canadian, national or topical reference in his work. He had a clarity and directness of expression which reflected his life-long appreciation of the ancient classics, and he was an accomplished rhetorical poet. Champion of republicanism and critical of urban life, he found during his last few years little stimulus to his imagination in the changing world around him. A note of pessimism and a preoccupation with the theme of his death are apparent in many of his poems. Arthur S. Bourinot, *Five Canadian Poets* (Montreal, 1954).

GRACE CAMPBELL (1895-1963). Born in Glengarry County, Ontario, Mrs. Grace MacLennan (Grant) Campbell graduated from Queen's University in 1915 and taught school for some years. Her first novel, *Thorn Apple Tree* (1942), was a historical romance set on the farm of her childhood and vividly portrays pioneer life. Her later novels are *The Higher Hill* (1944), *Fresh Wind Blowing* (1947), *The Tower and the Town* (1950) and *Torbeg* (1953). *Highland Heritage* (1962) describes a return pilgrimage of Mrs. Campbell to the storied land of her own ancestors.

WILFRED CAMPBELL (1858-1918). Born in Kitchener (then Berlin), Ontario, the son of a clergyman, William Wilfred Campbell was educated at the University of Toronto, Wycliffe College and the Episcopal Theological School of Cambridge, Massachusetts. Ordained in the Episcopal Church in 1885, he preached for three years in New England before going to St. Stephen, New Brunswick. While at St. Stephen he published his first volume of verse, *Lake Lyrics and Other Poems* (1889). In such lyrics as "Indian Summer," "The Winter Lakes" and "How Spring Came," Campbell depicted with simplicity and charm the changing aspects of season and mood of Georgian Bay and Lake Huron, as well as the countryside where he had roamed as a boy and first been inspired to write poetry. His "Lazarus" has a strong imaginative and warm sympathetic appeal.

Affected by Emersonian transcendentalism and his own study of mythology, Campbell retired from the church in 1891 and entered the Civil Service in Ottawa. Although discontented with the mundane drudgery of his work in the Dominion Archives Bureau, he remained there until his death and continued to produce in his spare time a wide variety of literary works. His second volume of verse

The Dread Voyage (1893) was a collection of rather sombre pieces with the note of tragedy and doom evident throughout. In 1893 he was elected F.R.S.C. During the nineties, along with Lampman and Scott, he wrote a literary and critical column, "At the Mermaid Inn" for the Toronto *Globe.*

Beyond the Hills of Dream (1899) contained several musical nature lyrics which were bright in spirit, as well as a moving threnody to Lampman, "Bereavement of the Fields." This publication was followed in 1905 by *The Collected Poems of Wilfred Campbell,* and the first of his two mediocre novels *Ian of the Orcades* (1906). *Poetical Tragedies* (1908) consisted of four verse dramas: "Mordred" and "Hildebrand," which had appeared earlier, and "Daulac" and "Morning."

Producing a poem for every occasion, from the death of Sir John A. Macdonald to the passing of Queen Victoria, Campbell continued his publications, although in much of his later work he did not maintain the quality of his earlier verse. His independent nature, his serious disposition, strong **convictions and** fascination by the Lake Country are revealed in both his poetry and prose. Some of his other publications include *A Beautiful Rebel* (1909), an historical novel of the 1812 era, *The Canadian Lake Region* (1910), a descriptive book, *Sagas of Vaster Britain* (1914), a collection of poems, *War Lyrics* (1915), and an edition of the *Oxford Book of Canadian Verse* (1913). *The Poetical Works of Wilfred Campbell* (1922) was published posthumously with a "Memoir" by W. J. Sykes. C. F. Klinck, *Wilfred Campbell: A Study in Late Provincial Victorianism* (Toronto, 1942).

JANEY CANUCK. *See* Murphy, Emily Gowan.

---

[22]

JUDITH CAPE. *See* Page, P. K.

JAMES CAPPON (1854-1939). Born in Scotland, Cappon was educated at the University of Glasgow (M.A. 1879). After several years of teaching in the United Kingdom, he emigrated to Canada in 1888. Joining Queen's University as a professor of English, he became its first Dean of Arts (1906), and editor of *Queen's Quarterly* to which he frequently contributed critical articles. *Roberts and the Influences of His Time,* which Cappon produced in 1905, as the first scholarly book on a native author, was a landmark in Canadian studies. He was elected F.R.S.C. in 1917. In 1925 he published a revised edition of the Roberts book, and in 1930 an important critical work, *Bliss Carman, and the Literary Currents and Influences of His Time.*

GABRIELLE CARBOTTE. *Voir* Roy, Gabrielle.

BLISS CARMAN (1861-1929). Born in Fredericton, New Brunswick, the son of a barrister and descended on his mother's side from Loyalist stock, William Bliss Carman was educated at the Collegiate School in Fredericton and the University of New Brunswick. After his graduation in 1881, he studied for two years at Edinburgh, where he wrote occasional verses.

It was not until his return to Canada that his first poem was published in 1883 in *The Week,* then under the editorship of his cousin, Charles G. D. Roberts. After teaching a year in Fredericton Collegiate, and wavering between a career in law or surveying or journalism (he contributed a few articles and poems to the *University Monthly* of U.N.B.), Carman went in 1886 to Harvard to read philosophy under Josiah Royce. Here he met Richard Hovey who became his collaborator in the Vagabondia series.

During this period Carman edited the *Chap Book* and his poems appeared in the *Harvard Monthly, The Atlantic Monthly* and *The Century.* In 1890 he went to New York where he did editorial work, first for *The Independent,* primarily a religious weekly, then for *Current Literature* and various other American magazines.

Carman's first volume of poetry *Low Tide on Grand Pré* was published in 1893. Its title poem was inspired by the Evangeline country of Nova Scotia near Windsor, where Carman spent many summers visiting with Roberts. In this volume of lyrical impressions, Carman is at his best. "Low Tide on Grand Pré" creates a haunting melody by the appropriate use of the tide's fretful ebb and flow along the Fundy coast as a symbol of the desolation felt by the poet recalling a lost love; "A Windflower" depicts with felicity of phrase the ephemeral, fragile and anxious life of man; "A Northern Vigil" evokes in the setting "of the eerie Ardise hills" a mood of hopeless longing for the wild sweet will "of a vanished Guendolen"; "The Eavesdropper," "Marian Drury" and "The White Gull" illustrate Carman's ability to project ecstatic feeling and touch the imagination by his suggestive use of imagery and melody.

In 1894 there appeared the first of the three series of *Songs from Vagabondia* written in collaboration with Richard Hovey (the other two were *More Songs from Vagabondia* in 1896, and *Last Songs from Vagabondia* in 1901). The best of these poems proved popular for their exuberance reminiscent of Whitman, their gaiety of description and swinging rhythm. Carman followed this series with another group of poems the theme of which—expressed in "The Pipes of Pan" of *From the Book of The Myths* (1902)—is the revival of natural love and beauty in a world growing old. *From The Green Book of the Bards*

(1903), *Songs of the Sea Children* (1904) and two other volumes of this period reiterate with occasional striking effect the concept of a universal brotherhood, rooted in a rich understanding of nature, and echo the nostalgia for a classical golden age.

Carman's theory of poetry, as explained in *The Friendship of Art* (1904), *The Kinship of Nature* (1904), *The Poetry of Life* (1905), and *The Making of Personality* (1908), with its stress on rapture and affinity with nature, is fundamentally romantic, although it embraces the classical view that poetry serves truth and goodness as well as beauty. In his own work, and partly because of his interest in unitrinianism (harmony of body, mind and soul), Carman was increasingly didactic; his later poetry for the most part lacks the sustained melody and haunting effect of his earlier lyrics. *Behind the Arras* (1895), however, with its allegories of the soul's quest for peace and love, *Ballads of Lost Haven* (1897), with its melancholy themes, *Sappho* (1905), with its subtle expansion of the extant Greek lyrics, and *Sanctuary* (1929), with its happy rendering in sonnets of the New England seasons, all contain pieces which excel in verbal magic and wistful mood.

Honoured in his later life as a distinguished poet and lecturer, Carman was elected a F.R.S.C. and received the Lorne Pierce Medal for his contribution to Canadian letters. He died suddenly in New Canaan, Connecticut. James Cappon, *Bliss Carman and the Literary Currents and Influences of his Time* (Toronto, 1930); H. P. Gundy, "The Bliss Carman Centenary," *Douglas Library Notes* [Queen's University], 10 (Summer, 1961); H. D. C. Lee, *Bliss Carman* (1912); Desmond Pacey, *Ten Canadian Poets;* Odell Shepard, *Bliss Carman* (Toronto, 1923); Donald Stephens, "A Maritime Myth," *Can. Lit.,* 9 (Summer, 1961).

EMILY CARR (1871-1945). Born in Victoria, British Columbia, Carr was educated at the local high school and then continued her studies at the Mark Hopkins' School of Art, San Francisco (1889-95) and Westminster School of Art, London, England (1899-1905). After graduation she returned to teach art in Vancouver. Despite the numerous hazards and discomforts of travel in that day on the Coast, she made innumerable trips to the villages of the West Coast where she sketched totem poles and Indian types and absorbed the regional culture and atmosphere which appeared in her later literary work. In 1910 she returned to Europe to further her studies at the Academy in Paris and to sketch extensively in Brittany. Her paintings were not financially successful. On her return to the West Coast, she was forced to support herself by raising dogs, running a boarding house and making pottery.

After giving up her work as an artist for fifteen years, she resumed painting the West Coast villages and developed a highly individualistic style in which the symbol of the totem pole was predominant. Although for many years she had been privately making notes of her impressions of the world around her, it was her failing health that gave the stimulus to her public literary career. She won the Governor General's Award for non-fiction with *Klee Wyck* (1941), a collection of twenty-one sketches mainly of life among the Indians of the West Coast with whom she was so familiar. The title of the book came from the name, Laughing One, given her by an old Indian woman. With simplicity of expression, rigid selectivity, and economy of detail and word, Miss Carr has sensitively expressed in her writings and in her paintings how intensely moved she was by the primitive sense of beauty which she found in the forest and which she discovered behind the life and art of the Indians. Without patronage or sentimentality, she presented the Indian as a human being, self-respecting, with a tradition and culture in which he could take just pride.

She continued writing and published *The Book of Small* (1942), concerning her childhood in Victoria, *House of All Sorts* (1944), about her woes as owner and keeper of a boarding house, breeder of dogs and pottery maker, and *Growing Pains* (1946), her auto-biography. *Emily Carr: Her Paintings and Sketches* (1945) and *The Heart of a Peacock* (1953) were edited by her literary executor, Ira Dilworth. All of Miss Carr's work, with its haunting sense of loneliness and frustration, represents uniquely the impact of impressions of people and place upon a sensitive artist. Roy Daniells, "Emily Carr" in *Our Living Tradition*, 4th Series (Toronto, 1962).

GEORGES CARTIER (1929-   ). Né à l'Assomption, il a étudié au Collège de l'Assomption, obtenu la licence ès lettres et le baccalauréat en biblio-théconomie à l'Université de Montréal. Bibliothécaire, il a été de 1961 à 1964 attaché au service de presse de l'UNESCO à Paris. Il est maintenant directeur de la Bibliothèque Saint-Sulpice à Montréal. Après quelques plaquettes de vers où le sentiment de la mort donne plus de prix aux beautés de la nature et à l'amour, il a obtenu le Prix du Cercle du Livre de France pour *Le Poisson pêché* (1964), évocation rétrospective de la vie médiocre d'un Canadien à Paris au moment où il hésite entre le retour et l'expatriation volontaire.

HENRI-RAYMOND CASGRAIN (1831-1904). Né à Rivière Ouelle, Casgrain étudia au Collège de Sainte-Anne de la Poca-tière et au Séminaire de Québec et fut ordonné prêtre en 1856. Vicaire à Québec, il s'intéressa vivement à la littérature, fréquenta Crémazie et ses amis et devint un des principaux mem-bres de l'Ecole patriotique de 1860. Il consacra la plus grande partie de son temps à l'histoire et fut un des membres fondateurs de la Société royale du Canada dont il fut président en 1889-1890.

Il a publié deux volumes de vers sans valeur, des *Légendes canadiennes* (1861) d'intérêt folklorique, une *Histoire de l'Hôtel-Dieu de Québec* (1878), une étude sur *Montcalm et Lévis* (1891) et quelques autres ouvrages historiques qui sont mal-heureusement déparés par un goût trop prononcé pour les développements lyriques. Il a aussi écrit de courtes bio-graphies sur quelques-uns des écrivains qu'il avait connus: Garneau, Crémazie, Aubert de Gaspé, Gérin-Lajoie, Park-man. En 1884, il a publié en quatre volumes des *Oeuvres complètes* qui ne sont pas complètes. Il a aussi édité la *Collection des manuscrits du maréchal de Lévis* (12 v., 1891) et les *Oeuvres complètes* de Crémazie. Il a participé à la fondation des *Soirées canadiennes* (1861) et du *Foyer canadien* (1864) et a été mêlé à toutes les manifestations de la vie littéraire à Québec de 1860 à 1900. On peut lire sur Casgrain Camille Roy, *Essais sur la littérature canadienne*.

CECILE CHABOT (1907-   ). Née à L'Annonciation, Cécile Chabot a étudié à l'Ecole des Beaux-arts de Montréal et elle illustre elle-même ses ouvrages. Publiciste et scripteur à la radio, elle a séjourné en France et elle est membre de la Société royale du Canada. Elle a débuté par des poèmes d'une sensibilité attendrie chantant avec naïveté et candeur, avec une pointe de ferveur de temps en temps, les beautés de la nature et les appels d'un coeur inem-ployé. Son *Vitrail* (1939) en vers réguliers la situait dans le prolonge-ment du romantisme féminin ranimé par Jovette Bernier et Simone Routier. Depuis, elle a adopté le vers libre et elle a célébré avec beaucoup de fraîcheur la *Légende mystique* de la fondation de Montréal (1942) ainsi que d'autres pages mystiques dans le goût de la Légende dorée. Ces textes ont été réédités en 1962 sous le titre *Contes du ciel et de la terre.* Elle a aussi publié des contes poétiques qui évoquent des souvenirs de son enfance, *Et le cheval vert* (1961).

PAUL CHAMBERLAND (1939-   ). Né à Longueuil, il a obtenu une licence en philosophie de l'Université de Montréal, a été professeur et est rédacteur à l'Hydro-Québec. Il est un des directeurs de *Parti pris.* Après un recueil de poésies pleines de mythes et de symboles obscurs où les choses sont le plus souvent évoquées comme des reflets de Dieu (*Genèses,* 1962), il a ramené sa poésie à des thèmes plus incarnés: patrie québécoise dont il se sent dépossédé et qu'il faut reconquérir par la révolte, la révolution et l'amour (*Terre Québec,* 1964). Cette poésie qui, partie du platonisme pour atteindre tôt à l'engagement, lui a inspiré aussi cette sorte de réquisitoire politique et poétique à la fois qu'est *L'afficheur hurle* (1965) où le langage se fait plus violent pour souligner la détresse d'un homme qui se sent comme un étranger chez lui.

THOMAS CHAPAIS (1859-1946). Né à Saint Denis (Kamouraska), fils de Jean-Charles Chapais, Sir Thomas a étudié au Collège de Sainte-Anne de la Pocatière et à l'Université Laval dont il était licencié en droit. Avocat, il fut journaliste, directeur du *Courrier du Canada* (1884-1901) et fut un des principaux personnages du parti conservateur pendant plus d'un demi-siècle. Conseiller législatif dès 1892, il fut ministre dans plusieurs administrations provinciales et fut nommé au Sénat en 1919. Membre de la Société royale du Canada, il en fut président général (1923/4); il fut aussi président de la Canadian Historical Association (1925/6). Il fut créé chevalier (Knight) en 1925.

Dès 1879, il avait été nommé professeur d'histoire du Canada, à l'Université Laval et il est resté toute sa vie intéressé aux recherches historiques. Il est l'auteur de deux biographies qui font encore autorité, *Jean Talon* (1904) et *Le marquis de Montcalm* (1911), ainsi que d'un *Cours d'histoire du Canada* en huit volumes (1919-1934) qui fut professé à l'Université Laval et qui est surtout l'histoire du Canada depuis 1760 jusqu'à 1867. Son oeuvre écrite porte malheureusement la marque de son éloquence souvent excessive, et on retrouve son ton solennel dans les articles qu'il a publiés dans *La Presse,* la *Revue canadienne* et le *Courrier du Canada* et dont quelques-uns ont été réunis dans *Mélanges* (1905). Il a aussi publié quatre volumes de *Discours et conférences* (1911-1943). Il est resté, par ses idées farouchement conservatrices comme par son style ampoulé, un homme d'un autre âge. Jean-Charles Bonenfant a publié un *Thomas Chapais* dans la collection Classiques canadiens de Fides (1957). Julienne Barnard a publié trois volumes de *Mémoires Chapais* qui évoquent l'histoire de cette famille depuis les origines jusqu'à Sir Thomas.

WILLIAM CHAPMAN (1850-1917). Né à Saint-François de Beauce d'un père anglais et d'une mère française, Chapman étudia au Collège de Lévis et entreprit à l'Université Laval des études de droit qu'il n'acheva pas. Il fut journaliste, notamment à *La Minerve,* puis fonctionnaire provincial et, en 1896, il ouvrit une librairie à Ottawa où il devint en 1902 traducteur au Sénat. Il a publié quelques recueils de poèmes, *Les Québecoises* (1876), *Les Feuilles d'érable* (1890), *Les Aspirations* (1904), *Les Rayons du nord* (1909) et *Les Fleurs de givre* (1912).

Ses dernières poésies ont paru dans le *Bulletin du parler français*. Presque toute sa poésie est de style romantique, souvent déclamatoire et inspirée surtout par l'histoire du Canada et les moeurs populaires. Jaloux de la célébrité de Fréchette, il l'attaqua dans deux pamphlets d'une grande violence, *Le Lauréat* (1892), et *Deux copains* (1894).

JEAN CHARBONNEAU (1875-1960). Né à Montréal, Charbonneau étudia le droit à l'Université de Montréal et fut avocat et traducteur. Il fit aussi du théâtre et fut plus tard professeur de diction.

Avec quelques amis, il fonda l'Ecole littéraire de Montréal à l'automne de 1895. Cette école n'avait pas de doctrine officielle, elle réunissait de jeunes poètes et prosateurs attirés vers les lettres et leur seul caractère commun fut d'avoir voulu réagir contre la littérature apologétique et patriotique dont Québec avait été le centre depuis 1860. Charbonneau a écrit une histoire de *l'Ecole littéraire de Montréal* (1935) dont certaines pages sont sujettes à caution, et des essais mal composés sur *Les Influences françaises au Canada* (3 v., 1917, 1918, 1920).

Il fut lui-même un des poètes de l'école, un poète ambitieux qui a repris les grands mythes religieux de plusieurs nations dans un style grandiloquent. Ses poèmes métaphysiques sont obscurs. Il a publié *Les Blessures* (1912), *L'Age de sang* (1921), *Les Prédestinés* (1923), *L'Ombre dans le miroir* (1924), *La Flamme ardente* (1928), *Tel qu'en sa solitude* (1940) et *Sur la borne pensive* (1952). Il a aussi écrit un roman et des pièces de théâtre qui sont restés inédits.

ROBERT CHARBONNEAU (1911-1967). Né à Montréal, Charbonneau étudia au Collège Sainte-Marie et à la faculté des sciences sociales de l'Université de Montréal. Journaliste à *La Patrie*, au *Droit* puis au *Canada*. Il a fondé en 1940, avec Claude Hurtubise, les Editions de l'Arbre. Depuis 1950, il fut à l'emploi de la Société Radio-Canada, d'abord comme journaliste puis, depuis 1955, comme directeur du service des textes. Membre de l'Académie canadienne-française, il a été président de la Société des éditeurs de la province de Québec (1945-1947) et fut président de la Société des écrivains canadiens. En 1934, il avait fondé avec Paul Beaulieu la revue *La Relève* qui est devenue ensuite *La Nouvelle Relève* (1941-1948) et qu'il a dirigée avec Claude Hurtubise. En 1946, il a reçu le Prix Duvernay, et en 1965 la médaille Chauveau.

Charbonneau est un romancier d'analyse dont le premier roman, *Ils posséderont la terre* (1941), est une date dans l'histoire du roman canadien français. L'auteur n'a jamais plus atteint à la même qualité dans ses trois autres romans: *Fontile* (1945), *Les Désirs et les jours* (1948) et *Aucune créature* (1961). Il a repris les personnages de son premier roman et il y a une grande unité d'atmosphère dans cette oeuvre romanesque. *Ils posséderont la terre* est le roman de la liquidation de l'adolescence et l'auteur a réussi à évoquer ici, avec un rare sens du spirituel et du mystère, les états d'âme successifs de jeunes hommes qui doivent faire un choix et s'engager pour la vie. Le drame intérieur qui résulte de la découverte de l'écart qui existe entre les rêves de l'adolescence et les réalités de la vie est la vraie matière du romancier; lorsqu'ils vieillissent et deviennent adultes, ses personnages deviennent caricaturaux et perdent leur densité. Cette oeuvre austère et tragique, d'une écriture cursive, est une contribution importante au roman d'analyse canadien. Le décor a ici une importance secondaire, c'est le drame intérieur des personnages qui compte.

Charbonneau a écrit des essais remarquables sur des romanciers et dramaturges (Dostoïewsky, Bernanos,

Mauriac, Ibsen, etc.) qu'il a réunis dans *Connaissance du personnage* (1945). Il a aussi eu une retentissante polémique avec des écrivains français sur l'orientation de la littérature canadienne française au carrefour des influences française et américaine: *La France et nous* (1947). Il a aussi publié de *Petits Poèmes retrouvés*. Marie-Blanche Ellis lui a consacré un petit livre (1948). Il y a aussi un essai sur lui par Allan McAndrew dans le *University of Toronto Quarterly* d'octobre 1946.

P. J. O. CHAUVEAU (1820-1890). Né à Québec, Pierre Joseph Olivier Chauveau étudia au Séminaire de Québec, devint avocat en 1841, fut député à la législature de 1844 à 1855 et fut membre de divers gouvernements provinciaux avant de devenir premier ministre du Québec au moment de la Confédération. Il fut nommé sénateur en 1873, mais résigna l'année suivante et il devint plus tard doyen de la faculté de droit de l'Université Laval. De 1855 à 1867, il fut surintendant de l'instruction publique de la province de Québec et, en 1857, il fonda le *Journal de l'Instruction publique*. Président de la Société littéraire et historique de Québec, de l'Institut canadien de Québec et de l'Institut canadien français de Montréal, il fut un des membres fondateurs de la Société royale dont il fut président en 1883/4. Il fut un des meilleurs orateurs de son temps et il a aussi écrit de nombreuses pièces de vers (qu'on peut retrouver dans le *Répertoire national* de Huston), des études littéraires dont la plus remarquable est celle qu'il a consacrée à Garneau; plusieurs essais sur l'éducation dont le plus important est *l'Instruction publique au Canada* (1876) ainsi qu'un de nos premiers romans de moeurs, *Charles Guérin*, paru dans *l'Album de la Minerve* en 1846, et en volume en 1853. Son oeuvre a vieilli, mais son influence a été considérable et il a été un des personnages littéraires les plus importants du pays pendant près d'un demi-siècle. Une médaille de la Société royale du Canada porte son nom.

PHILIP CHILD (1898-). Born in Hamilton, Ontario, Philip Albert Child received his early education in Germany, Switzerland and Canada. He left school to join the Canadian army during World War I and served overseas in the artillery. After the war he received his B.A. (1921) from Trinity College, Toronto, and spent the following year at Cambridge University. Returning to Canada he taught at Trinity College, the University of British Columbia and then for some years at Harvard. While there he brought out his first book *The Village of Souls* (1933), a historical novel which admirably presents the excitement, loneliness and clash of cultures and values in New France during the seventeenth century.

Leaving Harvard in 1936, he returned to Canada where he published *God's Sparrows* (1937), a novel set in Canada and in the scenes of the first World War. In a multiplicity of episodes and characters, the psychological turmoil of the narrative is convincingly portrayed.

In 1945 he brought out two novels *Blow Wind—Come Wrack* and *Day of Wrath,* which won a Governor General's Award. Set in Nazi Germany, *Day of Wrath* treats the struggle of man to maintain his honesty and human dignity in the midst of barbaric cruelties. Although the characters and scenes are sometimes overdrawn, the episodes are exciting and the author's compassion and faith in man are evident. Child won another Governor General's Award with *Mr. Ames Against Time* (1949), an allegorical novel concerned with the struggle of an ordinary man to preserve human dignity in the hostile environment of the Toronto underworld.

Interested in the Canadian Institute for International Affairs, Child produced *Post-War Organization* (1940) and, in collaboration with John W. Holmes, *Dynamic Democracy* (1941). His poems are principally long narratives: *The Victorian House and Other Poems* (1951), concerning memories of his family home, and *The Wood of the Nightingale* (1965), dealing with experiences in World War I. William H. Magee, "Philip Child, a Re-Appraisal," *Can. Lit.*, 24 (Spring, 1965).

RENE CHOPIN (1885-1953). Né à Sault-au-Récollet, Chopin étudia au Collège Sainte-Marie et à la faculté de droit de l'Université de Montréal. Notaire, il pratiqua sa profession à Montréal tout en faisant un peu de journalisme et en écrivant ses poèmes, après avoir espéré un moment faire une carrière de ténor de concert.

Il a publié deux recueils, *Le Coeur en exil* (1913) et *Dominantes* (1933), le premier de facture plus classique, le second manifestant que le poète a été influencé par les verlibristes. Chopin est surtout un poète de la nature, et un poète de l'hiver, ce qui lui donne une note typiquement canadienne. Mais il est aussi un artiste du vers qui sait user avec habileté des procédés usuels, et c'est pourquoi il a été si souvent apparenté à son ami Paul Morin. Il y a chez lui un pessimisme désabusé qui donne à son oeuvre une gravité qu'on ne retrouve pas chez le poète du *Paon d'émail*; moins parfait technicien que Morin, il est plus original que lui et son oeuvre est plus personnelle.

ADRIENNE CHOQUETTE (1915-). Née à Shawinigan Falls, Adrienne Choquette a étudié au couvent des Ursulines de Trois-Rivières et est publiciste au ministère de l'Agriculture de Québec. En 1939, elle a recueilli des *Confidences* *d'écrivains canadiens français*; elle a publié en volume quelques nouvelles, *La nuit ne dort pas* (1954), et deux romans qui sont pour ainsi dire l'envers l'un de l'autre: *La coupe vide* (1948) qui analyse le trouble que sème dans l'âme de quatre adolescents une femme séduisante, et *Laure Clouet* (1961), sa meilleur oeuvre, qui analyse le bouleversement qu'éprouve une vieille fille en découvrant l'amour réciproque que se portent deux jeunes mariés. Ce dernier roman, bref et discret, est un des récits les mieux écrits qui aient paru récemment en français au Canada.

ROBERT CHOQUETTE (1905-). Né à Manchester, New Hampshire, aux Etats-Unis, Choquette est arrivé au Canada à 8 ans et a étudié au Collège de St-Laurent et au Loyola College de Montréal. Journaliste, rédacteur en chef de la *Revue Moderne* (1928-1930), bibliothécaire de l'Ecole des Beaux-Arts de Montréal (1929-1931), Choquette a ensuite gagné sa vie en écrivant des romans pour la radio et la télévision. En 1942/43, il fut professeur invité au Smith College de Northampton, Massachusetts. Lauréat de nombreux prix, il est membre de l'Académie canadienne-française et de l'Académie Ronsard (Paris). En 1963, il a été nommé sous-commissaire de la Commission du Centenaire et, en 1965, consul général du Canada à Bordeaux.

Choquette est surtout connu comme poète, mais il a aussi publié des romans, *La Pension Velder* (1927), *Le Curé de village* (1936), *Les Velder* (1941) et *Elise Velder* (1958), qui sont des romans d'observation des moeurs canadiennes. Son oeuvre poétique comprend *A travers les vents* (1925), *Metropolitan Museum* (1931), *Poésies nouvelles* (1933) et *Suite marine* (1953): le tout a été réédité en 1956 sous le titre d'*Oeuvres poétiques,* avec quelques poésies inédites.

Choquette est un poète lyrique inspiré

par la force, la jeunesse, l'enthousiasme qui créé les oeuvres et pousse à l'aventure. Son oeuvre est celle d'un romantique impénitent et fougueux qui aime les sujets épiques ou, du moins, grandioses. Il a quelque peu atténué l'éclat excessif de ses poèmes de jeunesse dans l'édition définitive de 1956, mais il reste néanmoins un poète souvent grandiloquent qui abuse encore des procédés factices et usés dont Hugo fut le maître. Il y a dans cette oeuvre beaucoup de pages d'une emphase creuse, mais Choquette a souvent trouvé des images neuves pour chanter la nature canadienne, ou encore les grandes époques de l'humanité dans *Metropolitan Museum* et enfin tous les aspects de la mer un des plus considérables poèmes du Canada français, *Suite marine,* auquel il a travaillé vingt ans. Cet immense poème a de très belles parties, mais le poète a trop souvent développé laborieusement des thèmes usés avec des procédés conservateurs. On en trouvera l'essentiel dans le choix qu'en a fait André Melançon dans le Choquette de la collection des Classiques canadiens (1959).

EUGENE CLOUTIER (1921-   ). Né à Sherbrooke, il a étudié au Collège Saint-Charles Borromée, à l'Université Laval et à l'Université de Paris. Il a été successivement journaliste, réalisateur à Radio-Canada, directeur de la Maison Canadienne à Paris, et il écrit maintenant pour la radio et la télévision. Dans *Les Témoins* (1953), il analysait les réactions d'un meurtrier méditant sur son crime et le jugeant de divers points de vue. Son deuxième roman, *Les Inutiles* (1956) fait le procès de la civilisation matérialiste en évoquant avec ironie des personnages que leur attachement aux valeurs spirituelles ou à l'art gratuit rend inadaptés, inutiles. Le goût de l'analyse, de l'introspection, de la dissection qui rendait ses deux récits difficiles à suivre est poussé à la limite dans *Croisière* (1964) où les

mêmes thèmes sont abordés d'abord dans le rêve, puis dans la réalité d'une croisière propice aux poursuites amoureuses. Les romans d'Eugène Cloutier défient les règles du genre. Ils sont eux-mêmes des aventures où il peut arriver à chacun de se perdre dans la forêt des énigmes.

CHARLES NORRIS COCHRANE (1889-1945). Born in Omemee, Ontario, Cochrane graduated from Toronto and Oxford Universities and returned to teach Classics at Toronto. After service in the Tank Corps overseas during the First World War, he rejoined the University of Toronto in 1919. Although he published a biography, *David Thompson, The Explorer* (1924), and *Thucydides and the Science of History* (1929), he is best known for an interpretative philosophical work, *Christianity and Classical Culture: A Study of Thought and Action from Augustus to Augustine* (1940). Cochrane's range of scholarship and vigorous presentation of his views on Graeco-Roman civilization are an important contribution to Canadian letters.

EMILE CODERRE (1893-   ). Né à Montréal, Coderre a fait ses études au Séminaire de Nicolet et à l'Université de Montréal dont il a obtenu une licence en pharmacie et il a été longtemps secrétaire du Collège des pharmaciens de la province de Québec. Influencé par les symbolistes, il a d'abord écrit des poèmes en alexandrins traditionnels inspirés par l'amour et par la nature et réunis dans *Les signes sur le sable* (1922). Puis, influencé par les poètes populistes, et surtout par Jehan Rictus, il a écrit des pièces en langage populaire pour souligner les misères des petites gens et leur rêves toujours déçus et il a publié sous le pseudonyme de Jean Narrache: *Quand j'parl' tout seul* (1932), *Histoires du Canada* (1937), *Bonsoir les gars* (1948), *J'parl'*

tout seul quand Jean Narrache (1961)
et *Jean Narrache chez le diable* (1963).

FRED COGSWELL (1917-   ). Born in
East Centreville, New Brunswick,
Frederick William Cogswell served in
the Canadian army from 1940 to 1945.
On his return, he took his B.A. (1949)
and M.A. (1950) from the University of
New Brunswick. On receiving his Ph.D.
(1952) from the University of Edinburgh, he returned to teach English in
the University of New Brunswick. As
editor of *The Fiddlehead,* a principal
"little magazine" of Canadian verse
since 1945, he has been a leader among
the poets of the Maritimes. Several of
his books have appeared: *The Stunted
Strong* (1954), *The Haloed Tree* (1955),
a translation of *The Testament of
Cresseid* (1957) and *Lost Dimension*
(1960). His best poems, collected in
Descent from Eden (1959), concern the
people of the region around Fredericton
which is his home. His ballads and
fantasies, sonnets, epigrams and satires
and lyrics partly record, as he says,
"the struggle in [his] own mind between
an environmentally acquired Puritanism
and an outgoing nature which collided
with it." His collection of *Five New
Brunswick Poets* (1962) includes some
twenty of his own poems.

LEONARD COHEN (1934-   ). Born in
Montreal, Cohen was educated at
McGill and Columbia Universities. In
the best poems of *Let Us Compare
Mythologies* (1956) and *The Spice Box
of Earth* (1961), he writes with vigour
and perception on a wide range of
themes. Although his main concern
is love, he restricts his lyricism by
hobbling his metre to achieve not
dramatic colloquialism but a mixture
of the sensuous, the pedestrian and the
ornate. His novel *The Favourite Game*
(1963) records a Montrealer's revolt
against the culture of the Jewish community in which his family is

prominent. He has lived in recent years
on the island of Hydra off Greece, and
in Montreal. *Flowers for Hitler* (1964),
his third book of poems, is experimental, disturbing, and evidently
another step toward Cohen's self-
discovery. Another novel, *Beautiful
Losers*, appeared in 1966. A. W. Purdy,
"Leonard Cohen, a Personal Look,"
Can. Lit., 23 (Winter, 1965).

W. E. COLLIN (1893-   ). Born in County
Durham, England, William Edwin
Collin was educated at the Universities
of Toulouse (L. ès L. 1922) and Western Ontario (M.A. 1925) and was a
professor of Romance Languages at the
University of Western Ontario until his
retirement in 1960. A contributor to
The Canadian Forum, Collin won
recognition as an outstanding critic of
Canadian letters with his publication of
The White Savannahs (1936), including
pioneer studies of E. J. Pratt and the
contemporary Montreal poets. For
many years he wrote the annual survey
of French-Canadian publications in
The University of Toronto Quarterly.
Collin has produced a small volume
of poetry, *Monserrat and Other Poems*
(1930). He was elected F.R.S.C. in
1950.

LAURE CONAN (1845-1924). Née à La
Malbaie, Félicité Angers étudia chez les
Ursulines de Québec, puis vécut toute
sa vie à La Malbaie chez ses parents
d'abord, puis avec son frère. Sa vie est
celle de son oeuvre qu'elle a publiée tout
entière sous le pseudonyme de Laure
Conan. Elle fut la première femme de
lettres canadienne française et elle fut
surtout romancière, quoique elle ait
écrit quelques biographies. Ses romans
les plus connus sont des romans historiques d'une psychologie sommaire où
abondent tous les bons sentiments; *A
l'oeuvre et à l'épreuve* (1891), *L'Oublié*
(1900) et *La Sève immortelle* (1925)
nous donnent une vision idyllique du

passé. Elle avait publié dès 1884 le premier roman d'analyse canadien français, *Angeline de Montbrun,* roman épistolaire dont l'héroïne, à qui l'amour humain est refusé, trouve dans la contemplation mystique le remède à sa solitude désespérante. Ce roman a été réédité en 1950 avec une importante préface de Bruno Lafleur.

RALPH CONNOR. *See* Gordon, Charles William.

THOMAS B. COSTAIN (1885-1965). Born and educated in Brantford, Ontario, Thomas Bertram Costain became a reporter for the Brantford *Courier* and later for the Guelph *Daily Mercury.* After some years as editor of *Maclean's,* he left Canada in 1920 to join the staff of the *Saturday Evening Post.* In the mid-thirties, after some fourteen years with the *Post,* he became an editor of Doubleday, leaving that employ in 1946 to spend all his time in writing.

Costain's historical romances, beginning with *For My Great Folly* (1942), rapidly became best sellers. *Ride With Me* (1944), *The Black Rose* (1945), *The Moneyman* (1947), *The Silver Chalice* (1952, *Le calice d'argent,* 1955), *The Tontine* (1955, *La Tontine,* 1956), *Below the Salt* (1957), *The Darkness and the Dawn* (1959) and other books appeared in succession, all exhibiting Costain's ability to tell exciting stories fortified by painstaking historical research. His dramatic technique has been described as "centering his story around an outstanding figure neglected in the historical records." This method also is succesful when applied to more formal history, as in *The Magnificent Century* (1951).

In *High Towers* (1949), the setting is near Montreal and the adventures belong to the "fabulous Le Moyne family [Charles; Pierre, Sieur d'Iberville; and Jean-Baptiste, Sieur de Bienville] who became the heroes of French

Canada and founded the storied city of New Orleans." *Son of a Hundred Kings* (1950) is a novel of the 1890's, full of life and scenes in Balfour, a city which may be identified as Costain's own Brantford. *Chord of Steel* (1960) is the story of the telephone, which was invented by another resident of Brantford, Alexander Graham Bell. This volume, like many of his novels and the series on Canadian history which he edited for Doubleday, reflected Costain's particular interest in Canada's past.

JOHN COULTER (1888-   ). Born in Belfast, Ireland, John William Coulter attended the School of Art and School of Technology there as well as in Manchester. He was associated with John Middleton Murry in editing *The New Adelphi* from 1927-1930.

Since coming to Canada in the 'thirties, Coulter has published several plays and radio dramas, librettos for two operas with music by Healey Willan —*Transit Through Fire* (1942) and *Deirdre of the Sorrows* (1944), a biography, *Churchill* (1944), a novel, *Turf Smoke: A Fable of Two Countries* (1945), and a volume of poems, *The Blossoming Thorn* (1946). Among his earlier plays, *The House in the Quiet Glen* (1937) and *The Family Portrait* (1937), reveal his typically skilful use of Irish setting and legend. In *Riel,* first produced in 1950 and since revised for radio, Coulter presents the controversial "father of Manitoba," Louis Riel, with excitement and power.

ISABELLA VALANCY CRAWFORD (1850-1887). Born in Dublin, Ireland, Isabella Crawford emigrated with her family to Canada in 1858. Her father practised medicine at Paisley, then at Lakefield on the Kawartha Lakes, and later at Peterborough. After his death in 1875, Miss Crawford moved with her mother to Toronto. Here she wrote not only

[32]

poems but also short stories and novels on such popular subjects as cowboys, Indians and the opening of the great Northwest, which were designed to attract the readers of Toronto newspapers. In 1884 she published at her own expense a little book in cheap paper covers entitled *Old Spookses' Pass, Malcolm's Katie, and Other Poems*. Although the volume received some favourable comment from British reviewers, it was a financial failure. In 1886 her novel *The Little Bacchante* appeared in serial form in the Toronto *Evening Globe* a year before her sudden death.

It was not until a collected edition of her poems appeared in 1905 that Isabella Crawford's poetic merit was recognized. Further manuscripts in the Lorne Pierce Collection at Queen's University are attracting literary critics. Widely read in ancient and modern European—and even in Oriental—literature, she wrote, with a strong sense of the past and a steady view of life, of her new country, its bushland, cities and westward growth. Her poems are powerfully conceived, varied and fresh in their adaptation of Indian imagery for Canadian scenes. She ranges through the presentation of a cattle stampede in "Old Spookses' Pass," the haunting note of brief love lyrics like "The Rose" and the moving settlers' idyll of "Malcolm's Katie." Although many of her presentations of pioneer life are implausible and even melodramatic, her poetry is invariably exciting. As James Reaney remarks, "She was one of the first to translate our still mysterious melancholy dominion into the releasing apocalyptic dominion of poetry." J. W. Garvin, editor, *The Collected Poems of Isabella Valancy Crawford* (Toronto, 1905); Katherine Hale, *Isabella Valancy Crawford* (Toronto, 1923) James Reaney, "Isabella Valancy Crawford" in *Our Living Tradition*, 3rd series (Toronto, 1959).

DONALD CREIGHTON (1902-   ). Born in Toronto, Donald Grant Creighton graduated from the Universities of Toronto and Oxford, returning to the history department at Toronto in 1926. Winner of Guggenheim, Rockefeller and Nuffield Fellowships from 1940-1951, he published during this period several historical books and articles including *The Commercial Empire of the St. Lawrence* (1937), *British North America at Confederation* (1940; rev., 1963) and *Dominion of the North* (1944; revised 1957). He was elected F.R.S.C. in 1946 and for his outstanding contributions received the Society's Tyrrell Medal in 1951. He was given a Governor-General's Award for each volume of his definitive biography of John A. Macdonald: *The Young Politician* (1952) and *The Old Chieftain* (1955). In 1964 he published *The Road to Confederation: The Emergence of Canada 1863-1867*. Creighton has won recognition for his literary as well as his historical achievement. William Kilbourn, "The Writing of Canadian History," *Literary History of Canada* (1965).

OCTAVE CREMAZIE (1827-1879). Né à Québec, Claude Joseph Olivier (dit Octave) Crémazie fit ses études au Petit Séminaire de Québec, puis devint l'associé de ses frères Jacques et Joseph, libraires à Québec. A partir de 1854, il publia des poésies dans le *Journal de Québec* et, en peu de temps, acquit une petite gloire locale. Il se rendit plusieurs fois à Paris pour y acheter des livres pour la librairie, y dépensa largement et, devenu insolvable, fabriqua des faux. Menacé de poursuites judiciaires, il s'embarqua clandestinement pour la France en 1862 où, sous le nom de Jules Fontaine, il vécut pauvrement, à l'emploi d'un libraire, jusqu'à sa mort en 1879.

En 1882, Henri-Raymond Casgrain publia ses *Oeuvres complètes,* qui contiennent la plupart de ses poèmes, un *Journal du siège de Paris* qui n'est pas sans intérêt, et une partie de sa correspondance. C'est comme poète que Crémazie est célèbre au Canada et sa réputation lui vint de ce qu'il fut le premier à exprimer avec un certain art la nostalgie de la vieille France dans des pièces historiques et patriotiques qui sont presque du folklore. Il a exercé une grande influence sur les poètes de la deuxième moitié du dix-neuvième siècle, influence beaucoup plus considérable que ne le justifiait la qualité médiocre de son oeuvre. Le tome V des *Lettres canadiennes d'autrefois* de Séraphin Marion lui est consacré et Pierre-Georges Roy a écrit sa biographie (1945).

LOUIS ARTHUR CUNNINGHAM (1900-). Born in Saint John, New Brunswick, Cunningham graduated from St. Joseph's College, New Brunswick, where he took his B.A. and M.A. degrees. He did postgraduate work at the University of Washington and at Notre Dame.

Cunningham has been a prolific writer of romantic and historical novels and short stories. Of these, *Yvon Tremblay* (1927), a skilful story of French Canadian inhabitants of an Acadian village, and *Tides of the Tantramar* (1935), a love-story complicated by a family feud, are perhaps his best-known works. In addition to further novels, he has continued to produce short stories and articles for Canadian, English and Australian periodicals from his New Brunswick home.

ROY DANIELLS (1902-). Born in London, England, Daniells came to Canada in 1910 and was educated at the Universities of British Columbia (B.A. 1930) and Toronto (M.A. 1931, Ph.D. 1936). He has taught English at Victoria College, the University of Manitoba and the University of British Columbia, where he is Professor of English. He spent 1965-66 on leave in Italy.

Daniells has contributed scholarly articles and reviews to learned journals in Canada and the United States, and he has edited Thomas Traherne's sermons. His extraordinary sensitivity and taste, as well as his graceful style, give distinction to his articles and to his two books of verse, *Deeper into the Forest* (1948) and *The Chequered Shade* (1963). The first of these very thoughtfully deals with "the way in which we live, endure life, attain to life." The "green shade" of the "deep forest" is "the fortress heart of life." *The Chequered Shade* repeats the key word of shade. It employs the sonnet form with practised art and shows a deeply moved—but restrained—soul's responses to a changing world, to literature, and to a year of residence abroad, near the centres of classical culture. Daniells also completed *Milton, Mannerism and Baroque* (1963). In 1964 he received an honorary LL.D. from the University of Toronto. He was one of the editors of the *Literary History of Canada* (1965). Hugo McPherson, "Roy Daniells: Humanist," *British Columbia Library Quarterly*, 24 (July, 1960).

LOUIS DANTIN (1865-1945). Né à Beauharnois, Eugène Seers étudia au Séminaire de Montréal, passa un an au Séminaire d'Issy et, après avoir visité la France, l'Italie et la Belgique, entra chez les Pères du Très Saint Sacrement et fut ordonné prêtre. Etudiant à Rome, il y perdit la foi et y eut une liaison amoureuse. Secrétaire du supérieur de sa Congrégation, il vécut quelques années en Europe puis il rentra à Montréal; il passa encore quelques années au couvent et fréquenta l'Ecole littéraire de Montréal et s'y lia d'amitié avec Nelligan dont il publia les poésies en 1903 avec une importante préface.

Quelques-uns de ses propres poèmes parurent alors dans *Le Petit Message—du Très Saint Sacrement* sous le pseudonyme de Serge Usène. Mais il dut quitter la Congrégation et il s'exila aux Etats-Unis. Il eut une nouvelle aventure amoureuse et un fils lui naquit qu'il prénomma Adéodat. Employé par l'imprimerie de l'Université Harvard, il vécut le reste de sa vie à Boston où il mourut aveugle. Il avait peu à peu renoué des liens intellectuels avec le Canada et, de 1920 à 1940, il publia de nombreuses chroniques littéraires dont un grand nombre ont été recueillies en volumes. Il fut à cette époque un des principaux guides des jeunes poètes canadiens français et aucun critique n'a eu une influence égale à la sienne sur les poètes de la génération de Desrochers, Choquette et Simone Routier.

Dantin a écrit des nouvelles réunies dans *La Vie en rêve* (1930) et plusieurs de ses poèmes qui sont inspirés par son drame personnel ont été réunis dans *Le Coffret de Crusoë* (1932). La partie de son oeuvre qui a le moins vieilli, c'est toutefois son oeuvre critique qui a été recueillie dans quatre volumes: *Poètes de l'Amérique française* (1928, 1934) et *Gloses critiques* (1931, 1935). Mais plusieurs chroniques sont encore éparses dans les journaux et revues et seront sans doute rééditées par Gabriel Nadeau qui a entrepris la publication des papiers de Dantin dont le premier volume paru en 1962 contenait les poésies non reproduites dans *Le Coffret de Crusoë*. Lorsque tous ces papiers auront été édités, il sera possible de mieux juger de l'étendue et de la profondeur de l'action de Dantin sur l'évolution des idées littéraires au Canada français, surtout de 1920 à 1940. Il fut un des premiers critiques à juger des oeuvres selon leurs qualités littéraires et il a ainsi contribué à libérer la littérature d'un moralisme souvent superficiel et abusif.

En 1951, a paru *Les Enfances de Fanny,* roman autobiographique posthume qui manifeste sa profonde sympathie pour les noirs de Boston auxquels il s'était intéressé. Le Dr Gabriel Nadeau a publié un ouvrage sur Dantin (1948) qui renferme une partie de son intéressante correspondance.

PIERRE DAVIAULT (1899-1964). Né à Saint-Jérome, Daviault fut journaliste à *La Presse* et courriériste parlementaire à Ottawa avant de devenir traducteur (1925) et, depuis 1954, surintendant du Bureau des traductions du governa- ment du Canada. Ses travaux portent sur l'histoire, *La Grande Aventure de Lemoyne d'Iberville* (1935), *Le baron de Saint-Castin* (1939), et sur les problèmes de langage et de traduction, *Langage et traduction* (1961), *Dictionnaire militaire* (1945) et *Dictionnaire canadien* (1962), ces deux derniers en collaboration. En 1952, il fonda *La Nouvelle Revue canadienne* qu'il dirigea jusqu'à sa disparition en 1955. Membre de la Société royale du Canada, il en fut président en 1958-59. Il fut aussi président de la Société des Ecrivains canadiens de 1958 à 1961.

ROBERTSON DAVIES (1913-   ). Born in Thamesville, Ontario, William Robertson Davies was educated at Upper Canada College, Queen's University and Balliol College, Oxford (B.Litt. 1938). Remaining in England after graduation, he joined the Old Vic Repertory Company and did stage managing, some acting and directing as well as teaching in the Old Vic Theatre School. While in England he began his literary career with the publication of *Shakespeare's Boy Actors* (1939). On returning to Canada in 1940, Davies was appointed literary editor of the *Saturday Night* and in 1942 became editor and later publisher of the Peterborough *Examiner*. That same year he brought out his second work, *Shakespeare for Young Players* (1942).

A prolific writer, Davies continued his publication with *The Diary of Samuel Marchbanks* (1947) and *The Table-Talk of Samuel Marchbanks* (1949), two books of essays, originally begun as a series of articles in the Peterborough *Examiner,* full of wit and humour, satirizing and mocking contemporary Canadian morality and manners. Marchbanks, like Dr. Johnson, "loved tea, conversation and pretty women, and had not much patience with fools." Fascinated with the theatre, and having an intimate knowledge of the specific requirements of dramatic art, Davies produced in 1949 his witty and provocative *Fortune My Foe*, set in Kingston, *Eros at Breakfast and Other Plays,* comedies ridiculing stupidity and dullness, for which Tyrone Guthrie wrote an introduction, and *At My Heart's Core* (1950), based on the Rebellion of 1837 in Upper Canada.

In 1951 he brought out the first of a trio of novels built around the mythical town of Salterton and the local inhabitants. Entitled *Tempest-Tost* (1951), this amusing satire relates the efforts of the Salterton Little Theatre to produce Shakespeare's *The Tempest. Leaven of Malice* (1954), which won the Stephen Leacock Medal for Humour, was the second of the series and revolved around the life of a newspaper editor. Although its principal characters are different, many of the familiar figures from the first story reappear. Both of these novels are satires on Canadian provincialism and complacency, which the author attempts to discredit and ridicule by light-hearted raillery and caricature. In the third book, *A Mixture of Frailties* (1958), after beginning with the familiar setting and characters, Davies shifts his locale to London, Paris and Wales, and his heroine, the gifted but vulgar village soprano, is transformed into a sophisticated woman of the world. Although thoroughly entertaining, this story is less closely knit in construction and more diffuse than his previous novels.

Davies continued to write plays and collaborated with Tyrone Guthrie and Grant McDonald on three books, *Renown at Stratford* (1953), *Twice Have the Trumpets Sounded* (1954) and *Thrice the Brinded Cat Hath Mew'd* (1955), describing the Stratford Shakespearean Festival's objectives, productions and achievements from its inception in 1953. Appropriately he presented the lecture on Stephen Leacock in *Our Living Tradition* (1957). In *A Voice from the Attic* (1961), he published a further collection of essays, the theme of which he announced as "reading," directed to the "clerisy" who read with some pretention to taste. The style of these essays on a variety of subjects is characterized by Davies's shrewd observation and exuberant humour. In 1961 he was awarded the Lorne Pierce Medal for his contribution to Canadian literature.

In addition to his lectures at Trinity and University Colleges of the University of Toronto, and his numerous articles on literary criticism and social comment in *Saturday Night*, Kingston's *Whig-Standard* and the Peterborough *Examiner,* Davies wrote for some time a monthly column "A Writer's Diary" which appeared in several Canadian newspapers and *The Philadelphia Bulletin.* He was appointed Master of Massey College, University of Toronto, in 1962, and in 1963 published a children's play *A Masque of Mr. Punch.* Hugo McPherson, "The Mask of Satire," *Can. Lit.*, 4 (Spring, 1960); [Samuel Marchbanks], "The Double Life of Robertson Davies," *Liberty* (April, 1954) and *Canadian Anthology* (1966); Ivon Owen, "The Salterton Novels," *Tamarack Review,* 9 (Autumn, 1958); M. W. Steinberg, "Don Quixote and the Puppets," *Can.Lit.*, 7 (Winter, 1961).

WILLIAM ARTHUR DEACON (1890-   ). Born at Pembroke, Ontario, Deacon matriculated at Stanstead College, P.Q., attended the University of Toronto for two years, and graduated with an LL.B. from the University of Manitoba in 1918. He practised law in Winnipeg until 1922, when he was appointed literary editor of the Toronto *Saturday Night,* and subsequently launched its famous supplement "The Bookshelf." During this period he published *Pens and Pirates* (1923), *Peter McArthur* (1924), *Poteen* (1926) and *The Four Jameses* (1927).

As bookman, essayist and journalist, Deacon has contributed articles and reviews to national and foreign magazines and journals. He is best known as literary editor of the *Mail and Empire* (1928-1936) and *The Globe and Mail* (1936-1961) in which his column "The Fly Leaf" appeared. His books include *My Vision of Canada* (1933), *Literary Map of Canada* (1935) and *SH-H-H . . . Here Comes the Censor* (1940).

GUY DELAHAYE (1888-   ). Né à Saint-Hilaire, Guillaume Lahaise étudia au Séminaire de Saint-Hyacinthe et à la faculté de médecine de l'Université de Montréal. Médecin, il fit un stage d'études à l'Institut Pasteur de Paris. Aliéniste, il a pratiqué à Saint-Jean de Dieu et il a enseigné à la faculté de médecine de l'Université de Montréal.

Sous le pseudonyme de Guy Delahaye, il a publié deux recueils de poésies: *Les Phases* (1910), un des meilleurs livres de poésie du Canada français, fait de très brefs poèmes d'un symbolisme hardi et d'une concision de forme qui touche au prodige; et *Mignonne, allons voir si la rose* (1912), divertissements saugrenus indignes de son talent. S'il a continué à écrire, il n'a cependant rien publié depuis cinquante ans. Il y a un bon article sur lui dans Marcel Dugas, *Littérature canadienne* (1929).

MAZO DE LA ROCHE (1885-1961). Born in Toronto, Mazo de la Roche was an only child of Irish, French and English United Empire Loyalist background. She was educated at various schools in Toronto and in Galt and later, when prevented by ill health from entering the University of Toronto, she attended classes at the School of Art. A period of some years spent with her family on a fruit and stock farm on the shore of Lake Ontario between Toronto and Hamilton was an important formative influence on the future novelist, as were the games of fantasy peopled with richly imagined characters in which she and her beloved cousin, Caroline, constantly engaged.

Miss de la Roche began her writing career with short stories and one-act plays, the former published in various American magazines, the latter performed in Toronto's Hart House Theatre. Three of these—*Low Life, Come True* and *The Return of the Emigrant*—were collected and published in 1925.

Three early books—*Explorers of the Dawn* (1922), a collection of stories, *Possession* (1923), a first novel in which she experimented with the Ontario lakeside setting, and *Delight* (1926), in which she manipulated various eccentric characters—were followed by *Jalna* (1927), which won an *Atlantic Monthly* prize from among twelve thousand entries. *Jalna* established its characters, the Whiteoak family, and its setting, a spacious lakeside Ontario farm, firmly in the minds of a large reading public. It is well-constructed: the setting is meticulously and evocatively described; all the characters are strongly individualized and at least two of them, the matriarchal Adeline and her grandson Renny, must be counted among memorable characters in twentieth-century fiction, in charm and brilliance if not in depth of portrayal. *Jalna* presents an attractive, if non-existent, rural squirarchal way of life

maintained in spite of the encroach-
ments of democratic materialism.

In the subsequent novels of the
series, Miss de la Roche spun out the
lives of her characters and their
descendants, with *Whiteoaks of Jalna*
(1929), *Finch's Fortune* (1931), *The
Master of Jalna* (1933), *Young Renny*
(1935), *Whiteoak Harvest* (1936),
Whiteoak Heritage (1940), *Wakefield's
Course* (1941), *The Building of Jalna*
(1944), *Return to Jalna* (1946), *Renny's
Daughter* (1951), *Variable Winds at
Jalna* (1954), and *Morning at Jalna*
(1960). All are available in French
translation.

The series' success does not depend
solely on the loyalty of a reading public
who were as enchanted by the Whiteoaks as was Miss de la Roche herself.
Skilful characterization, setting and
description raise some of them,
particularly *Whiteoaks of Jalna* and
The Building of Jalna, close to the
distinction of *Jalna* itself. No Canadian
novelist of her time has been more
popular in Europe.

The sequence was interrupted from
time to time for other works: *Portrait
of a Dog* (1930), a series of animal
sketches; *Lark Ascending* (1932), a
novel with a Sicilian setting; *Beside
a Norman Tower* (1934), children's
tales; *Growth of a Man* (1938) and
The Two Saplings (1942), both novels
of a predominantly psychological bent.

For some years, Miss de la Roche
lived in England with her lifelong
companion and the young brother and
sister whom she had adopted. From
time to time she returned to Canada for
lengthy visits, and in her later years
"Windrush Hill" at York Mills became
her permanent home. A major source
of pleasure to the authoress was the
adaptation of *Whiteoaks of Jalna* for
the stage and its successful runs in
London and New York, with Nancy
Price and then Ethel Barrymore playing
the role of Adeline Whiteoak.
E. K. Brown, "The Whiteoaks Saga,"

The Canadian Forum, XII (October,
1931); Mazo de la Roche, *Ringing the
Changes* (Toronto, 1957); Dorothy
Livesay, "The Making of Jalna, A
Reminiscence," *Can. Lit.,* 23 (Winter,
(1965); B. K. Sandwell, "The Work of
Mazo de la Roche," *Saturday Night,*
LXVIII (Nov. 8, 1952).

JAMES DE MILLE (1836-1880). Born in
Saint John, New Brunswick, the son of
a merchant and long-time governor of
Acadia College, De Mille was educated
at Horton Academy, Acadia College
and Brown University. His own life
as a young schoolboy was later captured in his entertaining stories for
boys, the "B.O.W.C." (Brethren of the
White Cross) and the Young Dodge
Club series, produced over a period of
several years.

De Mille spent some years in business before becoming Professor of
Classics at Acadia (1861) and of
English Literature at Dalhousie (1864).
He was the prolific author of some
thirty books, the first of which was
Martyr of the Catacombs (1865). His
works of melodrama and comedy were
both popular and profitable in his lifetime. *The Dodge Club* (1869), which
tells of the visit he made as a student
to Italy, and is similar in treatment to
Twain's later *Innocents Abroad,*
illustrates De Mille's genial manner.
Better known perhaps is *A Strange
Manuscript Found in a Copper Cylin-
der* (1888), a vividly Gothic satire on
society's vulgar pursuit of wealth and
fame, which was published posthumously. His only poetic venture,
Behind the Veil: A Poem (1893), a dull
descriptive vision of the world, was
unsuccessful.

De Mille's fictional style is engagingly
rapid-fire and daringly extravagant.
Like Twain and later Leacock, he
endeared himself to his readers by such
spontaneously witty and exaggerated
sketches as "Minnehaha Mines." His

reputation in this vein won him the distinction of being included in Twain's "Library of American Humour." W. G. MacFarlane, *New Brunswick Bibliography* (Saint John, 1895); A. Mac-Mechan, "De Mille the Man and the Writer," *Canadian Magazine,* XXVII (Sept. 1906).

EDMOND DE NEVERS (1862-1906). Né à la Baie-du-Febvre, Edmond Boisvert dit de Nevers étudia au Séminaire de Nicolet. En 1888, il partit pour Berlin et y étudia l'histoire, l'anthropologie, la sociologie et l'économie. Disciple de Mommsen, il s'intéresse à tout, voyage en Italie, en Espagne et au Portugal et apprit, outre l'italien, l'espagnol, le portugais et l'allemand, le russe et le norvégien. De 1892 à 1900, il fut rédacteur à l'Agence Havas à Paris et y poursuivit ses recherches et ses travaux. Il y a traduit deux pièces d'Ibsen et, plus tard, rentré au Canada, *Civilization in the United States* de Matthew Arnold. Il nous a laissé deux ouvrages curieux, pleins d'aperçus originaux, brillants ou faux sur *L'Avenir du peuple canadien-français* (1896) *et sur L'Ame américaine* (1900). Sa pensée était souvent confuse, mais il fut un des premiers à étudier systématiquement la condition nord-américaine des Canadiens français à la lumière de l'histoire, des pressions sociales, des facteurs économiques et des valeurs culturelles. Beaucoup de ses pages sont encore pleines d'actualité.

MERRILL DENISON (1893-   ). Born in Detroit, Denison studied at the Universities of Toronto, Pennsylvania and Paris. After service with the French and American armies during the First World War, he returned to Toronto where he participated in the activities of the Hart House Theatre. His *Brothers in Arms* (1923), a hilarious presentation of a pompous business man stuck in the northern bush, and his collection of four realistic comedies in *The Unheroic North* (1923) did much to encourage the development of native drama.

Denison has written many plays as well as various works in the field of economic history dealing with Canadian subjects. Among these, *Boobs in the Woods* (1927), sixteen dramatic sketches satirizing backwoods life, *Henry Hudson and Other Plays* (1931), a collection of six historical plays written for the radio, his biographical *Klondike Mike* (1943), and several well-documented histories of corporations like Massey-Harris (1946) and Molsons (1955) are his most familiar publications.

GONZALVE DESAULNIERS (1863-1934). Né à Saint-Guillaume (Yamaska), Désaulniers a étudié au Collège Sainte-Marie et à l'Université de Montréal dont il est sorti licencié en droit. Avocat, il a dirigé un journal radical *Le National* (1889-1896) et s'est toujours occupé de littérature et des relations culturelles entre la France et le Canada. Membre de l'Ecole littéraire de Montréal, longtemps président de l'Alliance française de Montréal, il a été membre de la Société royale du Canada et, en 1923, il a été nommé juge à la Cour Supérieure de Québec. En 1918, il avait publié un poème patriotique *Pour la France,* et il a recueilli ses poèmes dans *Les Bois qui chantent* (1930).

Cette poésie est toujours d'inspiration romantique et l'auteur a été visiblement marqué par Vigny et surtout par Lamartine. Poète de la nature, il chante les bois et la mer avec sentimentalité et, parfois, il évoque avec tendresse les vicissitudes des indigènes délogés par les Blancs. Son lyrisme annonce celui qu'on allait retrouver dans les grands poèmes d'Alfred DesRochers.

ALFRED DESROCHERS (1901-   ). Né à
Saint-Elie d'Orford, Desrochers
exerça divers métiers manuels avant
d'entreprendre des études secondaires
interrompues au bout de trois ans. Il
exerça alors d'autres métiers avant de
devenir journaliste à *La Tribune* de
Sherbrooke. En 1942, il s'engagea dans
l'armée canadienne et, en 1944, il fut
quelque temps traducteur à Ottawa. Il
habite maintenant Montréal.

Desrochers est l'auteur d'un grand
nombre de poèmes parus dans les
journaux et revues ou encore inédits.
Il n'a publié que deux recueils,
L'Offrande aux vierges folles (1928) et
A l'ombre de l'Orford (1929), ce
dernier réédité en 1948 avec treize
sonnets, *Le Cycle du village,* inspirés
par les métiers manuels du pays. Il
y a dans cette oeuvre deux manières:
des sonnets parnassiens d'un réalisme
pittoresque et d'une rare perfection de
forme; de longs poèmes lyriques où
s'entremêlent le sentiment de la nature
et les émotions religieuses du poète.
Desrochers est non seulement un des
plus parfaits techniciens du vers au
Canada français, il atteint par moments
à une grandeur qui en fait un des plus
puissants poètes d'aujourd'hui. S'il y
a dans son oeuvre de nombreuses pièces
inspirées par l'amour, et d'autres qui
sont des petits tableaux de moeurs, de
grands poèmes comme l'*Hymne au
Vent du nord, Je suis un fils déchu* ou
Prière ont un souffle qui s'accorde aux
grands espaces vierges dont il a senti
l'appel et qui donne à sa poésie une
santé, une force, une virilité uniques ici.
La littérature dite du *terroir* est dépas-
sée ici; cette poésie est spécifiquement
nord-américaine, mais elle l'est d'une
manière qui débouche sur l'universel.
Elle ne l'est pas seulement par le choix
des sujets traités, mais aussi et surtout
par la sensibilité de l'auteur qui est
celle des pionniers. On a publié en 1963
des fragments de son *Retour de Titus,*
65 stances royales inspirées par l'amour
de l'empereur pour Bérénice.

Desrochers a aussi publié des critiques littéraires, *Paragraphes* (1931).
L'Office national du Film a réalisé un
documentaire sur lui (1960).

LEO-PAUL DESROSIERS (1896-1967). Né
à Berthierville, Desrosiers a étudié au
Séminaire de Joliette et à l'Université
de Montréal dont il était licencié en
droit. Journaliste, il a été courriériste
parlementaire du *Devoir* à Ottawa,
rédacteur du feuilleton et des procès-
verbaux de la Chambre des communes
et, de 1941 à 1953, conservateur de la
Bibliothèque municipale de Montréal.
Depuis dix ans, il prit sa retraite en
1955 et vécut l'hiver à St-Sauveur-des-
Monts et, l'été, en Gaspésie. Il a épousé
Antoinette Tardif, romancière qui a écrit
sous le nom de Michelle Le Normand.
Membre de l'Académie canadienne-
française, il a été membre de la Société
royale du Canada de 1942 à 1953.

Desrosiers est l'auteur des meilleurs
romans historiques écrits en français au
Canada. Il s'est d'ailleurs toujours
intéressé à l'histoire et a publié
L'Accalmie (1937) sur l'influence de
Durham; *Commencements* (1939)
études sur les postes de traite et sur
les relations des Blancs et des Indiens,
et *Iroquoisie* (1947). Membre des Dix,
il a aussi publié plusieurs études dans
leurs cahiers. Ses nouvelles *Ames et
paysages* (1922) et *Le Livre des mys-
tères* (1936) ne valent pas ses romans.
Le premier, *Nord-Sud* (1931) évoque le
malaise économique du milieu du
dix-neuvième siècle et révélait un
écrivain de qualité. Le second est sans
doute son oeuvre la plus forte: *Les
Engagés du Grand Portage* (1938)
reconstitue la lutte des grandes com-
pagnies de fourrures au début du
dix-neuvième siècle et analyse la
montée de l'ambition dans l'âme de
Nicolas Montour. C'est un roman dur
et puissant. Il y a a plus de poésie dans
Les Opiniâtres (1941) qui raconte les
débuts de Trois-Rivières sous la menace
iroquoise. En général, ses romans histo-

riques sont parfaitement documentés, mais ils sont aussi vivants, ils font revivre une époque et ils sont d'une écriture précise et forte.

Ses romans de moeurs contemporaines (*Sources*, 1942, et *Vous qui passez,* 1958-1961) sont moins bons malgré de bons passages. Le récit lyrique qui est presque un poème en prose *L'Ampoule d'or* (1951) est une exception dans son oeuvre qu'il a voulue réaliste et objective. Ce récit d'inspiration mystique renferme des pages d'une poésie intense. Desrosiers reste, en définitive, le maître du roman historique au Canada français.

RICHARD DIESPECKER (1907-   ). Born in England, Richard E. Alan Diespecker came to Canada in 1908. Educated in South Africa and British Columbia, he graduated from the University of British Columbia and for a number of years was a reporter for several British Columbia papers. *Prayer for Victory* (1943) and *Between Two Furious Oceans, and Other Poems* (1944) reflect his experiences during World War II. On his return from overseas service, he resumed his connection with broadcasting and was active in writing and producing radio dramas and Jubilee shows for Vancouver, Nelson, Trail and Burnaby. Among the later works to win him recognition are the documentary *Battle of the Fraser* (1949) and two novels *Elizabeth* (1950) and *Rebound* (1953).

ALBERT DREUX (1887-1949). Né à Sainte-Thérèse-de-Blainville, Albert Maillé a étudié au Séminaire de Sainte-Thérèse et à l'Ecole des Hautes Etudes commerciales de Montréal; journaliste, il collabora à plusieurs journaux de Montréal et fut pendant vingt ans directeur de *L'Action médicale.* Sous le pseudonyme d'Albert Dreux, il a publié deux recueils de poèmes, *Les Soirs* (1910) et, beaucoup supérieur au pre-

mier, *Le Mauvais Passant* (1920). Il fut un des premiers poètes canadiens à utiliser le vers libre et il reste un de ceux qui y ont le mieux réussi. Dreux fut surtout le poète idéaliste qui chante la hantise d'un monde parfait dans un univers où règne le laid.

WILLIAM HENRY DRUMMOND (1854-1907). Born in Ireland, Drummond emigrated to Canada with his family at an early age. By his own effort and ambition, he put himself through high school and university, graduating from Bishop's College with his M.D. in 1884. Although his writing was done during the course of a successful medical practice in Montreal, it was his early experience as a telegraph operator and later as a country doctor that made him familiar with the life of rural Quebec which he portrays in his poetry.

A member of the then fashionable school of the regional idyll, Drummond became its sole poetic exponent. In his poems he tried to express the humour, pathos and whimsicality of the Provincial French Canadian, who refused to be stirred out of his traditional values and ways of life despite the rising vigour of the nineties. His first volume of poems *The Habitant and Other French-Canadian Poems* appeared in 1897. It was given prestige by an introduction by the French-Canadian poet Louis Fréchette, who had high praise for this new genre of Canadian poetry; such poems as "De Bell of St. Michele" and "The Wreck of the 'Julie Plante'" won immediate popular success.

Although the dialect, or "patois," of his verse has been criticized as being no language at all, obviously Drummond was making a sincere attempt to represent and describe what he himself had observed of the Quebec habitant, and to do so with sympathy and understanding. Acutely aware of the racial barrier which existed between French- and English-speaking Canada, he felt that his presentations of the French-

[41]

Canadian people might serve in some way to lower this barrier. While some French-Canadians have considered his work an aspersion upon the intelligence of their race, there is no patronizing element in Drummond's affectionate portrayals, even though the modern reader may find their sentimentality naïve. *Johnny Courteau and Other Poems* (1901) and *The Voyageur and Other Poems* (1905) illustrate his ability to achieve dramatic effect by a skilful blend of humour and pathos. He was a lover of nature, particularly that of the Laurentian region, and his descriptions are direct and striking. The literary interest of Drummond's work lies in its particular quality of regional whimsicality. His collected poetical works were published in 1912 and 1926. R. H. Craig, "Reminiscences of W. H. Drummond," *Dalhousie Review,* 5 (July, 1925); Mary Harvey Drummond, Biographical Sketch of W. H. Drummond in *The Great Fight* (New York and Toronto, 1908); J. F. MacDonald, *William Henry Drummond* (Toronto, n.d.); R. E. Rashley, "W. H. Drummond and the Dilemma of Style," *Dalhousie Review* 28 (January, 1949).

MARCEL DUBÉ (1930-   ). Né à Montréal, Dubé étudia au Collège Sainte-Marie et à la faculté des lettres de l'Université de Montréal. Depuis 1951, il a écrit pour la scène et pour la télévision plusieurs pièces qui comptent parmi les meilleures du répertoire canadien. Il a publié *Zone* (1953), *Le Temps des lilas* (1958), *Un simple soldat* (1958), *Florence* (1960). Parmi les pièces qui ont été jouées mais qui n'ont pas été publiées, on relève: *Le bal triste* (1951), *De l'autre côté du mur* (1953), *Une nuit perdue* (1954), *Chambre à louer* (1955), *Le Barrage* (1956), *Le Naufrage* (1956) et *Les Beaux Dimanches* (1965). Dubé a fait un carrière d'écrivain de théâtre à laquelle nulle autre ne peut encore être comparée au Canada français.

Le sujet varie évidemment d'une pièce à l'autre mais, sauf dans *Le Temps des lilas* qui est une oeuvre de commande et qui est d'une tendresse et d'une poésie qui ne vont pas sans artifices, on retrouve dans toute l'oeuvre de Dubé la même atmosphère et le même style. Ces tranches de vie réalistes qui manifestent un sens aigu de l'observation mettent en scène des humbles, des petits que la vie a blessés et qui ont perdu leurs illusions en découvrant, en devenant hommes et femmes, que la vie est laide. Il y a chez tous ses jeunes personnages une révolte contre l'avilissement de l'homme qu'ils découvrent autour d'eux et leurs plus vives réparties sont les cris de l'animal blessé qui ne comprend pas pourquoi il est atteint. L'auteur éprouve à l'égard de ses personnages les plus déshérités une sympathie réelle et profonde, mais cet amour n'empêche pas son oeuvre d'être foncièrement pessimiste. Ses personnages ne parviennent pas à s'épanouir dans leur milieu et la seule solution que Dubé a trouvée à leur problème est la fuite, ce qui n'est pas une solution. Cette oeuvre révèle chez l'auteur un sens inné du théâtre et l'art du dialogue qui est juste de ton; on aimerait parfois que le langage des personnages soit moins vulgaire et plus correct: la vérité est parfois l'ennemie de l'art.

Dubé a aussi publié quelques nouvelles et il a écrit de nombreux poèmes qui sont encore presque tous inédits. Jean-Paul Vanasse a étudié son théâtre dans *Liberté* (novembre-décembre 1959).

RODOLPHE DUBE. *Voir* Hertel, François.

LOUIS DUDEK (1918-   ). Born in Montreal of Polish-Canadian parents, Dudek was raised in the industrial East End of the city. He attended McGill, and published his early poems while a graduate student at Columbia University. One of the poets included in *Unit of Five* (1944), he brought out his own *East of the City* in 1946. From 1946 to 1951 he served as an instructor of English at City College, New York. His association with the poets Irving Layton and Raymond Souster resulted in the collaboration of the three in the publication of the collection *Cerberus* (1952). The group also promoted and published experimental poetry through the medium of Contact Press.

The Searching Image, Twenty-Four Poems and an excellent anthology *Canadian Poems: 1850-1952* appeared in 1952. *Europe,* a series of ninety-nine brief "cantos" describing a journey back to the European roots of our culture, was published in 1955, the year of its author's graduation from Columbia with a Ph.D. in English and Comparative Literature. Continuing his academic career as an Assistant Professor at McGill University, he published *The Transparent Sea* (1956), a further volume of poetry.

Dudek's early work places some emphasis on Marxist ideas, but in general his poetry has little of the harshness and didacticism usually associated with social criticism. Nor is there a marked intellectual quality in his writing; the over-all effect is one of lyrical simplicity. He depends largely on a sensitive power of observation which is expressed directly, often in a single image, with a kind of wistful naïveté. There is a distinct similarity to Ezra Pound in much of his work. As an admirer of Pound, he tends to emulate the mannerisms of the older poet, particularly in the style of the "travelogue" poem *Europe.* Dudek displays, however, an individual skill and strength and a capacity for arousing emotion through the melodic use of words.

Predominant in *The Transparent Sea* are poems on love. Dudek excels when he is portraying either mood or movement, as he does in many of these love-songs. There is an immediacy in his imagery, and a personal flavour of great loneliness and longing.

A regular contributor of critical articles and studies to various literary publications, he has produced one full-length critical work *Literature and the Press* (1960). In 1957 he became editor and publisher of *Delta,* a poetry magazine, and in 1958 published two volumes of poetry: *En México,* a single poem of about 1,000 lines, is a meditative "travelogue" similar to *Europe,* but in over-all quality less successful than the earlier work; and *Laughing Stalks,* a light literary and social satire, including parodies of various Canadian poets and critics, which reveals a delightful and versatile sense of humour. Tony Emery, Review of *Literature and the Press* in *Can. Lit.,* 9 (Summer, 1961); Wynne Francis, "A Critic of Life: Louis Dudek as Man of Letters," *Can. Lit.,* 22 (Autumn, 1964); Northrop Frye, "Letters in Canada: 1956," *UTQ,* XXVI (April, 1957); Desmond Pacey, Review of *Laughing Stalks* and *En México* in *The Fiddlehead,* 40 (Spring, 1959).

MARCEL DUGAS (1883-1947). Né à Saint-Jacques-de-l'Achigan, il a étudié au Collège de l'Assomption et à l'Université Laval. Attaché aux Archives du Canada à Paris, il y a vécu la plus grande partie de sa vie, fréquentant les écrivains et leurs oeuvres autant que les documents historiques qui l'intéressaient peu. Avant tout esthète, influencé par la poésie symboliste, il a publié des proses lyriques souvent hermétiques, parfois alambiquées mais où se trouvent aussi des pages opulentes comme *Feux de Bengale à Verlaine glorieux* (1915) ou *Paroles en liberté* (1944); et des essais critiques impressionnistes, désordonnés et souvent gratuits qui nous éclairent plus sur lui-même que sur les écrivains dont il commentait les oeuvres: *Littérature canadienne* (1929), *Approches* (1942). Son *Louis Fréchette* (1934) est plus objectif.

ROGER DUHAMEL (1916-   ). Né à Hamilton, Duhamel a étudié au Collège Sainte-Marie et à l'Université de Montréal dont il est licencié en droit. Secrétaire du maire Camilien Houde (1938-1940), il opta ensuite pour le journalisme et fut rédacteur au *Canada* (1940-1942), au *Devoir* (1942-1944) et à *La Patrie* (1944-1947) avant de devenir directeur de *Montréal-Matin* (1947-1953), puis rédacteur en chef de *La Patrie* (1953-1959). Il est imprimeur de la Reine depuis 1960.

En plus de commenter quotidiennement les événements nationaux et internationaux, Duhamel n'a jamais cessé d'exercer son métier de critique littéraire avec goût et facilité et ses chroniques littéraires comptent parmi les meilleures des vingt dernières années. Il en a recueilli quelques-unes dans *Les moralistes français* (1947) et dans *Littérature* (1948). Ses *Lettres à une Provinciale* (1962) commentent l'actualité avec beaucoup de finesse et de modération. Il a aussi publié *Aux sources du romantisme français* (1964) et *Lecture de Montaigne* (1965).

Président de la Société Saint-Jean-Baptiste de Montréal (1943-1945), il fonda le Prix Duvernay; il fut président de la Société des Ecrivains canadiens de 1955 à 1958. Il est membre de l'Académie canadienne-française depuis 1949 et a été élu à la Société royale du Canada en 1959.

FERNAND DUMONT (1927-   ). Né à Montmorency, il a étudié à l'Université Laval où il enseigne la sociologie; et à l'Université de Paris. Esprit curieux de tout, il s'intéresse autant à la biologie, à la philosophie des sciences et à la littérature qu'à la sociologie et aux problèmes religieux. Il a publié en 1952 un recueil de poésies, *L'Ange du matin*, poésie tout intérieure, plutôt désincarnée, plutôt aride, sans nulle rhétorique, dans laquelle il exprime sa solitude, son inadaptabilité au monde, mais aussi une constante attente du miracle. Après diverses études éparses dans nos revues, il a publié en 1964 ce qui est peut-être le plus grand ouvrage religieux écrit au Canada français, *Pour la conversion de la pensée chrétienne,* dans lequel il fait la critique des institutions, analyse diverses attitudes devant le surnaturel et soutient que le christianisme authentique est une incarnation, sans cesse vécue et renouvelée, du pécheur dans le monde à tranformer. Ce grand livre est en voie de traduction dans plusieurs langues. Dumont est membre de la Société royale du Canada.

NORMAN DUNCAN (1871-1916). Born in Brantford, Ontario, Duncan entered the University of Toronto in 1891, where he participated in literary activities. After two years on the staff of the *Auburn Bulletin* (New York), he worked from 1897 to 1900 for the *New York Evening Post*. Then he spent four summers as correspondent for *McClure's Magazine* on the Newfoundland and Labrador coasts, which later furnished the most congenial material for his fictions. His first published book *The Soul of the Street* (1900) was a collection of short stories about the Syrian section of New York.

After teaching from 1901 to 1906 at Washington and Jefferson College, he went to the Middle East in 1907 as correspondent for *Harper's Magazine*. He returned to take a position as an English professor at Kansas University and then once more, in 1912/13, he travelled in the Far East for *Harper's*. In his short stories for boys—such as *Battle Royal* and *Down North*—Duncan excels in his descriptions of fishing villages on the Labrador coast. His best tales deal with fishermen and the sea: *The Way of the Sea* (1903) and *Doctor Luke of the Labrador* (1904). A prolific writer, he could produce magnificently realistic passages, but his works have an uneven quality. Influenced by Dickens and Bret Harte, Duncan is often sentimental and melodramatic in his style.

SARA JEANNETTE DUNCAN (1861-1922). Born in Brantford, Ontario, Miss Duncan was educated locally and at the Normal School in Toronto. For a while she taught school, and during the eighties became a journalist, writing a column for the Toronto *Globe*, Montreal *Star* and Goldwin Smith's *The Week*. In 1890 she published her first novel *A Social Departure: How Orthodocia and I Went Round the World by Ourselves*, a series of travel sketches which was acclaimed for its literary polish, humour, gentle whimsy and satire. In 1891 she married Everard Charles Cotes, Curator of the Indian Museum in Calcutta.

In India, Miss Duncan produced more than a dozen novels. *The Simple Adventures of Memsahib* (1893) reveals her keen observation of Indian life both inside and outside the English community there. In most of these novels the setting is foreign, although some like *Cousin Cinderella: A Canadian Girl in London* (1908) reflect her Canadian background. One novel in particular, *The Imperialist* (1904), is thoroughly Canadian and undoubtedly inspired by her early experiences in Brantford. As Claude T. Bissell has pointed out, it illustrates the belief of Miss Duncan in "the eternal irony created by the conflict between manners and customs, on the one hand, and human desires and aspirations, on the other." Her cosmopolitan and sophisticated treatment of this theme reflects her reading of Henry James, but she does a skilful switch by portraying the new world as having a salutary and corrective influence on old world concepts of social decorum. Despite some flaws in style, this novel—because of its lively tone, rich description and penetrating criticism of life—continues to retain its appeal.

After more than twenty years in India, and several trips around the world, Sara Jeannette Duncan eventually returned to England, where she lived in Chelsea and wrote plays. Manuscripts of these plays are now in the library of the University of Western Ontario. She died at Ashtead, Surrey, and is buried there beside the parish church. Claude T. Bissell, Introduction to *The Imperialist* (Toronto, 1961). Rae Goodwin, "The Early Journalism of Sara Jeannette Duncan, with a Chapter of Biography," U. of T. thesis, 1964; M.E.R. (Mrs. Sandford Ross), "Sara Jeannette Duncan, Personal Glimpses," in *Can. Lit.*, 27 (Winter, 1966).

MABEL DUNHAM (1881-1957). Born at Harriston, Ontario, Bertha Mabel Dunham graduated from the University of Toronto and McGill Library School and in 1908 became Librarian of the Kitchener Public Library. In 1924 she published *The Trail of the Conestoga* based on Ezra E. Eby's *The History of Waterloo Township*, which portrays with warmth and humour the migration of the Pennsylvania Mennonites to Waterloo County in the newly established colony of Upper Canada. *Toward Sodom* (1927) and a children's book *Kristli's Trees* (1948) are also devoted to the Mennonites, her mother's people. *The Trail of the King's Men* (1931), dedicated to the Dunhams, "whose Loyalist ancestors came to the St. John River on a refugee ship in 1783," tells the story of the Loyalist Johnsons of the Mohawk Valley. *Grand River* (1945) is a descriptive book full of regional history.

WILLIAM DUNLOP (1792-1848). Born at Greenock, Scotland, William ("Tiger") Dunlop became an Army Surgeon and served in Canada during the War of 1812 at Prescott, Gananoque, Cornwall, Niagara and the Penetanguishene Road. His *Recollections of the American War* (1905), which first appeared in the

[45]

Literary Garland (1847), is a lively account of this period of his life.

After spending some time as a journalist in Calcutta, India, he was invalided home as the result of a fever. *Blackwood's Magazine* published some of his articles, and he became one of the Edinburgh literary set and a popular lecturer in medical jurisprudence at the University. Then, in London, he edited *The Telescope*, a Sunday newspaper, through one exciting year. In 1826 he came to Canada with the title "Warden of the Forests" in the Canada Company venture under John Galt.

He and his brother Captain Robert Dunlop settled at Goderich where their home "Gairbraid" shortly became equally famous for its hospitality and its eccentric and colourful hosts. Under the *nom de plume* "A Backwoodsman," he published *Statistical Sketches of Upper Canada* in 1832, a vigorous and whimsical description of conditions in Upper Canada, written to mock distorted information given to prospective immigrants. During this period he was a frequent contributor to newspapers and journals and the most famous literary figure in the colony. War memoirs, travel literature and political journalism were refreshed by his contributions.

Violently opposed to the rebels who hoped to overthrow the government in 1837, Dunlop acted as leader of a loyal regiment from Huron County; his address to his troops on their disbanding is one of the most vivid examples of Canadian patriotic rhetoric. In 1841 he became a member of the Legislature for Huron, retaining his seat until 1846. At his death he left a wealth of legend centring around his home and his eccentricities, and a Will which is one of the curiosities of Surrogate literature. W. H. Graham, *The Tiger of Canada West* (Toronto, 1962); C. F. Klinck, *William "Tiger" Dunlop* (Toronto, 1958); Kathleen and Robina Lizars, *In the Days of the Canada Company* (Toronto, 1896); Robina and Kathleen Lizars, *Humours of '37* (Toronto, 1897).

EVELYN EATON (1902-   ). Born in Switzerland of Canadian parents, Evelyn Sybil Mary Eaton published her first book of collected poems *Stolen Hours* in 1923. Her first novel *The Encircling Mist* (1925) was based on her life as a writer for a Paris film studio. With *Quietly My Captain Waits* (1940), a historical romance about the conflict between the French and English colonists, she became popular with Canadian readers. Miss Eaton, who is a professor of French in California, became an American citizen in 1945 but spends her summers in Nova Scotia. Her published works include several historical romances, children's books, travel and personal essays, a collected volume of verse *Birds before Dawn* (1942) and two biographies *Every Month Was May* (1947) and *The North Star Is Nearer* (1949).

PELHAM EDGAR (1871-1948). Born in Toronto of a distinguished Canadian family, Oscar Pelham Edgar graduated from the University of Toronto in 1892 and took his doctorate at Johns Hopkins University in 1897 in modern languages. He was Professor of English at Victoria University from 1902 to 1938. His understanding of Classical, French and English Victorian principles of criticism was combined with genuine taste and acumen. These qualities helped him and others to make steady progress across the bridge to a modern and distinctive Canadian literature. Notable among his friends, colleagues and students were Carman, Roberts, D. C. Scott, Marjorie Pickthall, E. J. Pratt, J. D. Robins, Douglas Bush, Raymond Knister, E. K. Brown and Northrop Frye.

In addition to scholarly articles and reviews, Edgar wrote important studies of *Henry James, Man and Author* (1927) and *The Art of the Novel from 1700 to the Present Time* (1933). Founder of the Canadian Writers' Foundation, he was elected F.R.S.C. (1915) and received in 1936 the Lorne Pierce Medal for his contribution to Canadian letters. His memoirs *Across My Path* were edited in 1952 by Northrop Frye.

ROBERT ELIE (1915-   ). Né à Montréal, Elie étudia au Collège Sainte-Marie et à la faculté des lettres de l'Université de Montréal. Journaliste, il a collaboré à *La Presse,* au *Canada* avant d'entrer au service de la Société Radio-Canada. Critique d'art, il a publié une brochure sur *Borduas* (1943) et commenté maintes expositions d'abord dans *La Relève* dont il fut une des principaux collaborateurs, puis dans les journaux et revues auxquels il a été attaché. Directeur de l'Ecole des Beaux-arts de Montréal (1957-1961), puis directeur de l'enseignement des arts dans la province de Québec (1961), il est nommé en 1962 attaché culturel à la Maison du Québec à Paris. En 1966, il devient directeur associé du Bureau du bilinguisme au Conseil privé à Ottawa. Membre de la Société royale du Canada, il a publié avec Jean Le Moyne, les poésies complètes et le journal de Saint-Denys-Garneau auquel il a consacré plusieurs essais pénétrants.

Son premier roman *La Fin des songes* (1950, *Farewell My Dreams,* 1954) est un des meilleurs romans d'analyse parus au Canada français. C'est l'étude subtile et pleine de sympathie de la déchéance spirituelle et morale d'un homme impuissant à trouver une réponse à la question essentielle du sens de la vie et de son aboutissement au suicide. Le même sens du spirituel, le même besoin des êtres en quête de lumière et d'amour et la même douleur de se retrouver toujours seuls se retrouvent dans son deuxième roman *Il suffit d'un jour*

(1957) qui est un échec, ainsi que dans sa pièce *L'Etrangère* (*Ecrits du Canada français,* no 1). Il a aussi écrit des poèmes qui n'ont pas été recueillis en volume, non plus que ses essais.

EUDORE EVANTUREL (1854-1919). Né à Québec, Evanturel étudia au Petit Séminaire de Québec et fut tour à tour journaliste, secrétaire de Parkman et archiviste chargé de recueillir des manuscrits concernant l'histoire du Canada à Boston et à Washington. En 1878, il avait publié ses *Premières poésies* qui furent aussi les dernières et qui renferment quelques pièces réussies inspirées par la tristesse des hivers canadiens.

R. G. EVERSON (1903-   ). Born in Oshawa, Ontario, Ronald Gilmour Everson graduated in economics from the University of Toronto in 1927 and was called to the Ontario bar in 1930. He began publishing poetry as an undergraduate and has continued writing throughout his career as a lawyer and executive of a Montreal public relations firm. He has produced four significant volumes of poetry: *Three Dozen Poems* (1957); *A Lattice for Momus* (1958); *Blind Man's Holiday* (1963), with drawings by Colin Haworth; and *Wrestle with an Angel* (1965).

Everson's verse is characterized by compression, skilful use of metrics and whimsical humour. He artfully juxtaposes the disparities of contemporary life with unexpectedly apt analogies from the past to present the changeless aspects of human experience. His pervading outlook is explicitly stated in "credo":

Passionate human love, the scenes of
    nature,
agony of bringing into life
child, or thought, or sound, or shaped
    colour
—these triumph over our lives' horror.

CLAIRE FAUCHER. *Voir* Martin, Claire.

FAUCHER DE SAINT-MAURICE (1844-1897). Né à Québec, Narcisse Henri Edouard Faucher étudia au Séminaire de Québec et, en 1864, s'engagea dans l'armée de Maximilien et participa à la guerre du Mexique où il fut blessé. Rentré à Québec, il obtint un emploi de greffier au Conseil législatif qu'il résigna, en 1881 pour se faire élire député de Bellechasse à l'Assemblée législatif. En 1890, il redevint greffier au Conseil législatif. Il avait aussi été journaliste et il a beaucoup voyage aux Etats-Unis et en Europe. Il a représenté la Société des Gens de lettres au Canada et il fut un des membres fondateurs de la Société royale du Canada.

Il a publié un grand nombre d'ouvrages de toutes sortes: traités d'art militaire, biographies, récits de voyages, contes, essais littéraires, ouvrages de linguistique. Il a touché à tout avec facilité et sans rien approfondir. Ses meilleures pages se trouvent dans des récits de voyage et des mémoires (*Deux ans au Mexique,* 1878; *Loin du pays,* 1889) et dans ses contes (*A la veillée,* 1878); mais la plus grande partie de son oeuvre est gâtée par un romantisme artificiel.

ALBERT FERLAND (1872-1943). Né à Montréal, Ferland reçut une éducation privée sommaire et fut dessinateur d'abord à son compte, puis à partir de de 1910, pour le ministère des Postes. Un des premiers membres de l'Ecole littéraire de Montréal, il en fut président. Il fut élu membre de la Société royale du Canada.

Son oeuvre poétique est assez abondante, mais les bonnes pages y sont assez rares: les meilleures sont celles que lui inspirent la forêt et les Indiens. Il fut un des plus actifs représentants de l'école du *terroir* et son inspiration est essentiellement canadienne. Il a publié cinq recueils groupés sous le titre collectif *Le Canada chanté.* Ses autres recueils sont inférieurs.

JEAN-BAPTISTE ANTOINE FERLAND (1805-1865). Né à Montréal, il étudia au Collège de Nicolet où il enseigna l'histoire et la philosophie, après avoir été ordonné prêtre en 1828. En 1854, il fut nommé professeur d'histoire à l'Université Laval; il y fut plus tard doyen de la faculté des Arts. Son oeuvre principale est son *Cours d'histoire du Canada* en deux volumes (1861-1865). Ses oeuvres mineures sont plus vivantes.

JACQUES FERRON (1921-). Né à Louiseville, Ferron a étudié au Séminaire de Trois-Rivières et à l'Université Laval. Médecin, il a pratiqué d'abord dans l'armée (1945/6), puis en Gaspésie et, depuis 1949, à Ville Jacques Cartier. Il a écrit des pièces et des nouvelles dans lesquelles il a moqué avec humour les moeurs canadiennes dont il est un fin observateur. Esprit original et mordant, il s'est appliqué à combattre les idées reçues et toute son oeuvre a une saveur anarchique peu commune au Canada français. Ses pièces sont *L'Ogre* (1949), *Le Licou* (1953), *Le Dodu* (1956), *Tante Elise* (1956), *Le Cheval de Don Juan* (1957), *Les Grands Soleils* (1958), *La tête du roi* (1963). En 1962, il a publié d'excellents contes, *Cotnoir* et *Contes du pays incertain* qui lui valurent un Prix du Gouverneur général. Ses *Contes anglais et autres* (1964) sont pleins de traits désinvoltes et insolites. Ce moraliste est un satiriste impénitent. Mais dans *La Nuit* (1965) il y a du meilleur et du pire, comme dans *Papa Boss* (1966).

JEAN FILIATRAULT (1919-). Né à Montréal, Filiatrault est directeur des services français de l'agence de publicité Vickers et Benson de Montréal. Il a publié des romans d'analyse qui trahissent l'influence de Mauriac et dont les personnages se torturent réciproquement parce qu'ils s'aiment trop, notamment ses mères et ses fils. Il a publié *Terres stériles* (1953), *Chaines* (1955), *Le Refuge impossible* (1957) et *L'Argent est odeur de nuit* (1961). Il a aussi écrit une pièce *Le Roi David* qui a été représentée à la télévision. Président da la Société des écrivains canadiens en 1961-1962, il a été élu à la Société royale du Canada en 1961.

ROBERT FINCH (1900-   ). Born in Freeport, Long Island, Robert Duer Clayton Finch studied at the University of Toronto. As an undergraduate he received in 1924 the Jardine Memorial Prize for poetry. Following three years postgraduate study in Paris, he returned to Canada to lecture in French at the University of Toronto. He was one of the six poets represented in *New Provinces* (1936). The first collection of his own verse, entitled *Poems,* was published in 1946 and won a Governor General's Award. The poetry included in this volume shows a strong sense of form, ironic wit, an intellectual interpretation of modern urban life, and an intensity derived through economy and restraint of expression. Finch is at his best in sonnets and in brief, epigrammatic pieces which give adequate rein to his gift for satire, and at the same time require delicacy and precision.

Neatness of expression is again evident in *The Strength of the Hills,* his second volume of poems, which appeared in 1948. Here his affinity with the metaphysical poets is apparent, and although his use of word associations and conceits is occasionally too facile, his quiet assurance and accuracy maintain a simple dignity throughout.

Finch published *A Century Has Roots* (1953), a masque in commemoration of the hundredth anniversary of Toronto's University College, and in 1960 brought out two separate volumes of new poems. The first of these, *Acis in Oxford,* which earned him a second Governor General's Award, is a series of meditations on a performance of Handel's *Acis and Galatea* and uses the myth in relation to ethics, aesthetics and emotion. Nature and humanity are interpreted in terms of sensation; the impression conveyed is one of power and sincerity with academic fineness, gentle humour and elegant taste. Finch's interests and accomplishments in art and music are apparent in his poetry.

Dover Beach Revisited also appeared in 1960. A set of variations on the theme of Matthew Arnold's "Dover Beach," the collection is more varied in style than *Acis in Oxford* and ends with a group of religious poems. Less urgent in tone, the verse maintains the same poetic excellence. *Silverthorn Bush and Other Poems* (1966) is another notable collection of his elegant, penetrating and witty observations on life. Finch was elected F.R.S.C. in 1963. Roy Daniells, "Earle Birney et Robert Finch," *Gants du Ciel,* XI (Spring, 1946); John Peter, Review of *Dover Beach Revisited, Can. Lit.,* 12 (Spring, 1962); A. J. M. Smith, "Turning New Leaves," *The Canadian Forum,* XXVII (May, 1947); George Woodcock, Review of *Acis in Oxford, Can. Lit.,* 13 (Summer, 1962).

R. A. D. FORD (1915-   ). Born in Ottawa, the son of Arthur R. Ford, distinguished editor of the *London Free Press,* Robert Arthur Douglas Ford was educated at the University of Western Ontario and Cornell University. Since graduation he has served in many positions with the Canadian Department of External Affairs, and is now Ambassador to Russia. His book of poems, *A Window on the North* (1956), based on his intelligent and mature interpretation of aspects of life not only in Canada but also in South America and Russia, included early translations of Pasternak and won a Governor General's Award. Another collection of new poems and some translations of contemporary Russian poets is forthcoming.

JULES FOURNIER (1884-1918). Né a Coteau-du-Lac, Fournier étudia au Séminaire de Valleyfield et entra en 1903 comme journaliste à *La Presse*. En 1904, il passa au *Canada* comme courriériste parlementaire et, en 1908, devint directeur du *Nationaliste*. Poursuivi par Sir Lomer Gouin pour libelle diffamatoire, il fut emprisonné pour trois mois en 1909 et écrivit des *Souvenirs de prison*. En 1910, Bourassa fonda *Le Devoir* et Fournier et Asselin y devinrent rédacteurs. Partageant les vues nationalistes de Bourassa, il résigna néanmoins quelques mois plus tard en alléguant qu'il ne jouissait pas d'une entière liberté d'expression. Après un séjour en Europe, il fonda *L'Action* (1911-1916), un hebdomadaire qu'il dirigea cinq ans et qui est un des meilleurs journaux jamais publiés au Canada français. Nommé traducteur au Sénat en 1917, il travaillait à la fondation d'une revue littéraire lorsqu'il mourut en 1918. Il avait trente-trois ans.

Une partie de son oeuvre a été réunie par sa veuve dans *Mon encrier* (1922) et Asselin a publié en 1920 l'*Anthologie des poètes canadiens* compilée par Fournier. En 1904, il avait écrit un roman paru en feuilleton dans *Le Canada*. Fournier fut un des meilleurs journalistes que le Canada français ait produits. Il a écrit sur nos moeurs politiques et sur quelques personnages de son époque des articles d'une encre peu commune au pays. Polémiste de premier ordre, il avait le sens du ridicule au plus haut point et il savait trouver des mots qui frappaient pour abattre les fausses idoles. Il fut aussi un des meilleurs critiques littéraires que le Canada français ait encore eus et certains de ses articles sur des écrivains médiocres sont des modèles de satire et d'ironie. Adrien Thério lui a consacré un livre (1954).

WILLIAM SHERWOOD FOX (1878-1967). Born in New York State, Fox moved to Canada in 1889. Educated at McMaster University and the universities of Geneva and Johns Hopkins, he taught both in Canada and the United States before becoming Professor of Classics (1917), and later President (1927-1947) of the University of Western Ontario. In addition to his scholarly volume, *The Mythology of Greece and Rome* (1916), Fox has contributed numerous articles to various journals on educational, archeological, classical and botanical subjects. He is best known, however, for his works on Western Ontario, *'T Ain't Runnin' No More* (1946), *St. Ignace, Canadian Altar of Martyrdom* (1949), *The Bruce Beckons* (1952) and *Silken Lines and Silver Hooks* (1954). In these he described with charm and humour the colourful characters and events of local history. He was elected F.R.S.C. in 1922 for his literary contributions. His fostering of Western's French Summer School at Trois Pistoles and the School of Indian Archeology in the Penetanguishene area is further evidence of his broad scope of interest in Canadian culture and lore. *Sherwood Fox of Western* (1964) is an autobiography and a personal history of the University of Western Ontario during the years of expansion while he was President. He died on August 15, 1967.

LOUIS FRECHETTE (1839-1908). Né à Lévis, Louis Honoré Fréchette étudia au Séminaire de Québec, au Collège de Sainte-Anne de la Pocatière et au Séminaire de Nicolet avant d'entreprendre ses études de droit à l'Université Laval. Lorsqu'il fut admis au barreau en 1864, il avait déjà manifesté un goût très vif pour la littérature, il avait fréquenté la librairie Crémazie et il avait publié son premier recueil de poésies *Mes loisirs* (1863). Avec un frère, il lança à Lévis en 1865 deux journaux éphémères et devant son insuccès, il décida d'aller chercher fortune aux Etats-Unis et s'exila à Chicago en 1866. Déjà fasciné par Hugo qu'il imitera toute sa vie, il semble qu'il ait comparé son propre exil à celui du poète français et, de 1866 à 1869, il publia des *Voix d'un exilé* où il exprima sa rancoeur comme l'avait fait Hugo dans *Les Châtiments*. Il travailla pour l'Illinois Central Railway, fit du journalisme, puis décida de rentrer au pays et se mit à la pratique du droit à Lévis en 1871. Il fut élu député de Lévis à la Chambre des communes (1874-1878), mais sa carrière politique fut courte et il revint à la poésie. En 1889, il fut nommé greffier du Conseil législatif et, en plus de poursuivre son oeuvre littéraire, il collabora à divers journaux, notamment à *La Patrie* au temps de Beaugrand. Il fit quatre voyages en France, en 1880, 1887, 1894 et 1898 et, en 1882, il fut un des membres fondateurs de la Société royale du Canada dont il fut président en 1900. Il fut aussi président de l'Ecole littéraire de Montréal et fit ériger un monument à Crémazie en 1906. Il avait publié des contes, fait jouer des pièces de théâtre et surtout il était l'auteur de la somme poétique la plus importante du dix-neuvième siècle au Canada français. Il fut considéré par ses contemporains comme le poète lauréat du Canada français. On a publié en volume en 1961 ses *Mémoires intimes* qui avaient paru dans *Le Monde illustré* en 1900. C'est un document révélateur non seulement sur lui, mais sur son époque.

Ses premiers poèmes ne le distinguent guère des poètes du temps, et *La Voix d'un exilé* est une imitation trop servile de Hugo. Les pièces qu'il a recueillies dans *Pêle-Mêle* (1877) n'auraient pas suffi à établir sa renommée solidement. Mais il s'affirme déjà comme un poète de la nature et un chantre patriotique supérieur à ses prédécesseurs dans *Fleurs boréales* (1879) et *Oiseaux de neige* (1881). L'oeuvre, toutefois, qui

consacra son talent et sur laquelle repose sa gloire est sans contredit *La Légende d'un peuple* (1887), suite de poèmes épiques qui célèbrent les grandes dates de l'histoire du Canada, comme Hugo avait chanté *La Légende des siècles*. Il y a dans cette oeuvre beaucoup de pages gâtées par les défauts habituels de l'auteur—grandiloquence, emphase, rhétorique creuse, hyperbole —mais lorsqu'il est à son meilleur, il atteint à une beauté réelle comme il l'avait laissé prévoir par un des plus beaux poèmes des *Fleurs boréales: La Découverte du Mississippi*. Il atteint parfois à des mouvements poétiques d'une vigueur rare au Canada français et certaines de ses images laissent une forte impression. Il a aussi publié deux autres recueils de poésies: *Feuilles volantes* (1890) et *Epaves poétiques* (1908) qui ont les mêmes défauts sans toujours avoir les mêmes qualités. Il reste que Fréchette fut la grande voix poétique de sa génération.

Il a aussi publié des drames en prose et en vers qui tombent dans le ridicule, notamment *Véronica*; des oeuvres de polémique et surtout des contes dont les meilleurs plaisent par leur pittoresque et leur bonhommie: *Originaux et détraqués* (1892). Son oeuvre en prose a été étudiée par George A. Klinck (1955) et les meilleurs livres sur lui sont ceux de Henri d'Arles (1923) et de Marcel Dugas (1934). Les pamphlets de son rival Chapman, *Le Lauréat* (1892) et *Deux copains* (1894), sont trop inspirés par la jalousie pour être justes, mais ils ont constitué une page animée de la vie des lettres à la fin du dix-neuvième siècle dont la victime fut précisément celui qui avait été le plus grand homme de lettres de sa génération au Canada français. Fréchette est encore considéré communément comme le poète national du Canada français.

GUY FRÉGAULT (1918-   ). Né à Montréal, Frégault étudia au Collège de

Saint-Laurent, au Collège Jean-de-Brébeuf, à l'Université de Montréal dont il est licencié ès lettres, et à l'Université Loyola de Chicago où il prit un doctorat en histoire (1942). Il entra alors aux Archives de la province de Québec, mais accepta dès l'année suivante d'être professeur d'histoire à l'Université de Montréal. En 1946, il est nommé directeur de l'Institut d'histoire et, en 1950, devient vice-doyen de la faculté des lettres. En 1959, il accepte le poste de directeur du département d'histoire à l'Université d'Ottawa et, en 1961, il devient le premier sous-ministre du nouveau ministère des Affaires culturelles de la province de Québec. Membre de l'Académie canadienne-française, il reçut la médaille Tyrrell de la Société royale du Canada en 1961 et le Prix Duvernay en 1944.

En plus de compiler, avec Michel Brunet et Marcel Trudel, une *Histoire du Canada par les textes* (1952) Frégault a publié cinq ouvrages, tous importants: des biographies d'*Iberville le conquérant* (1944) de *François Bigot, administrateur français* (1949) et de Vaudreuil, *Le Grand Marquis* (1952), ainsi qu'une description de *la Civilisation de la Nouvelle France* (1944) à la veille de la conquête anglaise et une étude détaillée de *La Guerre de la conquête* (1955). Frégault croit que l'histoire est une science exacte et, comme les Allemands, aime à dépouiller toutes les sources et à multiplier les autorités pour chaque fait ou interprétation. Par là, son oeuvre a un caractère un peu lourd. Mais il possède le sens de la synthèse et sait dégager l'essentiel de la forêt des détails. Il possède aussi une langue robuste et vivante qui anime ses sujets. On a longtemps insisté dans l'étude de notre passé sur ses aspects militaire et politique; Frégault a su leur ajouter les aspects social, économique et culturel pour nous donner une idée plus globale de la vie aux époques qu'il a étudiées.

NORTHROP FRYE (1912-   ). Born in Sherbrooke, Quebec, Herman Northrop Frye graduated with honours from Moncton High School and entered a local business college. In Toronto for a typewriting contest, he decided to continue his education there. He entered Victoria College in 1929 and came under the influence of Pelham Edgar, John D. Robins and E. J. Pratt. In 1933 he graduated in Philosophy and English and entered Emmanuel College. Ordained in the United Church of Canada in 1936, Frye left Toronto for a preaching mission in Saskatchewan. After receiving a scholarship from the Royal Society of Canada, he was admitted to Merton College, Oxford, where he was tutored by the poet Edmund Blunden. He graduated from Oxford in 1940, and after a year in Canada returned to England for further study before joining the English Department of Victoria.

A contributor since 1936 to *The Canadian Forum,* and subsequently editor-in-chief for several years, Frye has published some hundred articles, essays and critical reviews in the learned journals of Canada, the United States and Great Britain. These writings deal with a variety of topics, notably painting, music and theories of literary criticism and cultural history. Some of these reflect Frye's particular interest in the mythopoeic. As he notes in "Yeats and the Language of Symbolism" (*UTQ,* XVII, 1947), "Just as the teacher of a language is a grammarian, so one of the functions of the literary critic is to be a grammarian of imagery, interpreting the symbolic system of religion and philosophy in terms of language." His first book *Fearful Symmetry, A Study of William Blake* (1947), dedicated to Pelham Edgar and offering "an explanation of Blake's thought and a commentary on his poetry," established Frye as a foremost authority on Blake.

From 1950 to 1960 he wrote the

annual survey of Canadian poetry for "Letters in Canada," *University of Toronto Quarterly*. In 1951 he was elected F.R.S.C. He edited *Across My Path* (1952), Pelham Edgar's Memoirs, in which one section is devoted to Frye's own contribution to creative criticism in Canada.

His second book, *Anatomy of Criticism* (1957), with its comprehensive examination of criticism under the headings of Historical (Modes), Ethical (Symbols), Archetypal (Myths) and Rhetorical (Genres), won Frye international recognition as one of the most influential critics in America. Distinguished visiting professor and foundation lecturer at many American universities, he was honoured with the Lorne Pierce Medal in 1958 for his outstanding contribution to Canadian Literature. In *The Arts in Canada* (1958), he wrote the section dealing with Canadian poetry since World War II. His editions include Blake's *Selected Poetry and Prose*, Pratt's *Collected Poems, Sound and Poetry* (English Institute Essays, 1956), Shakespeare's *Tempest*, a selection from Byron in *Major British Writers* and a text of Milton. He prepared for publication and edited in 1962 the late Peter F. Fisher's study of "Blake as Prophet and Revolutionary," *The Valley of Vision*. In 1963 he published three critical works: *T. S. Eliot* ("Writers and Critics" series); *Fables of Identity, Studies in Poetic Mythology;* and *The Well-Tempered Critic*. Two of his recent books are important studies of Shakespeare, *A Natural Perspective* (1965), and of Milton, *The Return of Eden* (1965). He was one of the editors of the *Literary History of Canada* (1965).

From 1959 until 1966 Frye was Principal of Victoria College, Toronto. His published addresses, *Culture and the National Will* (1957), *By Liberal Things* (1960) and *The Educated Imagination* (1963) reveal not only his pungent wit and powerful idiomatic style, but also his vast erudition, wisdom and understanding of the educational process. He is now University Professor of English in the University of Toronto. In his complete devotion to the arts and humanities he has had an incalculable influence in stimulating a new generation of Canadian poets. Pelham Edgar, "Creative Criticism in Canada," in *Across My Path* (Toronto, 1952); Eli W. Mandel, "Toward a Theory of Cultural Revolution," *Can.Lit.*, 1 (Summer, 1959); A. J. M. Smith, "The Critic's Task: Frye's Latest Work" [*The Well-Tempered Critic*], *Can. Lit.*, 20 (Spring, 1964).

JOHN GALT (1779-1839). Born in Ayrshire, Scotland, Galt was educated there and at Greenock. After some time in London, he travelled in the Near East and Europe, promoting trade for several British firms. During this period he wrote articles, a biography, plays and fiction. His power as a story teller won recognition with the publication in *Blackwood's Magazine* of *The Ayrshire Legatees* (1820), the adventures of a Scottish minister and his family in London, related in the form of a number of diverting letters. This was followed by his masterpiece *The Annals of the Parish* (1821) depicting with authenticity and humour the life of a Scottish pastor and his parish, and by other appealing studies of Scottish character. Other novels followed in quick succession, *The Provost* (1822), *Sir Andrew Wylie* (1822) and *The Entail* (1823). The full list is a long one. Galt also had popular success with his life of Lord Byron (1830).

Galt's contributions to literature in Canada were made between 1826 and 1829, while he was Superintendent of the Canada Company, operating chiefly in the Huron Tract between Guelph and Goderich. "But when my numerous books are forgotten," he wrote, "I shall yet be remembered. . . . I contrived the Canada Company, which will hereafter be spoken of among the eras of a nation destined to greatness." Some of his Canadian experiences are recorded in his *Autobiography* (1833) and *Literary Life and Miscellanies* (1834). Through his association with Dr. William "Tiger" Dunlop and his ceremonious founding of Guelph, he gained a place in Upper Canadian legend. Two of his novels, *Lawrie Todd* (1830) and *Bogle Corbet* (1831), both of which are set principally near the head of Lake Ontario, on the American or the Canadian side, display what Erik Frykman has called Galt's "conscious blend of social description and character-drawing." This fiction was also designed to give information and advice to self-reliant settlers, especially Lowland Scots, emigrating to western New York state and, preferably, Upper Canada. Jennie W. Aberdein, *John Galt* (London, 1936); R. K. Gordon, *John Galt* (Toronto, 1920); Carl F. Klinck, "John Galt's Canadian Novels," *Ontario History*, 49 (Autumn, 1957); Harry Lumsden, *The Bibliography of John Galt* (Glasgow, 1931); D. M. Moir, Memoir in *Blackwood's Standard Novels,* Vol. I; Hamilton B. Timothy, "Preamble to a Psychological Biography of John Galt," *Ontario History,* II, No. 4 (December, 1964).

ALFRED GARNEAU (1836-1904). Né à Québec, fils de l'historien, Garneau étudia au Séminaire de Québec et à l'Université Laval. Il fut admis au barreau en 1860 et s'intéressa dès lors aux lettres. Il écrivit des poèmes qui ne furent recueillis en volume qu'après sa mort, *Poésies* (1906). En 1874, il devint traducteur au Sénat et le resta jusqu'à sa mort. Il édita la quatrième édition de l'*Histoire du Canada* de son père. Garneau fut surtout un poète élégiaque, le premier au Canada dont l'oeuvre fut inspirée surtout par ses sentiments intimes à une époque où presque toute la poésie était patriotique

et historique. Il a le ton triste de Sully-Prudhomme et quelques-unes de ses poésies comptent parmi les meilleures du dix-neuvième siècle au Canada.

FRANCOIS-XAVIER GARNEAU (1809-1866). Né à Québec, Garneau étudia avec François-Joseph Perrault qui lui donna sans doute le goût de l'histoire. Il entra ensuite comme clerc chez Archibald Campbell qui s'intéressa à lui et lui ouvrit sa bibliothèque qui était une des plus considérables de la colonie. Un client de Campbell cherchant un compagnon pour un voyage qu'il allait entreprendre à Halifax, Saint John, Boston, New York, Albany, Buffalo et Toronto, le notaire lui recommanda d'amener Garneau et c'est ainsi que le futur historien visita le nord des Etats-Unis et les provinces maritimes. Ayant terminé son apprentissage, Viger qui y représentait l'assemblée Garneau devint notaire en 1830 et, l'année suivante, partit pour l'Europe. A Londres, il devint le secrétaire de l'Assemblée législative du Bas-Canada et il y resta deux ans, allant à Paris pendant les vacances. Il a raconté ce *Voyage en Angleterre et en France* (1855).

Rentré au Canada en 1833, il exerça le notariat tout en écrivant des poésies et en collaborant aux journaux de Québec. Il semble qu'il ait été tenté par la politique un moment et il participa à la rédaction des Quatre-vingt-douze résolutions. Il travailla dans une banque, fut traducteur à l'Assemblée législative et, en 1845, devint greffier de la ville de Québec, poste qu'il occupa jusqu'à 1864. En 1848, il fut nommé membre du Conseil d'instruction publique et en 1855, fut élu président de l'Institut canadien de Québec. Il souffrait d'épilepsie et, à la fin de sa vie, fut réduit à une activité limitée.

Garneau fut non seulement le plus grand historien canadien du dix-neuvième siècle, mais il fut le meilleur écrivain de sa génération. Ses poésies sont les meilleures qui aient été écrites au Canada français avant Crémazie. Son récit de voyage est un intéressant document sur sa formation et sur son temps. Mais ce qui lui a mérité sa gloire, c'est son *Histoire du Canada* à laquelle il travailla pendant plus de vingt-cinq ans, corrigeant jusqu'à la fin une oeuvre qui était pourtant déjà remarquable. Dès 1836, il commença à publier dans *Le Canadien* des récits historiques. Lorsque Durham écrivit que les Canadiens n'avaient pas d'histoire, il décida de le réfuter en prouvant le contraire et il entreprit la composition de son *Histoire du Canada* dont la première édition parut en trois volumes (1845-1848). Il en publia des éditions corrigées en 1852 et 1859 et il travaillait à une nouvelle édition au moment de sa mort.

Influencé par Montesquieu, Thierry, Macaulay et Gibbon, il en vint néanmoins à considérer Tacite comme le maître par excellence. En grande partie autodidacte, Garneau a néanmoins réussi à écrire un livre qui n'a guère vieilli. Sans doute, il n'a pu prendre connaissance des sources découvertes après lui et il n'a pas connu tous les détails du passé qui sont familiers à l'historien d'aujourd'hui. Mais il a saisi l'essentiel des personnages et il a, en général, découvert les lignes de force et les faiblesses de la colonie, ainsi que les principes de la politique impériale de la France et de l'Angleterre. Il a aussi apporté une attention considérable à la vie du peuple canadien lui-même. Il avait de plus le don de la synthèse et son histoire est une succession de tableaux qui font le tour d'un sujet ou d'une époque. Enfin, il écrivait une langue nettement supérieure à celle de la plupart des écrivains canadiens de son temps et son histoire est un des rares livres de cette génération qu'on puisse encore lire avec profit et plaisir.

Garneau fut le fondateur de la plus grande famille littéraire du Canada français. Son fils Alfred fut un poète de qualité et il compte parmi ses descendants, Saint-Denys-Garneau, Simone Routier, Anne Hébert et Sylvain Garneau. On a publié les communications faites lors de la célébration du *Centenaire de l'Histoire du Canada de Garneau* (1845) et on peut lire aussi à son sujet les livres de Gustave Lanctôt (1946) et de Georges Robitaille (1929).

RENE GARNEAU (1907-). Né à Québec, Garneau a étudié au Séminaire de Québec et à la Sorbonne dont il est licencié ès lettres. Journaliste, il devint secrétaire adjoint de la Commission royale d'enquète sur les Arts, Lettres et Sciences après avoir servi comme major dans l'armée canadienne durant la guerre. Il entra ensuite au ministère des Affaires extérieures et fut conseiller culturel à l'ambassade du Canada à Paris et à Bruxelles. Il est maintenant ambassadeur du Canada en Suisse. Membre de la Société royale, il a publié sporadiquement dans les journaux et revues, notamment dans *Les Idées* et *Le Canada,* des essais critiques qui comptent au nombre des plus pénétrants, des plus érudits et des mieux écrits du Canada français. Il serait souhaitable de les réunir en volume.

SAINT-DENYS-GARNEAU (1912-1943). Né à Sainte-Catherine de Fossambault, Hector de Saint-Denys-Garneau étudia au Collège Sainte-Marie et à l'Ecole des Beaux-Arts de Montréal. In 1934, il participa à la fondation de *La Relève*. Atteint d'une lésion cardiaque, il dut interrompre ses études et vécut au ralenti à Montréal et à Sainte-Catherine, peignant, écrivant son journal, quelques essais et ses poèmes. En 1937, il fit un bref voyage à Paris et, à son retour, s'enferma de plus en plus dans la solitude. Le 24 octobre 1943, on découvrit son cadavre dans un ruisseau près du manoir de Sainte-Catherine. Il avait publié *Regards et Jeux dans l'espace* (1937); on a publié après sa mort ses *Poésies complètes*

(1949) et son *Journal* expurgé (1954). Aucun poète canadien de notre temps n'a été autant étudié, commenté et discuté et il est devenu une figure poétique légendaire, un destin exemplaire.

Son *Journal* est le plus beau et le plus tragique témoignage qu'ait laissé un écrivain canadien sur l'angoisse que peut éprouver un homme qui se sent de plus en plus impuissant à accepter la vie quotidienne et à exprimer cette impuissance dans une oeuvre poétique. Le journal abonde en méditations sur les oeuvres d'art considérées surtout comme moyens d'enrichissement spirituel, comme instruments de salut personnel. Il jette une vive lumière sur l'auteur et sur le sens de son oeuvre poétique.

Cette oeuvre poétique est peu abondante et elle comprend les *Regards et Jeux dans l'espace* qu'il a publiés lui-même, et les poèmes posthumes groupés dans les *Poésies complètes*. Les premiers sont, en général, d'un style simple et pur et touchent comme par jeu aux sujets les plus graves: la joie, l'amour, le jeu, la solitude, la mort, l'inquiétude devant le silence des espaces infinis. On retrouve les mêmes thèmes dans les poésies posthumes, mais sur un ton plus grave, plus tragique: ici le dépouillement extrême de la forme est parfaitement accordé à la nuit des sens et de l'esprit dans laquelle le poète cherche la lumière et la joie, mais en vain. Le caractère révolutionnaire de cette poésie vient de ce que les considérations esthétiques ont fait place au message spirituel d'un homme qui ne fait rien d'autre que mettre son coeur à nu. C'est par sa valeur d'exemple plus que par sa beauté propre que cette oeuvre poétique marque un tournant dans l'évolution de la poésie canadienne.

On pourra consulter sur lui les ouvrages suivants: Marie-Blanche Ellis, *De Saint-Denys-Garneau, Art et Réalisme* (1949); Lévis Fortier, *Le message poétique de St-Denys-Garneau* (1954); Benoît Lacroix, *St-Denys-Garneau* (1956); Romain Légaré, *L'aventure poétique et spirituelle de St-Denys-Garneau* (1957). On consultera aussi Guy Sylvestre, *Situation de la poésie canadienne* (1941); Marcel Dugas, *Approches* (1942); Gilles Marcotte, *Un littérature qui se fait* (1962); les hommages de *La Nouvelle Relève,* décembre 1944, et de *Notre Temps,* 17 mai 1947; Albert Béguin, *Réduit au squelette* dans *Esprit* (novembre 1954); Jean Le Moyne, *Saint-Denys-Garneau témoin de son temps* dans *Ecrits du Canada français* VII, sans oublier la préface de Robert Elie et Jean Le Moyne aux *Poésies complètes* (1949). Jacques Blais a relevé et analysé les études consacrées au poète dans un article de la *Revue de l'Université Laval* (janvier 1964). Frank Scott a traduit quelques-uns de ses poèmes, *St-Denys-Garneau, Anne Hébert, Translations* (1962).

SYLVAIN GARNEAU (1930-1953). Né à Montréal, Sylvain Garneau a été journaliste, comédien et annonceur à la radio. On l'a trouvé mort en 1953. Il avait publié deux recueils de poésies: *Objets trouvés* (1951) et les *Trouble-fête* (1952) réédités sous le titre *Objets retrouvés* (1965). Garneau a écrit, selon les règles traditionnelles, des poèmes sentimentaux, pleins de couleurs et d'odeurs riches, de personnages légendaires et de rêves habitant un monde d'une souriante fantaisie dans lequel le poète s'est réfugié pour échapper au réel. Plusieurs de ses pièces sont des chansons charmantes ou de petits poèmes narratifs; Garneau allait contre le courant et contre la mode. Marcel Dubé lui a consacré un article dans *Amérique française* (décembre 1953).

HUGH GARNER (1913-   ). Born in Yorkshire, England, Garner came to Toronto in 1919. Educated at Danforth Technical High School, he worked during the depression years at various jobs. In 1937 he fought in Spain with the International Brigade as a machine-gunner. Although his first stories appeared in *The Canadian Forum* in 1936/37, he did not publish again until after World War II, in which he served briefly with the army and from 1940 to 1945 with the R.C.N. From his battle experiences came *Storm Below* (1949), a realistic novel about the navy. His intimate knowledge of and sympathy with working people is evident in his books like *Cabbagetown* (1950), *Present Reckoning* (1951) and *The Yellow Sweater and Other Stories* (1952). Another novel *The Silence On The Shore,* concerning a group of characters in a Toronto rooming house, appeared in 1962. *Hugh Garner's Best Stories,* which won a Governor General's Award in 1963, was followed by *Author, Author!* (1964), a collection of his humorous essays. Another volume of stories, *Men and Women,* appeared in 1966.

GRATIEN GELINAS (1909-   ). Né à St-Tite (Champlain), Gélinas a étudié au Collège de Montréal et à l'Ecole des Hautes Etudes commerciales. Agent d'assurances quelque temps, il devint bientôt comédien à la radio et, de 1938 à 1947, il a connu un immense succès populaire avec ses revues annuelles *Fridolinades.* Comédien, auteur dramatique et metteur en scène, il a écrit, dirigé et joué lui-même ses trois pièces *Tit-Coq* (1950), *Bousille et les Justes* (1960, *Bousille and the Just,* 1961) et *Hier les enfants dansaient,* qui n'a pas encore eté publiée. Depuis 1957, il dirige la Comédie canadienne de Montréal. Il est membre de la Société royale du Canada.

Ses deux premières pièces sont des drames qui mettent en scène des personnages humbles, déshérités aux prises avec des problèmes qui les écrasent: le bâtard qui ne parvient pas à se donner une famille, une famille qui ne parvient

à sauver son pauvre honneur qu'en tombant dans un déshonneur pire. L'auteur connaît son métier et il a su ménager ses effets scéniques avec habileté; on comprend facilement que ses pièces aient connu auprès du public canadien une aussi grande faveur. Toutes les émotions fortes y sont exploitées et le dialogue est aussi vivant et pittoresque que l'action est bien conduite. De plus, les moeurs y sont observées et peintes avec un réalisme puissant. Les personnages manquent néanmoins de complexité et ils ont quelque chose de caricatural. Les deux pièces—la seconde surtout—sont des réquisitoires durs, cruels contre l'hypocrisie sociale et les personnages essentiels—Tit-Coq et Bousille—sont des malheureux que la vie écrase, que le destin poursuit avec acharnement. On tombe par moments dans le mélodrame et, même lorsque l'auteur fait rire, on ne peut oublier la détresse profonde des protagonistes. Cette forme d'art populaire, si elle manque de raffinement, ne manque ni de force ni de vérité.

LEON GERIN (1863-1951). Né à Québec, fils d'Antoine Gérin-Lajoie et petit fils d'Etienne Parent, Gérin a étudié au Séminaire de Nicolet et à la faculté de droit de l'Université de Montréal. Reçu au barreau en 1884, il partit pour Paris où il étudia les sciences sociales. Revenu au Canada, il exerça quelque temps sa profession d'avocat, fut secrétaire de l'honorable A. R. Angers; il devint traducteur aux Débats de la Chambre des communes et, en 1919, chef de ce service. Il se retira en 1936 et passa le reste de sa vie à réviser les études sociologiques auxquelles il avait consacré ses temps libres depuis 1895. Une grande partie de son oeuvre est encore éparse dans les revues; deux volumes réunissent quelques-unes des plus importantes: *Le type économique et social des Canadiens: milieux agricoles* (1937) et *Aux sources de notre histoire* (1946) qui étudient respectivement le comportement des agriculteurs canadiens du vingtième siècle et celui des colons français au dix-septième. Léon Gérin fut un pionnier au Canada français dans le domaine des sciences sociales et plusieurs des ses monographies sont considérées par les spécialistes comme des modèles du genre. Gérin écrivait de surcroît une langue châtiée et il fut un des bons prosateurs canadiens de sa génération. Elu à un Société royale du Canada en 1898, il en fut président en 1933. Il a aussi reçu la médaille Lorne Pierce en 1941. A l'occasion du centenaire de la naissance de son père, il a publié *Antoine Gérin-Lajoie* (1925). Hervé Carrier lui a consacré un petit livre (1960).

ANTOINE GERIN-LAJOIE (1824-1882). Né à Yamachiche, Gérin-Lajoie étudia au Séminaire de Nicolet et fut successivement rédacteur à *La Minerve* (1844-1852), traducteur à l'Assemblée législative (1852-1856) et bibliothécaire adjoint du Parlement (1856-1880). Il avait aussi étudié le droit et avait été reçu avocat en 1848. Dès son séjour au Séminaire, il avait écrit des pièces de vers et une pièce en trois actes, *Le Jeune Latour* qui fut reproduit par Huston dans son *Répertoire national*. Auteur d'un *Catéchisme politique* (1851) et d'une chronique de dix années publiée après sa mort, *Dix Ans au Canada, 1840-1850* (1888), il est surtout connu comme l'auteur d'une chanson populaire, *Un Canadien errant*, et d'un roman à thèse en deux parties: *Jean Rivard le défricheur* publié en 1862 dans les *Soirées canadiennes*, et *Jean Rivard économiste* publié en 1864 dans *Le Foyer canadien*. Ce pseudo-roman est en fait un récit gauchement construit par le truchement duquel l'auteur a voulu faire connaître ses idées sociales et économiques. On peu consulter à son sujet les biographies critiques que lui ont consacrées Henri-Raymond Casgrain (1912), Louvigny de Montigny (1926) et Léon Gérin (1925).

DIANE GIGUERE (1937-   ). Petite fille de Jean-Charles Harvey, comédienne, speakerine à la radio et à la télévision, elle a obtenu le Prix du Cercle du Livre de France en 1961 pour *Le Temps des jeux,* analyse de la haine qu'une fille éprouve pour sa mère à qui elle ne pardonne pas d'être ce qu'elle est; l'enfer moral où les personnages se débattent est quelque peu allégé par la nostalgie de l'enfance, et le récit est sobre et dense. *L'Eau est profonde* (1965) est moins sobre, mais non moins dense. Ce court roman évoque l'enchantement d'une liaison entre une jeune fille et un quadragénaire en vacances aux Antilles, et le désenchantement de la jeune fille qui retrouve la solitude et le vide de l'âme lorsque, rentré à Montréal et revenu au quotidien, son amant ne voit plus en elle qu'une habitude dont il se défait peu à peu. Diane Giguère semble être la romancière des mal-aimés.

ROLAND GIGUERE (1929-   ). Né à Montréal, Giguère est diplômé de l'Ecole des Arts graphiques de Montréal et de l'Ecole Estienne de Paris. Il a fondé les Editions Erta et il dirige son atelier d'arts graphiques à Montréal. Il a écrit, illustré et imprimé ses propres poèmes ainsi que ceux de quelques autres jeunes poètes.

Cette oeuvre comporte une dose d'ésotérisme et il est assez difficile d'en toujours saisir le sens profond. Ses premiers poèmes—*Yeux fixes* (1951)— abondent en images violentes qui trahissent une révolte contre un univers ennemi, inacceptable. D'autre part, *Les Armes blanches* (1954) manifestent une réconciliation avec les choses et les hommes, tandis que *Le défaut des ruines est d'avoir des habitants* (1957) nous propose l'image d'un monde mythique semblable à celui de Michaux qui est la caricature du nôtre et qui est le résultat d'un effort magique pour exorciser l'homme de tous ses maléfices par le truchement de l'évasion. Mais la fuite n'est pas une solution et le poète reconnaît lui-même qu'au terme de ce voyage imaginaire il est revenu à son point de départ. Son dernier poème *Adorable femme des neiges* (1959) est un poème d'amour conjugal triomphant qui révèle une réconciliation avec la vie et il semble que l'itinéraire du poète l'ait conduit de la révolte à l'assentiment. Presque toutes ses plaquettes ont été rééditées, avec des poèmes inédits, dans *L'Age de la parole* (1965).

Gilles Marcotte lui a consacré un chapitre dans *Une littérature qui se fait* (1962).

CHARLES GILL (1871-1918). Né à Sorel, Gill fréquenta plusieurs collèges et fut mauvais élève. Intéressé par la peinture plus que par les études académiques, il partit pour Paris où il séjourna deux ans (1890-1892) et fréquenta l'atelier de Gérôme. Revenu au pays, il ouvrit un atelier et peignit de nombreux portraits et paysages, tout en écrivant des contes, des poèmes et des chroniques diverses. Il fut membre de l'Ecole littéraire de Montréal dont il devint président en 1912. En 1902, il épousa Georgine Bélanger (femme de lettres qui signait Gaétane de Montreuil) dont il se sépara en 1914. Son oeuvre en prose reste éparse dans les journaux, mais ses poèmes ont été recueillis en volume *Le Cap Eternité* (1919).

Gill avait conçu un immense poème en trente-deux chants sur *Le Saint-Laurent* qui devait être une sorte d'épopée lyrique inspirée par l'histoire nationale et religieuse du pays. Il en a écrit des fragments qui ont paru avec une trentaine d'autres poèmes, y compris des traductions d'Horace, dans son recueil posthume. On y trouve d'heureux passages—surtout des descriptions de paysages grandioses— mais son oeuvre est gâtée par une grandiloquence creuse et une imagerie usée; fasciné par Hugo et Lamartine, il a abusé de clichés romantiques. Il reste qu'il y a par moment des visions grandioses qui font oublier qu'elles sont des accidents dans une entreprise avortée. On peut lire l'article de Paul Wyczynski sur *Charles Gill intime* dans la *Revue de l'Université d'Ottawa*, 1959.

ANDRE GIROUX (1916-   ). Né à Québec, Giroux a étudié à l'Académie de Québec et est à l'emploi du gouvernement du Québec où il a occupé divers postes administratifs avant de devenir publiciste au ministère de l'Industrie et du Commerce. Il a été nommé à la Maison du Québec à Paris en 1963 et il occupe maintenant un haut poste au ministère des Affaires culturelles à Québec. Il a fondé et dirigé la revue *Regards* (1940-1942) et il a été élu à la Société royale du Canada en 1960. Il a publié deux romans, *Au delà des visages* (1948) et *Le Gouffre a toujours soif* (1953) et un volume de nouvelles, *Malgré tout, la joie* (1959) qui lui a valu un prix du Gouverneur général.

Giroux est un analyste de conflits spirituels intimes en même temps qu'un peintre des travers humains. *Au delà des visages* étudie l'angoisse d'un jeune homme qui a tué sa complice sous le coup du dégoût que lui inspire sa première expérience amoureuse coupable, et nous propose une série de portraits moraux en peignant les réactions qu'éprouvent ses concitoyens en apprenant le meurtre qu'il a commis. Il y a aussi dans *Le Gouffre a toujours soif* des pages satiriques et des portraits bien dessinés, mais toute l'action se réduit à la longue agonie d'un cancéreux qui fait la somme de sa petite vie au moment où elle s'achève; après quelques mouvements de révolte, il finit par se reposer dans l'espoir de la miséricorde divine. Dans un roman comme dans l'autre, le personnage principal est saisi au moment où il est hanté par l'idée de la mort prochaine, et la mort est à toutes les pages de *Malgré tout, la joie* un recueil de nouvelles d'intérêt inégal qui mettent en lumière l'absence d'amour entre les êtres et nous proposent de la vie une série d'images presque toutes très sombres.

Giroux n'a guère de souffle et ses oeuvres manquent de grandeur et de diversité; mais il possède le sens du spirituel, un style un peu sec mais propre et des intuitions qui donnent à ses écrits une résonance humaine profonde: la hantise de la mort et la conscience de la mesquinerie de la plupart des existences. Ses romans rélèvent chez lui une très haute conception du christianisme.

JOHN GLASSCO (1909-   ). Born in Montreal, John Glassco after attending McGill University lived in Europe from 1928 until 1931.

His first publication was a pamphlet of verse entitled *Conan's Fig* (1928) which appeared in *transition* in Paris. Since then, he has produced two more volumes of poetry, *The Deficit Made Flesh* (1958) and *A Point of Sky* (1964), translations of *The Journal of Saint-Denys-Garneau* (1962) and Leopold von Sacher Masock's *Venus in Furs,* as well as three fictional works: *Contes en Crinoline* (1930, under the pseudonym of Jean de Saint-Luc), *Under the Hill* (1959, the completion of an unfinished novel by Aubrey Beardsley); and *The English Governess* (1960, under the pseudonym of Miles Underwood).

In his poetry, which is artful in form and sophisticated in tone, Glassco presents realistic glimpses of rural Quebec around Foster where he has lived for some twenty years. His mood, while frequently reflecting the Horatian theme of *carpe diem,* has a pervading note of pessimism as man is shown striving for materialistic goals that Nature will eventually destroy. Glassco edited *English Poetry in Quebec* (1964).

JACQUES GODBOUT (1933-   ). Né à Montréal, Godbout a étudié au Collège Jean de Brébeuf et à la faculté des lettres de l'Université de Montréal. Professeur de littérature à University College à Addis Ababa de 1954 à 1957, il est cinéaste à l'Office national du Film depuis 1958. Il a participé à la fondation de la revue *Liberté* dont il a été le directeur en 1961. Il a été un des principaux artisans des Rencontres des poètes et un des fondateurs du Mouvement laïque de langue française. Il a aussi voyagé aux Etats-Unis, au Mexique, aux Antilles, en Grèce et en Egypte. Il peint et il a écrit plusieurs théâtres radiophoniques.

Godbout a publié trois minces cahiers de poésies: *Carton-pâte* (1956), *Les Pavés secs* (1958) et *C'est la chaude loi des hommes* (1960), ainsi que deux romans, *L'Aquarium* (1962) et *Le couteau sur la table* (1965). Les deux premiers cahiers renfermaient quelques brèves pièces d'une ironie et d'une désinvolture qui se rient de toutes choses. Le troisième est plus grave, il exprime surtout la tendresse du poète pour les hommes menacés d'extermination. Le poète est trop intelligent et il a trop peur de tomber dans un romantisme ridicule; il en est d'un laconisme et d'une pudeur qui empêchent trop souvent ses poésies de s'ouvrir et de s'épanouir. Ses romans sont, eux aussi, très brefs et l'auteur multiplie les scènes courtes. Il semble qu'il lui répugne de s'appesantir sur quoi que ce soit. Cependant, il y a dans *L'Aquarium* une atmosphère qui se retrouve la même partout et qui donne au roman son unité; cet ennui dans lequel baignent tous ces étrangers venus en ce lieu d'Afrique comme conseillers techniques et qui les en chassera, cet ennui ronge ces êtres et leur fait manifester leur vraie nature. Le roman manque d'épaisseur, de complexité, mais il compte quelques tableaux où les personnages sont dessinés de quelques traits forts par un écrivain original qui allie une tendresse souriante à une ironie dévastatrice.

Dans *Le couteau sur la table,* il a raconté l'histoire amoureuse d'un jeune Canadien français et d'une Canadienne mi-irlandaise, mi-juive, et ce récit rapide et brillant, a des résonances politiques inévitables dans le contexte historique actuel. Le cynisme des personnages qui se sentent inutiles dans un monde où règne l'absurde donne au récit une teinte pessimiste: il est difficile dans un tel univers de croire à l'avenir de l'homme et du pays. Ce récit témoigne de la révolte d'une génération contre des valeurs qu'elle n'accepte plus dans leurs formes traditionnelles.

OLIVER GOLDSMITH (1794-1861). Born in St. Andrews, New Brunswick, Goldsmith moved later with his family to Halifax. Sent out to work as a youth, he had very little formal education but this lack was later supplemented by private study and tutoring. For many years he was in the employ of the Commissariat Department of the British Army at Halifax. Apart from some brief trips abroad on official postings, Goldsmith spent the greater part of his life in the Maritimes.

A grand-nephew of the author of *The Deserted Village,* Goldsmith tried to emulate his famous ancestor with *The Rising Village* (1825), an epic poem depicting the triumphs of the Loyalists in Acadia over their trials and home-sickness, and the growth of their love and faith in Canada. It was the first poem of any length to be published in book form in Great Britain by a native Maritime author. Although the social documentation and warm emotion of *The Deserted Village* are lacking in *The Rising Village,* there is expressed a noteworthy recognition of the cultural possibilities of the new Nova Scotia. The poem's popularity

is evidenced by the publication of *The Rising Village, with Other Poems* (1834). In 1943 an *Autobiography* of Goldsmith was discovered and published by the Rev. W. E. Myatt. Desmond Pacey, "The Goldsmiths and their Villages," *UTQ,* XXI (October, 1951).

CHARLES WILLIAM GORDON (1860-1937). The son of a Presbyterian clergyman who came to Canada from Scotland in the 1840s, Gordon ("Ralph Connor") spent his early years in Glengarry County, the Eastern Ontario Scottish community which provides the setting for his famous Glengarry series.

The family moved to a charge in Western Ontario when Charles was eleven, and after attending St. Mary's High School he graduated from the University of Toronto (1883) and from Knox College (1887). As a student minister he spent some time in Southern Manitoba, and before accepting the ministry of St. Stephen's Church, Winnipeg, in 1894, was an ordained missionary at Banff for a three-year period. His apprenticeship also included some experience in teaching high school in Chatham, Ontario, and at Upper Canada College in Toronto.

The year 1898 marks Gordon's definite entry into the field of fiction-writing with *Black Rock* which first appeared serially in a church paper *The Westminster.* Like *The Sky Pilot,* which followed it in 1899, *Black Rock* is a story of missionary adventure in the west. It established a pattern from which its author rarely deviated in a long, successful writing career: its plot is fast-moving but shallow, filled with melodrama and coincidence; its characters are types, bold flat outlines in black and white only; its western setting serves as a picturesque backdrop for the exemplum which Ralph Connor was to repeat in each of his subsequent novels—the triumph of good over evil, the eventual winning through of the strong and faithful hero. In *The Man from Glengarry* (1901) and its two sequels, *Glengarry School Days* (1902) and *The Girl from Glengarry* (1933), Gordon produced works which won immediate success.

His own life simulated the action-packed existence of his typical hero. In 1915 he joined the Canadian Expeditionary Force as Chaplain of the Cameron Highlanders. He was with the battalion at Ypres and the Somme, was mentioned in despatches and became Senior Chaplain of the Canadian Forces in England, with the rank of Major. From 1919 until his death, he combined again the careers of the prolific writer and the conscientious clergyman, continuing his pastorate of St. Stephen's and producing some fifteen novels.

These works range over an impressive variety of settings: *The Patrol of the Sun Dance Trail* (1914) is concerned with the period of the Riel uprising; *The Major* (1917) and *The Sky Pilot in No Man's Land* (1919) reflect his experiences of the war years; *To Him that Hath* (1921) and *The Arm of Gold* (1932) are based on labour-management relations; *Torches through the Bush* (1934) and *The Rebel Loyalist* (1935) centre again on crises in Canadian history.

Ralph Connor's over-simplified ethic and his spendthrift use of richly potential settings in the service of second-rate plots and characters deny him a place among Canada's most creative writers. In any history of Canadian literature, however, his novels are significant; their great popularity points to an agreement between author and readers in stubborn optimism, strong evangelism and the ready acceptance of the challenge of the frontier west. Ralph Connor's autobiography *Postscript to Adventure* (1938) is probably the most impressive of his works, providing evidence of a lifelong integrity of purpose and of the involvement of his sincere beliefs in everything he wrote. S. Ross Beharriell, Introduction to *The Man from Glengarry* (Toronto, 1960); Edward A. McCourt, "The Sky Pilot" in *The Canadian West in Fiction* (Toronto, 1949); F. W. Watt, "Western Myth—The World of Ralph Connor," *Can.Lit.*, 1 (Spring, 1959).

PHYLLIS GOTLIEB (1926-   ). Born in Toronto, Phyllis Fay Bloom Gotlieb was educated at Victoria (B.A., 1948) and University College (M.A., 1950) of the University of Toronto where her husband is Director of the Institute of Computer Studies. She began writing poetry as a child and her early work appeared in secondary school and college magazines, as well as in a broadsheet of some thirteen poems entitled *Who Knows One?* (1962). *Within the Zodiac* (1964) is the first collected volume of her poems, most of which had already appeared in *The Canadian Forum, The Tamarack Review,* and *Queen's Quarterly*. These poems display great versatility in theme and mood—from the wild, childlike word-play in "A Bestiary of the Garden for Children Who Should Know Better" to the Jewish rhetorical extravagances of "Who Knows One." Phyllis Gotlieb's observations of the trivialities of affluent, domestic suburban life are characterized by an imaginative satiric insight and a style that is lively and unpretentious.

In addition to her poetry, Miss Gotlieb has published a science fiction novel *Sunburst* (1964), which earlier appeared in serial form in *Amazing Science Fiction*.

GWETHALYN GRAHAM (1913-1965). Born in Toronto, Gwethalyn Graham Erichsen-Brown was educated at Havergal College, Toronto, at Lausanne, Switzerland, and Smith College, Massachusetts. In addition to short stories and articles written for

Maclean's and *Saturday Night,* she published two novels, *Swiss Sonata* (1938), based on her own experiences in a Swiss boarding school, and *Earth and High Heaven* (1944, *Entre ciel et terre,* 1946), set in Montreal and concerned with the theme of anti-semitism. Both won Governor General's Awards. With Solange Chaput Roland, Miss Graham published *Dear Enemies* (1963, *Cher Ennemies,* 1963), an exchange of letters on French-English relations. Eli Mandel, Introduction to *Earth and High Heaven* (Toronto, 1960).

ALAIN GRANDBOIS (1900-   ). Né à Saint-Casimir (Portneuf), Grandbois étudia au Collège de Montréal, au Séminaire de Québec, à St. Dunstan University et à l'Université Laval dont il est licencié en droit. Issu d'une famille riche, il passa une grande partie de sa vie à parcourir le monde. Il fit de longs séjours en France et voyagea en Italie, en Espagne, en Autriche, en Allemagne, en Russie, en Afrique, aux Indes, en Chine et au Japon. La guerre le ramena au Canada en 1940 et, en 1944, il participa à la fondation de l'Académie canadienne-française. Il vit depuis dans une demi-retraite, écrivant parfois pour la télévision. Il a reçu le prix Duvernay et la médaille Lorne Pierce.

Grandbois fut un grand voyageur et ce n'est sans doute pas par hasard qu'il a écrit *Né à Québec* (1933), bio-graphie poétisée de l'explorateur Louis Jolliet et *Les Voyages de Marco Polo* (1942)—il a refait lui-même ces voyages avant d'écrire ce livre. Son recueil de nouvelles *Avant le chaos* (1945) est plein de souvenirs de ses voyages à travers le monde et l'auteur a visiblement la nostalgie des folles années de l'entre-deux-guerres: ses personnages sont des aristocrates et des artistes qui promènent leur désoeuvrement dans une Europe de convention. C'est comme poète surtout que Grandbois s'impose à l'attention et il est un des maîtres de la jeune poésie canadienne.

Il a publié trois recueils de poèmes: *Les îles de la nuit* (1944), *Rivages de l'homme* (1948) et *L'Etoile pourpre* (1957). Les trois ont été réunis en un seul volume en 1963: *Poèmes.* Les deux premiers comptent parmi les plus beaux livres du Canada français; le troisième n'a pas la même qualité que les précédents. Le thème central de toute cette oeuvre, c'est la mort, la mort toujours présente au coeur et à l'esprit du poète et qui donne son tragique caractère à la vie humaine. C'est cette conscience de la mort à venir qui donne son poids et sa saveur à la vie, car toutes choses deviennent plus désirables du fait même qu'elles sont périssables; cette oeuvre repose donc aussi sur l'intuition du caractère fragile et éphémère de toute joie. L'oeuvre poétique devient ainsi un effort pour perpétuer, immortaliser, éterniser ce qui est par nature éphé-mère; c'est pourquoi les souvenirs y occupent une si grande place, souvenirs multiples et divers d'un grand voyageur sur la terre.

Cette poésie est, par ses thèmes comme par son style, d'intérêt universel: elle n'a pas de caractères spécifique-ment canadiens. L'amour, la mort, les rêves et les souvenirs surgissent partout dans cette poésie d'un rythme si personnel et si pleine d'images et de symboles. Cet art est discontinu, il est fait d'une succession de temps forts et Grandbois ne sait pas toujours *com-poser* son poème; mais par la gravité de ses thèmes, par son refus de la narration et du discours, par son sens du mystère et par ce curieux mélange de dureté et de tendresse, par la co-existence dans son oeuvre de la joie et de l'angoisse, Grandbois est accordé à la sensibilité d'aujourd'hui et aucun poète canadien vivant n'exerce une aussi grande influence sur la jeune poésie canadienne.

Jacques Brault a préparé le *Grand-bois* des *Classiques canadiens* (1958) et il y a a de bons chapitres sur lui dans *Approches* de Marcel Dugas et dans *Une littérature qui se fait* de Gilles Marcotte. La revue *Liberté* lui a rendu hommage (mai-août 1960) et René Garneau a écrit un article remarquable dans les *Cahiers de l'Ouest* (juillet 1954).

ELOI DE GRANDMONT (1921-   ). Né à Baie du Fèvre, Eloi de Grandmont a étudié au Collège de Nicolet et à l'Ecole des Beaux-Arts de Montréal. Il a été journaliste quelque temps, critique dramatique au *Devoir* et, après un séjour d'études en France, il a consacré toute sa vie au théâtre. Secrétaire général du Théâtre du Nouveau Monde depuis sa fondation en 1951, il a aussi été comédien, a adapté des pièces pour la télévision et rédigé de nombreux textes pour la radio et la télévision. Il a aussi écrit et publié des pièces: *Un fils à tuer* (1950), *La fontaine de Paris* (1955) et des poèmes: *Premiers Secrets* (1951), *Plaisirs* (1953), *Dimanches naïfs* (1954) et *Une saison en chansons* (1963).

Eloi de Grandmont est le poète des réalités familières, des choses les plus humbles dont il parle avec tendresse et simplicité. Il chante à voix basse le soleil et le sommeil, les fruits et les rêves, les promenades lentes à travers les champs et les bois. Il est un bon poète mineur qui recourt avec beaucoup de succès aux techniques les plus conservatrices pour exprimer des sentiments vieux comme le monde. Et pourtant, il ne répète personne.

GREY OWL. *See* Belaney, Archibald Stanfeld.

ELDON GRIER (1917-   ). Born in London, England, of Canadian parents, Eldon Brockwell Grier has travelled extensively in Europe and Mexico.

After completing secondary school in Montreal where he makes his home, he became a painter for several years. He started writing poetry during a trip to Spain in 1954. Since then his volumes of published verse include *A Morning from Scraps* (1954), *Poems* (1955), *Manzanillo and Other Poems* (1957), *The Ring of Ice* (1959), and *A Friction of Lights* (1963). The poems of Grier, who calls himself a "poet-painter", reflect his interest in surrealism and are characterized by concreteness of imagery and intensity of personal feeling. Robin Skelton, "Canadian Poetry", *The Tamarack Review,* 29 (Autumn, 1963).

CLAUDE-HENRI GRIGNON (1894-   ). Né à Sainte-Adèle, Grignon étudia au Collège de Saint-Laurent mais interrompit ses études jeune et fut surtout un autodidacte. Grand liseur, il s'est donné une formation littéraire éclectique, puis s'est mis à l'école des pamphlétaires catholiques: Bloy, Huysmans, Bernanos et autres. Journaliste, il a collaboré à plusieurs journaux de Montréal, dont *L'Ordre* et *La Renaissance.* Asselin l'a aussi influencé. De 1937 à 1939, il a dirigé un hebdomadaire libéral *En avant.* En 1936, il avait lancé *Les Pamphlets de Valdombre* qu'il rédigea seul pendant sept ans. A partir de 1938, il écrivit pour la radio et, plus tard pour la télévision, une adaptation de son roman *Un homme et son péché* qu'il exploite interminablement. Il est membre de la Société royale du Canada.

Après un premier récit que gâte un lyrisme excessif, *Le Secret de Lindbergh* (1928), Grignon a écrit *Un homme et son péché* (1933), portrait d'un avare qui est un des meilleurs romans réalistes du Canada français. Il a réuni en volume des nouvelles inspirées par l'amour de la terre, *Le Déserteur* (1934), ainsi que des essais critiques d'une violence presque constante, *Ombres et clameurs* (1933). Il allait pousser la violence encore plus loin dans ses *Pamphlets* où il a attaqué régulièrement les chefs de l'Union nationale, ainsi que des écrivains qu'il jugeait sans talent. Absolu en tout, il n'a aucun sens de la justice, mais il a été un pamphlétaire souvent savoureux et un conteur au style vivant et imagé.

LIONEL GROULX (1878-1967). Né à Chenaux près de Vaudreuil, le chanoine Groulx étudia au Collège de Sainte-Thérèse de Blainville, au Grand Séminaire de Montréal, aux universités de Rome et de Fribourg. Ordonné prêtre en 1903, il enseigna les humanités au Séminaire de Valleyfield de 1901 à 1915, sauf de 1907 à 1909 alors qu'il étudia la philosophie et la théologie en Europe. En 1915, il fut nommé professeur d'histoire à l'Université de Montréal et le resta jusqu'en 1948. En 1946, il fonda l'Institut d'histoire de l'Amérique française et, en 1947, la *Revue d'histoire de l'Amérique française* qu'il dirige. Elu membre de la Société royale du Canada en 1918, il en résigna en 1952. Il était membre de l'Académie canadienne-française. Il reçut la médaille Tyrrell en 1948.

Le chanoine Groulx a étudié toutes les périodes de l'histoire du Canada, mais surtout les luttes constitutionnelles qui depuis la conquête britannique jusqu'à la confédération ont conquis au Canada le gouvernement responsable et à la minorité française la reconnaissance de droits fondamentaux: ces études l'ont amené à un nationalisme agressif qui fit de lui un des chefs de file de la jeune génération dans les années trente. Il a aussi publié des ouvrages sur *La découverte du Canada* (1934), sur *L'enseignement français au Canada* (1931-3), ainsi que trois séries d'études plus courtes sous le titre de *Notre maître le passé* (1924, 1936, 1944), avant de réunir et de synthétiser ses vues sur l'évolution du pays dans son *Histoire du Canada* en quatre volumes (1950-5). Il avait publié, sous le pseu-

donyme Alonié de Lestre, deux romans à thèse d'inspiration nationaliste: *L'Appel de la race* (1922) et *Au cap Blomidon* (1932). Ni l'un ni l'autre ne sont de bons romans. Il a aussi réuni en volume des essais et des conférences qui exposent ses vues sur des problèmes politiques, économiques, éducatifs et religieux: *Orientations* (1935), *Directives* (1937), *Pour bâtir* (1953), etc. On peut lire André Laurendeau, *L'abbé Lionel Groulx* (1939).

FREDERICK PHILIP GROVE (1871-1948). Born in Russia, from which his parents were returning to their home in southern Sweden, Grove was of British-Swedish descent. He spent his early years in extensive travelling throughout Europe. His education was informal but included a wide reading in various languages and intermittent attendance at the universities of Paris, Rome and Munich. He visited Russia and the Far East. In 1892, he journeyed to North America, travelling west across the United States and back east through Canada. At Toronto he learned that his father had died bankrupt in Sweden, and Grove was forced to work for the next twenty years as a harvest labourer. During the winter months of this period, he produced several manuscripts of realistic novels, but was unable to interest a publisher in his work, which did not receive the recognition it merited until many years later.

In 1912 he obtained a position as a school-teacher in Manitoba, and two years later married a young colleague, Catherine Weins, who was to give him inspiration and support to continue his writing.

Grove's first book *Over Prairie Trails* was published in 1922, and was followed by a similar volume of descriptive and narrative essays based on his Manitoban experiences *The Turn of the Year* (1923). The success of these books brought him to the attention of members of the faculty of Wesley College, Winnipeg. Through Lorne Pierce, editor of The Ryerson Press, they met Grove in 1924, recognized the value of his work and assisted him in the publication of his fiction. Because of increasing deafness, Grove retired from teaching in 1924 and devoted his full time to writing. He was invited to address meetings in Winnipeg, and following the publication of his most popular book *A Search for America* (1927), partly autobiographical and partly fictional, he was for a short time in great demand as a lecturer.

Grove's novels, however, were for the most part badly received. *Settlers of the Marsh* (1925) was promptly denounced as obscene by the critics. *Our Daily Bread* (1928), also set in the prairies, received a modicum of praise, but the popularity of further novels suffered because of poor reviews and the advent of the depression.

Following a brief period with the newly formed Graphic Press in Ottawa, Grove moved to Ontario, settling on a farm near Simcoe in 1931. *Fruits of the Earth,* a novel of pioneering in Manitoba, appeared in 1933. The next year he was awarded the Lorne Pierce Medal for his distinguished contribution to Canadian literature.

Two Generations (1939) deals with Ontario rather than Western rural life, and is quieter and more mellow than most of his other works. It was followed in 1944 by *The Master of the Mill,* an interesting depiction of Ontario industrial society and the conflict of generations, and by *Consider Her Ways* (1947), a parable on ant-life. His most powerful and enduring work, however, is contained in the earlier novels set and written on the prairies. His intimate knowledge and understanding of the exigencies of pioneer life lend to his writing a sober authenticity, while early training in French naturalism and in archaeology gave him a literary and philosophical background with which to approach life on the Western frontier. The disappointments and frustrations of his own life, the years of dogged writing despite financial desperation and the lack of recognition, instilled into his work a tragic vision of an implacable universe, indifferent to the plight of man. Like Hardy, Grove often expresses himself best when he describes the elements in concentrated attack upon his characters. His tragic view, however, extends to people as well as nature; often his characters are destroyed by conflicts within themselves and with other people.

Although the general tone of his work is one of pessimism, its bleakness is alleviated by Grove's belief in the value of moral integrity, even in the face of inevitable defeat. His realistic approach to fiction was unusual in a period when idyllic romances were popular. His major weakness is his use of English, characterized by a stiffness which detracts from the quality of his dialogue and obscures his depth and insight. Plots tend to be episodic, and a passion for exhaustive technical exposition often impedes the progress of a story. Although he depicts a few strong and convincing characters, his isolation from close human companionship during the greater portion of his life affects his ability to portray people with whom the readers can become involved.

Grove's own character penetrated his writing most effectively in such autobiographical sketches as *Over Prairie Trails.* The courage and integrity which pervaded his life raises his writing, despite its defects, to the level of near-greatness. In 1945, three years before his death, he received gratifying recognition in the form of an honorary Litt.D. from the University of Toronto, and his autobiographical *In Search of Myself* (1946) won the Governor General's Award. Grove's papers are deposited in the Library of the University of Manitoba. Wilfred Eggleston, "Frederick Philip Grove" in *Our Living Tradition* (Toronto 1957); Ruth Mackenzie, "Life In A New Land," *Can.*

Lit., 7 (Winter, 1961); A. E. McCourt, "Spokesman of a Race?" *The Canadian West in Fiction* (Toronto, 1949); Desmond Pacey, *Frederick Philip Grove* (Toronto, 1945); Desmond Pacey, "Frederick Philip Grove: A Group of Letters," *Can. Lit.*, 11 (Winter, 1962); M. G. Parks, Introduction to *The Fruits of the Earth* (Toronto, 1965); Malcolm Ross, Introduction to *Over Prairie Trails* (Toronto, 1957); R. E. Watters, Introduction to *The Master of the Mill* (Toronto, 1961).

GERMAINE GUEVREMONT (1900-). Née à Saint-Jérôme, Germaine Grignon étudia aux couvents de Sainte-Scolastique, Saint-Jérôme et Lachine. Mariée à Hyacinthe Guèvremont, elle habita Sorel où elle collabora au *Courrier de Sorel,* puis à *Paysana.* Venue à Montréal, elle devint secrétaire de la Société des écrivains canadiens. En 1942, elle publia des récits terriens, *En pleine terre,* qui attirèrent l'attention sur son talent. En 1945, elle publia *Le Survenant* qui fut aussitôt accueilli comme un des meilleurs romans du Canada français. C'était le premier volume d'une trilogie dont le deuxième *Marie-Didace* a paru en 1947. Ces deux romans ont été traduits en anglais et publiés en 1950 sous le titre *The Outlander* et *Monk's Reach* et lui ont valu le prix du gouverneur général pour le roman. Germaine Guèvremont a reçu plusieurs autres prix et est membre de l'Académie canadienne-française et de la Société royale du Canada.

Le roman paysan de Germaine Guèvremont est réaliste et poétique à la fois. L'histoire est celle de l'extinction d'une famille terrienne—comme celle de *30 arpents* de Ringuet—mais sans surcharge; les personnages sont parfaitement accordés à la nature et les dialogues sont d'un naturel rare. L'oeuvre est d'une sensibilité remarquable et fait de Germaine Guèvremont un des meilleurs romanciers de moeurs du Canada français en même temps qu'un

prosateur de haute qualité. On lira sur elle le livre de Rita Leclerc (1963).

RALPH GUSTAFSON (1909-). Born of Anglo-Swedish stock at Lime Ridge, Quebec, Ralph Barker Gustafson attended Bishop's University, where he studied English and History. Following his graduation from Bishop's with an M.A., he studied at Oxford for three years. He was awarded the Prix David by the Quebec government for his first volume of poems *The Golden Chalice* (1935).

A second book *Alfred the Great* (1937), a play in blank verse, was commissioned by the CBC. In *Epithalamion in Time of War* (1941) he began to employ more modern and experimental techniques. Under the influence of Gerard Manley Hopkins and Dylan Thomas, Gustafson adopted a style which became increasingly elliptical and played upon the emotional quality of word combinations.

Lyrics Unromantic (1942), acclaimed for its unity and subtlety of tone and theme, was published in the same year as the first *Penguin Anthology of Canadian Poetry,* which included five of his own poems. In 1944 he edited a further Penguin anthology *Canadian Accent,* a collection of short stories and poetry. Gustafson, while living in New York, published his poetry in literary periodicals at home and abroad, and his short stories and critical articles appeared in numerous anthologies, including *Best American Short Stories* (1948 and 1950), *A Book of Canadian Stories* (1952) and in a collection of his own, *Summer Storm* (1958). In 1958 he edited the second *Penguin Book of Canadian Verse,* and in 1960 published two further books of his own work: *Rivers Among Rocks,* in which his theme is the life-giving "rivers" that run among the chaotic "rocks" of modern civilization, and *Rocky Mountain Poems,* expressing the grandeur and challenge of the Rockies. In these poems, as in the volume of his collected poems *Flight Into Darkness* (1944), his style is often characterized by a startling and sometimes incongruous use of word associations. Language is reduced to such skeletal remains that the cursory reader has difficulty in reconstructing the form. For the careful and discriminating, his poems have a rich melodic and emotional quality. Gustafson is now the first Poet-in-Residence at Bishop's University. Louis Dudek, "Two Canadian Poets: Ralph Gustafson and Eli Mandel," *Culture*, XXII (June, 1961); Milton Wilson, "Letters in Canada: 1960," *UTQ*, XXX (July, 1961).

RODERICK HAIG-BROWN (1908-   ).
Born in Sussex, England, Roderick Langmere Haig-Brown was educated at Charterhouse School in Surrey. He came to British Columbia in his late teens and worked on the Pacific coast in logging camps. During a visit to England, he wrote his first book *Silver* (1931), the life-story of the Atlantic salmon, and began *Pool and Rapid* (1932) which was published on his return to Canada. His interest in fishing and the outdoor life led him to settle on a farm flanking the banks of the Campbell River on Vancouver Island. Here, apart from service in the Canadian Army from 1939 to 1945, he has spent his time writing, fishing, farming and acting as magistrate and Judge of the Juvenile Court for the community.

In his study of the sport of fishing, Haig-Brown has become established as an authority with such collections of essays as *The Western Angler* (1939) and *Return to the River* (1941). His exact, detailed knowledge of nature, coupled with his concern for social questions, has brought forth novels like *Timber* (1942), which treats problems of the logging industry, and stories for juveniles, *Starbuck Valley Winter* (1943) and *Saltwater Summer* (1948).

A River Never Sleeps (1946), a semi-autobiography, reveals his view of fishing as an "art, ephemeral, graceful, complicated, full of tradition yet never static." It is a symbol of life as it should be—the pleasurable experience of an intelligent individual. In *Measure of the Year* (1950) his pleasure in fishing is extended to all the experiences of life in the country. From *Fisherman's Spring* (1951), *Fisherman's Winter* (1954), *Fisherman's Summer* (1959) and *Fisherman's Fall* (1965) emerges, for the writer, a pattern of civilized life, for the reader, "thoughts and ideas that might otherwise have remained idle and forgotten in the back of the mind." Haig-Brown's style is as quiet and thoughtful as his approach to life.

ARTHUR HAILEY (1920-   ). Born in Luton, England, Hailey was educated there and served during World War II as a pilot in the R.A.F. He came to Canada in 1947 and since 1956 has been a leading writer of television drama and fiction.

Two early novels are *Runaway Zero-Eight* (1958) and *The Final Diagnosis* (1959). His *Flight Into Danger* (1959) was first written as a television drama and since then has been made into a novel and a popular movie. *In High Places* (1961, *En haut lieu*, 1962) about Canadian-American relations, is characteristically dramatic and suspenseful in the treatment of moments of crisis. In *Close-Up on Writing for Television* (1960), Hailey illuminates the theoretical problems of such writing by illustrating from his own work. His *Hotel* (1965), which is set in New Orleans and combines a fast-moving plot with a wealth of detail about hotel administration, became a best seller and movie. In 1966 Hailey moved to the environs of San Francisco where he is working on a novel concerned with aviation.

---

[68]

THOMAS CHANDLER HALIBURTON (1796-1865). Born in Windsor, Nova Scotia, of Loyalist background, Haliburton was educated at King's College where he received his B.A. degree (1815) and was called to the bar of Nova Scotia in 1820. After graduation, he began his law practice at Annapolis Royal. He was elected Annapolis' representative to the Legislative Assembly in 1826, and he succeeded his father in 1829 as judge of the Inferior Court of Common Pleas.

Although in 1823 he had published an anonymous pamphlet entitled *General Description of Nova Scotia,* the first literary effort to appear under his own name was a history of his province, *A Historical and Statistical Account of Nova Scotia* (1829). In 1835, however, Joseph Howe printed in *The Novascotian* the first of Haliburton's humorous sketches about Sam Slick. Three series of these papers were printed in book form under the title *The Clockmaker, or, the Sayings and Doings of Sam Slick, of Slickville* (1836, 1838 and 1840). The shrewd and witty Sam Slick, wise in the ways of "soft sawder" and "human natur," very quickly gained a wide popularity, and the volumes were pirated in the United States and translated into several languages. Though the first series is the best in humour and originality, Haliburton continued the sketches in answer to popular demand, publishing two series of *The Attaché, or, Sam Slick in England* (1843 and 1844) and *Sam Slick's Wise-Saws and Modern Instances* (1853).

Haliburton's genuine concern for the future of Nova Scotia and of Canada, lightly masked by humour in the Sam Slick collections, was explicitly voiced in such serious tracts as *The Bubbles of Canada* (1839) and *A Reply to the Report of the Earl of Durham* (1839). In 1841 he became a judge of the Supreme Court of Nova Scotia, a position he held until his retirement in 1856. *Rule and Misrule of the English in America,* the last of his serious works, was published in 1851.

He continued his writing of humorous fiction as an avocation and was popular with a widespread reading public, not only in Canada and the United States, but in England and on the Continent. *The Letter-Bag of the Great Western; or, Life in a Steamer* was published in 1840, *The Old Judge; or Life in a Colony* in 1849 and *Traits of American Humour, by Native Authors* in 1852. He spent his later years in England, and was a member of the British House of Commons from 1859 until his death. One of the earliest Canadian writers to win international recognition, Haliburton created in Sam Slick a comic figure of enduring appeal, and the sketches, although they have lost the immediacy of their satiric sting against both slippery Yankee commercialism and Nova Scotian lethargy and gullibility, still retain their power to entertain. R. P. Baker, *A History of English-Canadian Literature to the Confederation* (Cambridge, 1920); V. L. O. Chittick, *Thomas Chandler Haliburton* (New York, 1924); V. L. O. Chittick, "The Hybrid Comic: Origins of Sam Slick," *Can. Lit.,* 14 (Autumn, 1962); V. L. O. Chittick, "Many-Sided Haliburton," *Dalhousie Review,* XLI, (Summer 1961); Fred Cogswell, "Haliburton," in *Literary History of Canada* (1965); Northrop Frye, "Haliburton: Mask and Ego," *Alphabet,* 5 (December, 1962); J. D. Logan, *Thomas Chandler Haliburton* (Toronto, 1925); R. L. McDougall, "Thomas Chandler Haliburton" in *Our Living Tradition,* 2nd Series (Toronto, 1959).

RONALD HAMBLETON (1917-). Born in England, Hambleton came to Canada in 1924. After his education in Vancouver, he worked along the Pacific Coast and in the Toronto area. During travels in England, he met some of the young poets of the modern school. A contributor to *The Canadian Forum* and *The Partisan Review,* he edited an important collection of verse by Dudek, Page, Souster, Wreford and himself entitled *Unit of Five* (1944). His poetry in *Object and Event* (1953), intellectual and metaphysical, is facile and witty although frequently verbose. He treats from a socialistic viewpoint the economic problems of the war and postwar period. In recent years he has devoted himself to radio scripts, a comic novel dealing with British Columbia life *Every Man Is an Island* (1959) and an ironical tale of a sea voyage *There Goes MacGill* (1962).

W. G. HARDY (1896-   ). Born on a farm near Lindsay, Ontario, William George Hardy attended Victoria College and graduated from the University of Toronto in English and Classics. He took his M.A. at the University of Toronto and his Ph.D. from the University of Chicago. After service with the Canadian Expeditionary Force in World War I, he lectured at the University of Toronto before joining the Department of Classics at the University of Alberta.

Hardy's career has been distinguished for its breadth of interest. For a time he was business manager of *The Rebel,* now *The Canadian Forum,* and was president of the Canadian Authors Association (1950/51). The writing of historical fiction has been an avocation which has brought well-deserved recognition. He wrote many short stories, and a first novel *Son of Eli* was serialized in *Maclean's* in 1929. *Father Abraham* (1935), a novel based on the life of the biblical patriarch, demonstrated sound antiquarian knowledge and research, as well as an imaginative feeling for ancient history as a parallel to modern.

Turn Back the River (1938) treated the decadent Roman society of Catiline and Claudia in the same well authenticated manner, and *All the Trumpets*

Sounded (1942) returned to a biblical theme with the story of Moses. *The Unfulfilled* (1951), set in Toronto and New York, and *The City of Libertines* (1957), set in Rome, are both sociological and historical in theme; they imply the universality of human passions that distinguished the earlier novels, and they give modern significance to such recurring concerns as totalitarianism and a sense of national identity.

JEAN-CHARLES HARVEY (1891-1967). Né à La Malbaie, Harvey étudia au Séminaire de Chicoutimi et entra dans la compagnie de Jésus dont il sortit quelques années plus tard. Journaliste, il travailla à *La Presse* et à *La Patrie;* de 1926 à 1934, il fut rédacteur en chef du *Soleil.* Après un stage comme directeur du bureau de la Statistique du Québec, il fonda *Le Jour* qu'il dirigea de 1937 à 1946. Il a été ensuite à l'emploi du service international de Radio-Canada et a été quelques années directeur du *Petit Journal.*

Son oeuvre de journaliste, qui est considérable, n'a pas été recueillie en volumes, sauf des articles de critique littéraire réunis dans *Pages de critique* (1926) et dans *Art et combat* (1937). Il a aussi écrit des poèmes publiés sous le titre *La fille du silence* (1958), mais c'est comme romancier qu'il est surtout connu.

Dans *Marcel Faure* (1922) et dans *Les demi-civilisés* (1934), il a utilisé ses personnages pour exposer ses vues sur l'émancipation économique du Québec et sur les déficiences du système d'enseignement. Ce sont des romans à thèse qui ont déjà beaucoup vieilli. Son roman anti-communiste *Les Paradis de sable* (1953) est de la même veine. Ses meilleures pages sont des nouvelles inspirées par le sentiment de la nature ou par la vision idéaliste d'un monde où la liberté serait totale et son meilleur livre est *L'Homme qui va* (1929).

CHARLES HEAVYSEGE (1816-1876).
Born in England, Heavysege settled in
Montreal as a cabinet-maker and
carpenter in 1853. Later he worked as
a journalist for the Montreal *Daily
Witness* and the *Transcript*. His first
book *The Revolt of Tartarus* (1852), a
verse drama, was published anonymously in England, but he was so dis-
satisfied with this effort that he later
destroyed all the copies he could find.
This work was followed by *Saul: A
Drama in Three Parts* (1857, 1859,
revised in 1869), a philosophical verse
drama which drew its theme and
inspiration from the Bible. Heavysege's
work displays some striking characters,
a certain noble eloquence and also pompous passages of pseudo-Elizabethan
rhetoric. Coventry Patmore, in a
favourable review of *Saul* in *The North
British Review* (1858), thought that
Heavysege was entirely on the side of
the good angels, but Professor Thomas
R. Dale, in an unpublished University
of Chicago dissertation (1951), has
assembled evidence of the dramatist's
"rebellious and questioning spirit,"
more in accord with modern criticism
than with mid-Victorian didacticism.

Heavysege also published *The Revolt
of Tartarus* (a revised edition, Montreal,
1855); *Sonnets* (1855); *Count Filippo;
or The Unequal Marriage* (1860), an
Italian tragedy of love and intrigue;
The Advocate (1865), an unsuccessful
novel set in Montreal; and *Jephthah's
Daughter* (1865), another Biblical
dramatic poem. There are some minor
poems: *The Owl* (1864), imitative of
Poe's "The Raven," *The Dark Hunts-
man* (1864) and *Jezebel* (1867). L. J.
Burpee, "Charles Heavysege" in *Royal
Society Proceedings and Transactions*
(Ottawa, 1901); T. R. Dale, "The
Revolt of Charles Heavysege," *UTQ*,
XXII (October, 1952).

ANNE HEBERT (1916-   ). Née à Ste
Catherine (Portneuf), fille du critique
Maurice Hébert et cousine de Saint-
Denys-Garneau, Anne Hébert a eu une
enfance maladive et une éducation
privée. Récemment, elle a éte employée
par l'Office national du Film comme
scénariste et elle a fait de longs
séjours en France. Membre de la
Société royale du Canada, elle a publié
des poèmes, des nouvelles, un roman
et des pièces de théâtre.

Son premier recueil, *Les Songes en
équilibre* (1942) a tout de suite retenu
l'attention. Poèmes fort simples faits
des rêves d'une enfant recluse qui se
joue des mots et des choses pour se
libérer de la solitude. Dans *Le Tombeau
des rois* (1953), le ton est devenu grave,
tragique; le style est d'un dépouillement
extrême pour s'accorder à la solitude
intérieure que le poète éprouve devant
le monde dont il se sent dépossédé. Le
thème du mur est ici central, il repré-
sente la solitude, l'incommunicabilité des
êtres, solitude qui est préfiguration de
la mort symbolisée ici par le couteau.
Les poésies récentes qui occupent la
dernière partie des *Poèmes* (1960)
chantent, au contraire, la réconciliation
du poète avec le monde et avec la vie;
le mur a été franchi, la poétesse habite
la terre et l'eau, elle rompt le pain et le
mange avec ses semblables, la poésie est
devenue habitable comme l'univers. Le
ton reste viril, voire dur, mais apparaît
pour la première fois une certaine
chaleur humaine.

Les contes et nouvelles réunis dans
Le Torrent (1950, réédité en 1963) sont
en général des récits charmants, sauf
Le Torrent qui a une force, une
intensité bouleversante. Cette histoire
d'un être dépossédé de tout, frustré,
bouillant de désirs inassouvis est un
des brefs récits les plus forts de toute
la littérature canadienne. Son unique
roman, *Les chambres de bois* (1958),
écrit dans une langue poétique d'une
belle qualité, est peut-être une autre
expression de la réconciliation du poète
avec la vie. Ses personnages ont quelque
chose de légendaire et d'irréel et ils
s'agitent dans un univers de rêve; mais
Catherine en sort en se donnant à un

garçon simple et fort et s'évade ainsi des chambres de bois où elle étouffait.

Les personnages du théâtre d'Anne Hébert étouffent aussi. *La Mercière assassinée (Ecrits du Canada français,* IV) est une pièce policière que l'auteur a écrite sans doute pour se faire la main; la seconde, *le Temps sauvage (Ecrits du Canada français,* XVI) lui est nettement supérieure et reprend dans un autre style les thèmes essentiels de sa poésie et de ses récits. Ces conflits qui s'élèvent entre une mère qui rêve de maintenir sa famille dans un monde d'une pureté idéale et ses enfants qui veulent répondre à l'appel de la vie sont la matière de dialogues d'une beauté et d'un sens profonds. Ce n'est peut-être pas du théâtre selon les règles habitu-elles; c'est en tout cas un texte d'une richesse peu commune dans les lettres canadiennes.

Sur Anne Hébert on peut consulter Guy Robert, *La poétique du songe* (1962); Gilles Marcotte, *Une littérature qui se fait* (1962); Maurice Blain, *Anne Hébert ou le risque de vivre (Liberté,* septembre-octobre 1959); Paul Wyczynski, *L'Univers poétique d'Anne Hébert (L'Enseignement secondaire,* mars-avril 1963); F. R. Scott, *St-Denys-Garneau, Anne Hébert, Translations* (1962): Albert Béguin, *Anne Hébert et la solitude (Le Devoir,* 3 octobre 1953); Jeanne Lapointe, *Mystère de la parole par Anne Hébert (Cité libre,* avril 1961); P. Purcell, *Agonizing solitude: the poetry of Anne Hébert (Canadian Literature,* fall 1961).

MAURICE HEBERT (1888-1960). Né à Québec, Hébert a étudié au Collège de Sainte-Anne de la Pocatière, au Séminaire de Québec et à l'Université Laval. Il fut directeur de l'Office du tourisme de la province de Québec et, disciple de Mgr Camille Roy, il a publié de nombreuses études critiques, notamment dans *Le Canada français,* qui ont ensuite été réunies dans *De*

livres en livres (1929), et *D'un livre à l'autre* (1932) et *Les lettres au Canada français* (1936). Il fut un tenant de l'ordre et de la clarté et un défenseur du classicisme. Membre de la Société royale du Canada, il était le père d'Anne Hébert.

ARTHUR HEMING (1870-1940). Born in Paris, Ontario, Arthur Henry Howard Heming studied art in Hamilton, New York and London. He returned as a teacher to the Hamilton Art School and contributed illustrations to various Canadian and American magazines. His first book, *Spirit Lake* (1907), written when another author failed to produce a manuscript for illustrations already drawn, is filled with his intimate knowledge of wood-craft and animal life. As in other books, *The Drama of the Forests* (1921) and *The Living Forest* (1925), Heming is a careful craftsman and tells his stories clearly and simply. Bold yet mysterious illustrations, repro-duced from his own paintings, accom-pany the text and are a distinctive feature of his northern books.

GILLES HENAULT (1920-). Né à Saint-Majorique, Hénault a fait des études primaires supérieures et suivi les cours de la faculté des sciences sociales de l'Université de Montréal. Journaliste, il a fait partie du personnel du *Jour,* du *Canada,* de *La Presse* et du *Devoir,* particulièrement comme critique dramatique et chroniqueur littéraire. Après de minces recueils où se mani-feste l'influence du surréalisme, *Théâtre en plein air* (1946) et *Totems* (1953), il a atteint à une plus grande plénitude poétique dans les poèmes en prose du *Voyage au pays de mémoire* (1960) réédités avec ses poèmes récents dans *Sémaphore* (1962).

Il semble que Hénault cherche à exprimer un irrésistible désir de re-trouver, par delà la civilisation, l'homme primitif avec ses instincts premiers et sa poésie est souvent une sorte de cri orchestré et rythmé inspiré par les joies telluriques éprouvées au milieu d'un dur paysage de rochers, de glace et de neige. Cette poésie a un accent nettement nord-américain et donne l'impression qu'un Blanc cherche à exprimer les sensations et les désirs des Peaux-Rouges incapables de s'exprimer eux-mêmes. En tout cas, il y a dans cette poésie un accent sauvage qui heurte et émeut.

FRANCOIS HERTEL (1905-   ). Né à Rivière Ouelle, Rodolphe Dubé a étudié au Collège de Ste-Anne de la Pocatière, au Séminaire de Trois-Rivières et est entré chez les Pères Jésuites obtenant ses licences en philosophie et en théologie au Scolasticat de l'Immaculée Conception à Montréal. Ordonné prêtre, il a enseigné les lettres et la philosophie au Collège Jean de Brébeuf. Il est sorti de la compagnie de Jésus a habité Paris longtemps où il dirigeait les Editions de la Diaspora. Il est maintenant professeur de littérature française à la Queen's University. Il est membre de l'Académie canadienne-française et collabore à divers journaux canadiens. Il a touché un peu à tout, publiant poésies, romans et essais.

Après des débuts d'un romantisme sentimental, *Les Voix de mon rêve* (1934), il a publié des poésies d'inspiration religieuse et de style abstrait: *Axe et parallaxes* (1941), *Strophes et Catastrophes* (1943), *Cosmos* (1945), puis des poèmes de facture plus classique dans lesquels il exprime son angoisse, sa solitude et son désespoir: *Mes naufrages* (1950) et *Poèmes européens* (1961). De même, son premier roman, *Le Beau Risque* (1939) était le récit banal d'aventures de jeunesse, puis ses récits postérieurs, *Mondes chimériques* (1940), *Anatole Laplante, curieux homme* (1944) et *Journal d'Anatole Laplante* relatent

les aventures intellectuelles de deux personnages loufoques, Charles Lepic et Anatole Laplante, dans des pages pleines de blagues et de paradoxes. Dans *Leur inquiétude* (1936) il avait cherché à analyser les sentiments et les idées des jeunes des années '30 et il a tenté de se construire une philosophie personnelle dans *Pour un ordre personnaliste* (1942). Dans *Vers une sagesse* (1965) il s'explique sur son agnosticisme et son nihilisme. Hertel fut surtout un éveilleur et, par son goût du paradoxe et de l'humour, il a été un semeur d'inquiétude pour beaucoup de jeunes et il a exercé, surtout de 1940 à 1950, une influence considérable sur les écrivains en herbe. A lire: un article de Jean-Ethier Blais dans *L'Action Nationale* (mai 1947).

PAUL G. HIEBERT (1892-   ). Born in Pilot Mound, Manitoba, Paul Gerhard Hiebert was educated at the Universities of Manitoba (B.A. 1916), Toronto (M.A. 1917, M.Sc. 1921) and McGill (Ph.D. 1924). In 1924 he joined the Department of Chemistry of the University of Manitoba from which he resigned in 1953 to pursue his interests in gardening and philosophy at Carman, Manitoba.

In 1947 he published the novel *Sarah Binks*. The plot of this witty satire, a merciless parody of the style of a serious literary critic and biographer, is centred about some hundred poems supposedly written by "The Sweet Songstress of Saskatchewan," Sarah Binks. "Unschooled but unspoiled, this simple country girl has captured in her net of poesy the flatness of that great province . . . in deathless lines so much of its elusive spirit, the baldness of its prairies, the alkalinity of its soil, the richness of its insect life." Hiebert is working on another spoof of Saskatchewan poetry, the *School of Seven*.

In *Tower in Siloam* (1966) he turned

his attention to a serious probe of the inter-relation of science, philosophy, and religion. Lloyd Wheeler, Introduction to *Sarah Binks* (Toronto, 1964).

DARYL HINE (1936-). Born in Vancouver, British Columbia, Hine was educated at McGill University. He has published four volumes of poetry, *Five Poems* (1954), *The Carnal and the Crane* (1957), *The Devil's Picture Book* (1960, 1964) and *The Wooden Horse* (1965). An academic poet, versatile in prosody and fluent in the language of symbol and myth, Hine presents in his vivid and haunting lyrics disparate aspects of experience. His novel *The Prince of Darkness* (1961), with its satire of the mythical fantasies of Robert Graves, is less successful than Hine's poetry. *Polish Subtitles* (1963) is a picture of the circle in which he moved during a visit to Warsaw. Now living in New York and writing radio plays, he is also working on another novel.

HUGH HOOD (1928-). Born in Toronto of an English-speaking father from Nova Scotia and a French-Canadian mother, Hugh John Blagdon Hood was educated at the University of Toronto where he received his Ph.D. degree in 1955.

His first book, *Flying a Red Kite* (1962), is a collection of eleven short stories which reveal his narrative talent as well as his understanding of both French- and English-Canadian language and milieu. In his novel *White Figure, White Ground* (1964), Hood presents a brilliant painter Alexander MacDonald against a background of three locales—Nova Scotia, Montreal, and Toronto—at a turning point in his career as he searches for the secret of his father's past and its effect on himself.

Hood, who teaches English at the University of Montreal, continues to publish short stories, has finished a second novel entitled *Goody Two Shoes,* and is working on a series of semi-fictional memoirs to appear in magazines as "Scenes from Montreal Life."

JOSEPH HOWE (1804-1873). Born in Halifax, Nova Scotia, Howe was the son of a Loyalist journalist and printer from Boston who held for many years the offices of King's Printer and Postmaster General for the Maritime provinces. At thirteen, Howe was apprenticed to the printing trade and in 1829, after a year's experience as part-owner of *The Acadian,* became the proprietor and editor of *The Novascotian.* During the next eight years he travelled frequently throughout the province learning to know its people and becoming well-known himself. Founder of "The Club," which met at his home from 1828 to 1832 to discuss literature and politics, he printed in his paper the satirical and witty writings of various members of the group.

In 1835, Howe published in *The Novascotian* a letter accusing the magistrates of Halifax, who were crown appointees, of misappropriation of public funds and general incompetence. Indicted for libel, he defended himself and won his case by a six-and-one-half-hour speech, a rhetorical masterpiece and a successful plea for the freedom of the press in British North America. Following Howe's acquittal, all the magistrates of Halifax resigned, and he himself was elected to the Provincial Legislative Assembly the next year, to continue his fight for responsible government. In 1835 he published in *The Novascotian* the first of Thomas Chandler Haliburton's Sam Slick papers, which won for their author an international reputation.

A journalist, a patriot and a public-spirited citizen, Howe held various posts in the government of the Maritimes. Though he had opposed the Confederation of the provinces, in 1869 he accepted office first as President of the Council and then as Secretary of State in the Dominion Government under Sir John A. Macdonald, and was elected member of the House of Commons. In May, 1873, he retired from politics and shortly before his death became Lieutenant-Governor of Nova Scotia.

His publications consist largely of public papers and speeches, some travel sketches, a lampoon and one posthumous volume of *Poems and Essays* (1874). The latter includes such diverse works as "Acadia," a long unfinished narrative poem in heroic couplets, celebrating the beauties of Acadia and the brave struggle of early Nova Scotians against the Indians and natural hardships; "To Mary," a charming and wryly humorous love-lyric; and his patriotic "The Flag of Old England." Like his contemporary Goldsmith, Howe sought in his descriptive poetry to show the new world gaining in urbanity and politeness; and his editorial encouragement of literary merit did much to create a cultural atmosphere in Nova Scotia. R. P. Baker, *A History of English-Canadian Literature to the Confederation* (Cambridge, 1920); J. M. Beck, "Joseph Howe" in *Our Living Tradition,* 4th Series (Toronto, 1962); J. A. Roy, *Joseph Howe; A Study in Achievement and Frustration* (Toronto, 1935).

BRUCE HUTCHISON (1901-   ). Born in Prescott, Ontario, William Bruce Hutchison was educated in Victoria, B.C., and began his career in journalism at the age of nineteen. In 1925 he joined the Press Gallery in Ottawa, where he gained much of the experience which has made him a recognized authority on Canadian economic and political affairs.

His first book, *The Unknown Country* (1942), an enthusiastically patriotic survey of Canada and her people, received the Governor General's Award for creative non-fiction. It was followed in 1944 by a novel *The Hollow Men* based on his own experiences as a young journalist, and interesting for its intimate political revelations.

Hutchison became Associate Editor of the Winnipeg *Free Press* in 1944, and continued his extensive travels throughout the Dominion, gaining a familiarity with Canada which is reflected in his writing. In 1950 he published *The Fraser,* his contribution to the "Rivers of America Series," and in the same year took over the editorship of the Victoria *Daily Times.* He is now editor of the Vancouver *Sun.*

His biography *The Incredible Canadian* (1952) is the exciting story of the life and career of William Lyon Mackenzie King. *Canada: Tomorrow's Giant* (1957) is another social documentary in the same ardent spirit of Canadianism typical of Hutchison's work. *Mr. Prime Minister,* 1867-1964 reviews Canada's prime ministry from its creation to the present incumbent. Alexander Brady, "Letters in Canada: 1955," *UTQ,* XXV (April, 1956); J. R. MacGillivray, "Letters in Canada: 1944," *UTQ,* XIV (April, 1945).

MAURICE HUTTON (1856-1940). Born in England, Hutton was educated at Oxford. Elected a fellow of Merton College on completion of his studies, he taught Classics in England until 1880 when he joined the faculty of Toronto University. A learned humanist, teacher and educator, Hutton was elected F.R.S.C. in 1913. He published such scholarly studies as *The Greek Point of View* (1925), *Many Minds* (1927), *All the Rivers Run into the Sea* (1928) and *The Sisters, Jest and Earnest* (1930), which are notable for their clarity of presentation, robust humour and intelligent consideration of classical virtues.

HAROLD A. INNIS (1894-1952). Born near Otterville, Ontario, Harold Adams Innis was educated in Woodstock and graduated from McMaster University. He joined the Canadian Army in 1916 and served overseas in the artillery. On his return, he took his doctorate at the University of Chicago in 1920. That year he joined the faculty of the University of Toronto where his keen insight and scholarly approach soon won him recognition as a leading authority in the social and political sciences in Canada. His volume *The Fur Trade in Canada, An Introduction to Canadian Economic History* (1930), which traced the relationship of agencies of communication to the development of the trade, introduced a radically new approach in Canadian history. He followed this with several economic studies of both primary and secondary industries in Canada. Such penetrating and scholarly works as *Political Economy in the Modern State* (1946), *Empire and Communications* (1950), *Bias of Communication* (1951) and *Changing Concepts of Time* (1952) won him international as well as national fame. Elected in 1934 F.R.S.C., he served as the Society's President, as well as a member of several Royal Commissions. His career and influence are presented with insight in Donald Creighton's lively biography, *Harold Adams Innis: Portrait of a Scholar* (1957).

CHARLES ISRAEL (1920-). Born in the United States, Israel began his literary career by writing script for a radio detective series in Hollywood. In 1954 he moved to Toronto, where he was employed by the CBC. His first novel *How Many Angels* (1956) is concerned with political questions in the Sudetenland. *The Mark* (1958), which was filmed, is a psychological study set in California, and treats with quiet compassion the sensational question of sexual assault. Israel's creation of character, sympathetic and convincing, emphasizes the pitiable vulnerability of humanity. His third novel, *Rizpah* (1961), a fictionalized account of the career of Saul's concubine, does not fulfil the promise of *The Mark. Who Was Then The Gentleman?* (1963) is a historical novel dealing with the Peasants' Revolt in mediaeval England. *Shadows on a Wall* (1965) explores the complex social and personal relations which result when a Californian white couple adopts a seventeen-year-old African girl. In *The Hostages* (1966) Israel uses the resistance of right-wing fanatics to China's entry into the United Nations as the idea for a taut and suspensive tale.

ANNA JAMESON (1794-1860). Born in Ireland, the eldest of five daughters of Denis Murphy, a miniature painter who emigrated to England in 1798, Anna Brownell Murphy Jameson was a bright and domineering child, eager to teach herself and her sisters, and responsible in considerable part for their education as well as her own. A combination of family need and personal ambition led her, at sixteen, into a governess' "career," in which she served intermittently for the next fifteen years.

In 1825 she was married to Robert Jameson, a young barrister who had been a boyhood friend of Hartley Coleridge and who was to become Attorney General of Upper Canada and later its first Vice-Chancellor. Jameson had the friends and influence which his wife lacked, and her first book *The Diary of an Ennuyée* was published with his enthusiastic patronage.

The *Diary*, a fictionalized autobiography which showed the influence both of Mme de Staël's *Corinne* and of Byron's *Childe Harold,* was an account of a continental trip taken in 1821/22 while Anna was governess to the Rowles family. Though not received with universal critical enthusiasm, it was a popular work and launched its author on a writing career which she followed diligently until the end of her life.

Her works range over a diversified field. *Memoirs of the Loves of the Poets* (1829) and *Memoirs of Celebrated Female Sovereigns* (1831) are collections of lively, informative but unimpressive essays, graceful in expression rather than profound in thought. *Visits and Sketches at Home and Abroad* (1834), a second travel diary, but this time without the lachrymose heroine mask, is forthright in its observations and remarkable for its introduction of a wide range of German life, literature and art to the English reading public, at a time when an interest in Germany was awakening. *Characteristics of Women* (1832), a series of essays in the psychological criticism of Shakespeare's heroines, was a major triumph: from the time of its publication, Anna Jameson was an accepted—even a renowned—writer both in England and on the continent.

In 1836/37, she joined her husband in Upper Canada. While her coming did nothing to repair an already broken marriage, her brief stay inspired *Winter Studies and Summer Rambles in Canada* (1838), an engaging and precise, if sometimes caustic, account of Toronto and of a trip from Toronto to Sault Ste. Marie, combined with chapters of comment on German literature, art and music. Although it is the product of a stay of only eight months, Anna Jameson's picture of Upper Canada in 1837 is memorable both for its scope and for the keenness of its observations.

In the forties, with her reputation firmly established, Mrs. Jameson directed her energy mainly to the criticism of art. Between 1848 and her death in 1860, she compiled a massive history of Christian art: *Sacred and Legendary Art* (1848), *Legends of the Monastic Orders* (1850), *Legends of the Madonna* (1852) and *The History of Our Lord,* the latter completed posthumously in 1864 by Lady Eastlake, wife of the director of the National Gallery.

The position and rights of women is an important theme in all of Anna Jameson's writing. Her *Sisters of Charity* (1855) and *The Communion of Labour* (1856) are pamphlets reporting on specific fields of feminine endeavour as found in Europe and suggesting their adoption and adaptation to English needs.

By a combination of driving ambition, writing talent and acuteness in assessing public taste, Anna Jameson rose to a position of prominence with the literary élite as well as popularity with the reading public of her day. Mrs. Stewart Erskine, *Anna Jameson* (London, 1915); G. H. Needler, editor, Introduction to *Letters of Anna Jameson to Ottilie von Goethe* (London, 1939); Clara Thomas, Introduction to *Winter Studies and Summer Rambles in Canada* (Toronto, 1965).

CLAUDE JASMIN (1930-   ). Né à Montréal, il a étudié au Collège Grasset et à l'Ecole des Arts appliqués dont il est diplômé. Il a été tour à tour, et est simultanément, céramiste, comédien, professeur et critique d'art, décorateur à Radio-Canada, dramaturge et romancier. De 1960 à 1965, il a publié une pièce et cinq romans, dont le second, *La Corde au cou* (1960) lui valut le Prix du Cercle du Livre de France, et dont les meilleurs semblent être *Délivrez-nous du mal* (1961) et *Ethel et le terroriste* (1964). Jasmin écrit en phrases rapides et syncopées des récits haletants dans lesquels les personnages fuient la société et se fuient eux-mêmes et cherchent dans l'amour et la violence l'oubli de leur milieu. Ses dialogues et descriptions abondent en termes grossiers dans le but de faire choc. Gilles Marcotte lui a consacré une importante conférence publiée par la faculté des Lettres de l'Université de Montréal (1965).

PAULINE JOHNSON (1861-1913). Born on the Six Nations Indian Reserve, Brant County, Upper Canada, daughter of a hereditary Mohawk Chief and an English mother, Emily Pauline Johnson (Tekahionwake) had little formal education. She was an avid reader and had read Byron, Scott, Longfellow, Shakespeare and the great essayists of England before the age of twelve, when she began writing creditable verse. During her teens, many well-known periodicals in England, Canada and the United States, such as *Gems of Poetry, The Week, Saturday Night, The Athenaeum, The Academy, Harper's Weekly,* were publishing her verses. Although she was fascinated with the thought of becoming an actress, it was not until 1892 that she was invited to participate in an evening of Canadian literature with national authors reading from their own works. Miss Johnson's "A Cry from an Indian Wife"—a poem depicting the Indian's side in the North-West rebellion—was enthusiastically received. After several such successful evenings, for one of which she wrote her best-known poem "The Song My Paddle Sings," Miss Johnson began a series of recitals across Canada. In 1894, she left for a tour in England. While there she published her first book *The White Wampum* (1895) which was a great success. With her influential letters of introduction, London society and literary circles were delighted to receive her. On returning to Canada, she toured from coast to coast, reciting

her verse in a buckskin dress and the traditionally colourful costume of an Indian princess. In 1903 she brought out her second very popular volume of verse *Canadian Born.*

After two more visits to England, one to the United States and a final tour of Canada, Miss Johnson settled in Vancouver where she continued her writings and published *Legends of Vancouver* (1911), prose tales of the Indians of the Pacific Coast, and her collected poems *Flint and Feather* (1912). In theme these poems indicate her transition from the protagonist of a wronged people, through a Canadian patriotism, to a cosmopolitan interest in humanity. Further tales *The Moccasin Maker,* much of which is a fictional treatment of her own mother's life, and *The Shagganappi,* a collection of boys' stories about Indians, appeared in 1913. Her immense popularity during her lifetime was due to her colourful appearance, the sentimental appeal of her heredity, and the nationalistic flavour of her early poems. Her picturesque descriptions of simple natural scenes to which every imagination can respond, her singing rhythms and warm blend of pathos and humour are likely to insure her continuing popular acceptance. Mrs. W. Garland Foster, *The Mohawk Princess* (Vancouver, 1931); Dorothy Keen and Martha McKeon as told to Mollie Gillen, "Pauline Johnson: Canada's Passionate Poet," *Chatelaine,* XXXIX (February and March, 1966); Walter J. McRaye, *Pauline Johnson and Her Friends* (Toronto, 1947); Norman Shrive, "What Happened to Pauline?" *Can.Lit.,* 13 (Summer, 1962); Marcus Van Steen, *Pauline Johnson; Her Life and Work* (Toronto, 1965).

GEORGE JOHNSTON (1913-). Born in Hamilton, Ontario, George W. Johnston graduated in English and Philosophy from the University of

Toronto (B.A. 1936). Before World War II, in which he served as a pilot in the R.C.A.F., he wrote verse and stories. His poetry, articles and short stories have appeared in *London Mercury, Atlantic Monthly, Queen's Quarterly* and *The Tamarack Review.* His first book *The Cruising Auk* (1959) is a delightful collection of unpretentious poems bubbling with the vitality of everyday life, in which the consciousness of death is ever present and playful fantasy is combined with pungently witty satire. *Home Free* (1966), characterized by the same wisdom and ironic wit, is his second volume of light verse. A Professor of English at Carleton University, Johnston translated with Peter Foote *The Saga of Gisli* (1963), an Icelandic epic of the thirteenth century.

D. G. JONES (1929-   ). Born at Bancroft, Ontario, Douglas Gordon Jones was educated at McGill and Queen's Universities. His poems first appeared in various Canadian publications, including the anthology *Poets 56.* His first volume *Frost on the Sun* came out in 1957, and was followed in 1961 by *The Sun Is Axeman.* His poems treat a wide variety of subjects, but he seems particularly interested in landscapes, birds and animals. His second volume still shows the influence of Eliot, Thomas, Auden and the imagists; in it, however, he also seems to be developing a characteristic meditative style, to be seen at its best is section IV of "Soliloquy to Absent Friends." Jones is with the Department of English at the University of Sherbrooke.

LEO KENNEDY (1907-   ). Born in England, Kennedy emigrated to Montreal with his family in 1912. He attended St. Patrick's Academy and the University of Montreal. From 1926 to

1928 he was associated with a group of poets which included F. R. Scott and A. J. M. Smith who ran *The McGill Fortnightly Review.* With the cessation of this magazine, Kennedy became one of the editors in 1928 of *The Canadian Mercury,* a short-lived journal publishing experimental Canadian writing. He produced poems, articles and several short stories.

His sole book of poetry *The Shrouding* (1933), preoccupied with the characteristically dominant theme of death, is rich and suggestive in its use of metaphysical tension and imagery. Some of his poems appear in the anthology *New Provinces* (1936) edited by F. R. Scott. W. E. Collin, "This Man of April" in *The White Savannahs* (Toronto, 1936).

BASIL KING (1859-1928). Born in Charlottetown, Prince Edward Island, William Benjamin Basil King studied in the Maritimes where he took his Master's degree at King's College, Nova Scotia. From 1884 to 1892, he was rector of St. Luke's Cathedral, Halifax, and from 1892 to 1900, of Christ Church, Cambridge, Massachusetts. Failing eyesight caused him to resign from the ministry and devote himself to writing and travelling. *Griselda* appeared in 1900, but *The Inner Shrine* (1909) was the first real success for this prolific writer who wrote some thirty-two best selling novels and books on morality during his lifetime. His style is didactic and sentimental, but to readers of his day his heroes and stories were exciting and satisfying. *The Conquest of Fear* (1921) was perhaps the most popular of his philosophical efforts.

WILLIAM KIRBY (1817-1906). Born in England, Kirby emigrated with his family to the United States in 1832. Because of his intense desire to live under British rule, he came to Canada in 1839, and after visiting Quebec, Montreal and Toronto settled in Niagara where he edited the Niagara *Mail* until he became Collector of Customs in 1871. His first book, *U.E., A Tale of Upper Canada* (1859), a narrative poem divided into twelve cantos of heroic couplets, was based partly on historical events in the Niagara district.

During his visit to Quebec in 1839, he became interested in a historic tablet inscribed "Le Chien d'Or," and the legends surrounding it were the foundation for his later masterpiece *The Golden Dog* (1877, *Le Chien d'or*, 1884). This historical romance of old Quebec in the days of Montcalm and Bigot, subtitled "A Romance of the Days of Louis Quinze in Quebec," is the product of almost eleven years of research. While the accuracy of some of the historical facts and figures is questionable, the plot is a skilful blending of three main stories, and the characters are credible individuals. Criticized at times for sensationalism or even melodrama, Kirby, with his fine artistic sense and detailed physical descriptions of rural and urban scenes, presents a vivid picture of the closing years of the old regime in New France. His book achieved great fame, was published in some thirty editions and translated into French by Pamphile LeMay and Louis Fréchette.

Kirby wrote several other books during his lifetime, including *The United Empire Loyalists of Canada* (1884), *Canadian Idylls* (1894), long patriotic poems modelled after the pastoral style of Goldsmith, and *Annals of Niagara* (1896), historic sketches of Newark, the ancient capital of Upper Canada, and of the Niagara Peninsula. None of these had the interest of *The Golden Dog*, which in its successful use of native material had a considerable influence on later Canadian fiction. A charter member of the R.S.C., Kirby was familiar with the leading English and Canadian literary and political figures of his day. Lorne Pierce, *William Kirby, The Portrait of a Tory Loyalist* (Toronto, 1929); W. R. Riddell, *William Kirby* (Toronto, 1923).

WATSON KIRKCONNELL (1895-   ). Born in Port Hope, Ontario, Kirkconnell graduated with distinction from Queen's University in 1916. Following war service, he studied music for two years in Toronto and in 1922 went on to Lincoln College, Oxford. He joined the staff of Wesley College, first as Professor of English and later of Classics. A prolific writer in many fields, he first ventured into literary scholarship with *An Outline of European Poetry*, published serially in 1927, and in the following year *European Elegies*, a book of translations. He produced his first volume of original verse, *The Tide of Life* in 1930, along with another volume of European poems *The European Heritage* and two books on Iceland, *The North American Book of Icelandic Verse* and *Canada to Iceland*. Pursuing his interest in Eastern European literatures, he published *The Magyar Muse* (1933), *Canadian Overtones* (1935), *A Golden Treasury of Polish Lyrics* and *The Death of King Buda* (1936), a translation from the Hungarian, and *A Primer of Hungarian* in 1938.

Titus the Toad (1938), Kirkconnell's only attempt at fiction, was followed by *Lyra Sacra* (1939), a set of four "occasional hymns." *The Flying Bull and Other Tales* (1940) is a collection of seventeen verse narratives set out in Chaucerian style in a Manitoba hotel.

In 1940, Kirkconnell became Head of the Department of English at McMaster University, and at the same time turned his attention temporarily from the arts to social studies. *Canadians All, A Primer of National Unity* was published in that year, and was followed in rapid sucession by

Our Communists and the New Canadian, Red Foe of Faith and *Future of European Freedom.* He collaborated with A.S.P. Woodhouse on *The Humanities in Canada* (1947).

In 1952 Kirkconnell published *The Celestial Cycle,* a study of the Paradise Lost theme as it has appeared in world literature. In 1962 he translated the epic *Pan Tadeusz* from the Polish. *Centennial Tales and Selected Poems* (1966) is a collection of his work in various genres. His unusual facility in many languages is demonstrated in his annual survey of "Publications in Other Languages" which appeared in the *University of Toronto Quarterly* from 1937 to 1966. Kirkconnell is President Emeritus of Nova Scotia's Acadia University which he headed from 1948 to 1964.

A. M. KLEIN (1909-   ). Born in Montreal, Abraham Moses Klein received a secular and Jewish education there. In 1926 he entered McGill University, where three years later he published in *The Canadian Mercury* his first poem, a sonnet entitled "Business." In the same year, while still an undergraduate, he contributed a total of thirty poems to various literary publications including the *Menorah Journal* and *The Canadian Forum.* From his early years he was interested in Talmudic studies, and had at one time studied for the rabbinate. After graduation from McGill in 1930, he enrolled in a law course at the University of Montreal. He was called to the Bar in 1933, and subsequently entered upon a full-time law practice.

Klein's first published volume was *Hath Not a Jew* . . . (1940). An authority on Jewish history, literature and religion, and one of the leading Talmudists in Canada, Klein reveals in this first collection an intense consciousness of his race. The lyrics, enriched by the exotic flavour of Judaic symbolism, reflect the Old Testament psalmists' arts of lamentation and praise, as well as their suggestive diction, and have a pervasive quality of exultation. *The Hitleriad* (1944) is a bitter invective on the Nazi persecution of the Jews. Although it displays his gift for satire, it contains little of the power and subtlety of his best work. *Poems* (1944) is also written within a Jewish frame of reference, and marks the end of this first period of his work.

His association with the Montreal group of poets, which included A. J. M. Smith, F. R. Scott and Leo Kennedy, influenced Klein to abandon temporarily purely Jewish themes. In his years at the University of Montreal, he gained an acquaintance with the French-Canadians in Quebec, and he drew upon this knowledge in his fourth and most successful collection of poems, *The Rocking Chair and Other Poems* (1948), which won a Governor General's Award. His effective use of symbolism, apt portraiture, vigorous expression, warm sympathy and humour are all revealed.

His novel *The Second Scroll* (1951) is a symbolical story of the Jewish search for a Messiah in this modern world. Klein's careful study of the writings of James Joyce is reflected in the method and the emphasis upon language and myth. The title of the book is significant: the Old Testament is considered the First Scroll. The story is set in the period between 1917 and 1949, and the dominant theme involves the return of the Jews for religious and national reasons to the Holy Land. The central character, Uncle Melech Davidson, is developed to represent a "mirror . . . of the events of our time," and ultimately symbolizes the Hebrew concept of the Messiah. Contemporary Jewish history is interpreted in the light of Old Testament tradition and prophecy. As Professor M. W. Steinberg remarks, "Through meaningful Biblical allusions and symbols in the text of the novel, Klein suggests the reconciliation of good and evil, necessary for the acceptance of God." Some of the novel is written in verse, and the prose itself displays much of the finely wrought power of high poetry.

In 1952, Klein published *Of Jewish Music, Ancient and Modern,* consisting of translations from the Yiddish. He was awarded the Lorne Pierce Medal in 1957 for his outstanding contributions to Canadian Literature. "A Symposium on A. M. Klein," *Can. Lit.,* 25 (Summer, 1965); W. E. Collin, "The Spirit's Palestine" in *The White Savannahs* (Toronto, 1936); Louis Dudek, "A. M. Klein," *The Canadian Forum,* 12 (May, 1932); Leon Edel, "Poetry and the Jewish Tradition," *Poetry: A Magazine of Verse,* 58 (April, 1941); Desmond Pacey, *Ten Canadian Poets* (Toronto, 1958); M. W. Steinberg, "Twentieth Century Pentateuch," *Can. Lit.,* 2 (Autumn, 1959); Milton Wilson, "Klein's Drowned Poet," *Can. Lit.,* 6 (Autumn, 1960).

RAYMOND KNISTER (1900-1932). Born near Blenheim, Ontario, where he spent many years working on an Essex farm, Knister graduated from Toronto University and Iowa State University. For a while in the early twenties, he lived in the mid-western United States, and for more than a year he was associate editor of *The Midland.* He contributed many rural stories and poems to this and other *avant-garde* magazines both Canadian and American. In 1928 he edited *Canadian Short Stories,* an anthology with an excellent critical introduction. The first and better of his two novels, *White Narcissus* (1929), about a city writer returning to the country and his old love, shows the influence of such Americans as Theodore Dreiser and Sherwood Anderson. *My Star Predominant* (1931)

is a fictional treatment of the last four years of Keats' life.

Knister was drowned in 1932 just when his reputation as a poet, short story writer and critic was becoming established. Both his poetry and prose were concerned mainly with rural life in Ontario. Although there is some sombreness and morbidity in his work, his attempt to develop an independent style lends a realistic atmosphere to his stories and a sharpness and clarity of presentation to his poetry. Knister was one of the first in Canada to accept the imagist movement. Leo Kennedy, "Raymond Knister," *The Canadian Forum,* XII (Sept., 1932); Dorothy Livesay, "Memoir," *Collected Poems of Raymond Knister* (Toronto, 1949); Peter Stevens, "The Old Futility of Art, Knister's Poetry," *Can. Lit.,* 23 (Winter, 1965).

HENRY KREISEL (1922-   ). Born in Vienna, Henry Kreisel received his early schooling there. After the Nazi occupation of 1938, he escaped to England, was interned during the war and sent to Canada. Released in 1941, he entered the University of Toronto and graduated with an M.A. After completing a Ph.D. at London, he joined the English Department of the University of Alberta. He is now head of that department.

In addition to numerous short stories published in various Canadian magazines and journals, and scripts written for CBC, Kreisel published *The Rich Man* (1948), a novel of a moderately succcesful immigrant to Canada who returns to his native Austria posing as a wealthy man who is inevitably exposed. Another novel, *The Betrayal* (1964), set in Edmonton, concerns the discovery of a former Austrian traitor by one of his embittered countrymen. The subsequent conflict, presented with a craftsmanship reminiscent of Conrad, depicts vividly the dilemma of conscience and expediency in the face of Nazi evil. John Stedmond, Introduction to *The Rich Man* (Toronto, 1961).

ALBERT LABERGE (1871-1960). Né à Beauharnois, Laberge étudia au Collège Sainte-Marie dont il fut chassé; il étudia ensuite le droit, puis fut journaliste de 1896 à 1932 à *La Presse* où il fut rédacteur sportif et critique d'art. Retraité, il voyagea en Europe en 1932, fit une croisière aux Antilles en 1937 et, vivant à la campagne, il publia à compte d'auteur et à tirage limité tous ses ouvrages, dont *La Scouine,* roman paru en 1918.

Agnostique et pessimiste, il a écrit un roman et des nouvelles qui sont d'un naturalisme unique au Canada français. *La Scouine* est un roman de la terre aussi sombre que ceux de Zola et plus noir que *30 arpents*. La plupart de ses nouvelles sont des évocations directes et sans fard des aspects les plus sordides de la vie. D'autre part, dans ses chroniques d'art, Laberge est habituellement trop élogieux à l'égard des artistes et écrivains qu'il a connus et dont il évoque le souvenir. Il n'a guère de sens critique. Ses nouvelles ont été recueillies dans *Images de la vie et de la mort* (1936), *La Fin du voyage* (1942), *Scènes de chaque jour* (1942), *Le Destin des hommes* (1950), *Fin de roman* (1951), *Images de la vie* (1952) et *Le Dernier Souper* (1953). Il a aussi publié *Peintres et écrivains d'hier et d'aujourd'hui* (1938), *Journalistes, écrivains et artistes* (1945). Gérard Bessette a publié une *Anthologie d'Albert Laberge* (1963) précédée d'une préface.

GUSTAVE LAMARCHE (1895-   ). Né à Montréal, le Père Gustave Lamarche étudia au Collège Bourget de Rigaud, à l'Institut catholique de Paris et aux universités de Montréal, Paris et Louvain, se spécialisant en littérature. Entré chez les Clercs de Saint-Viateur,

il fut ordonné prêtre et il a fait une longue carrière de professeur au Séminaire de Joliette (1927-1931), au Collège Bourget (1931-1934) et au Scolasticat des Clercs de Saint-Viateur à Joliette depuis 1937. En 1936, il a fondé les *Carnets viatoriens*, revue littéraire et religieuse qu'il a dirigée jusqu'en 1945. Il a écrit surtout pour le théâtre et ses pièces, toutes d'inspiration religieuse, sont d'un symbolisme difficile et d'un lyrisme mal freiné. Ses pièces principales sont *Jonathas* (1935), *Notre-Dame des Neiges* (1942) et *Les Gracques* (1945). Il a aussi publié des poèmes religieux *Palinods* (1944) d'une technique souvent compliquée mais où se trouvent quelques brefs poèmes d'une belle densité spirituelle et verbale. Il est membre de l'Académie canadienne-française.

BLANCHE LAMONTAGNE (1889-1958). Née aux Escoumains, Blanche Lamontagne a étudié dans divers couvents et a suivi des cours de littérature à l'Université de Montréal. Mariée à Hector Beauregard, elle a vécu en Gaspésie et à Montréal, mais toute sa biographie est celle de son oeuvre abondante qui en fait une des principales représentantes de la poésie d'inspiration régionaliste au début du vingtième siècle. Elle a écrit des poèmes historiques d'une grande banalité, mais elle a surtout chanté sa Gaspésie natale sans toutefois parvenir à faire sentir ce que cette région a de particulier. Elle a réussi à écrire quelques poèmes d'une tendresse émouvante perdus dans une foule de pièces sans caractère. Ses recueils sont: *Visions gaspésiennes* (1913), *Par nos champs et nos rives* (1917), *La Vieille Maison* (1920), *Les Trois Lyres* (1923), *Moisson nouvelle* (1926) et *Ma Gaspésie* (1928).

ARCHIBALD LAMPMAN (1861-1899). Born at Morpeth, Ontario, the son of a scholarly Anglican clergyman, Lampman moved with his family in 1867 to Gore's landing on Rice Lake. Here at the age of seven he suffered an acute attack of rheumatic fever which probably left his heart permanently weakened and made it necessary for him to receive his early education at home. Under his father's tutelage, he was early instructed in the love and art of poetry, and from his mother he learned to play the piano. As his health improved, he entered a private school in 1870, where he was thoroughly grounded in Latin and Greek, and later attended Trinity College School in Port Hope and Trinity College, Toronto. He graduated in Classics in 1882, and after a few months teaching in the high school at Orangeville, he joined the Post Office Department of the Civil Service in Ottawa, where he remained until his death.

His early poems appeared in Trinity's *Rouge et Noir*, in *The Week* and in other literary journals. In 1888, a volume entitled *Among the Millet* was financed by his wife's little legacy. These early poems reflect the influence of his reading in English poetry: Swinburne's phrasal extravagance and paganism; Keats's sensuous and often superfluous if colourful adjectives, and in a poem like "The Monk" or "Easter Eve" Gothic atmospherics and melodrama; Wordsworth's weighty moral tone; and Arnold's high-seriousness and hellenism. Everywhere, too, are examples of Lampman's disposition to dream—not only in such deliberately wistful pieces as "An Athenian Reverie," but also in his varied poems on rural life. In his accurate descriptions of the Ontario countryside, where in walking and on canoe trips he found life and adventure, he expresses his love and harmony with nature. "April" and "The Frogs" depict the "calm-eyed peace" of spring's flower buds, songbirds, dreaming frogs, ploughing horses and maple-sugar time, set in

contrast with "the loneliness, perplexity and pain" of the city; "Heat," presenting the hot glare of a summer's sun beating down on a dusty road with its solitary hay-cart, on flowers and cattle and crickets in fields through which runs a cool brook, is a poem rich in image, sensation, contrast and tension. In the ending of "Heat," where the effect of "the full furnace of this hour" is to heighten and clarify the poet's thought, as in many poems in which the landscape is so evocatively portrayed, the reader is always conscious that for Lampman, trained in the classics, human nature in action or contemplation is the proper subject of a poem. External nature, however, is more than a background, and like Wordsworth or Emerson, Lampman finds in the presence of nature not only beauty and comfort but also stimulus to dreams in which comes intuitive wisdom concerning himself and mankind.

During 1892, Lampman, together with his close friend Duncan Campbell Scott and William Wilfred Campbell, contributed to *The Globe* a weekly column on books called "At the Mermaid Inn." His criticism for the most part echoes Arnold's emphasis on humanity yet at the same time ironically reveals Lampman's own increasing disposition to escape from humanity into nature and reverie. His second volume of poems *Lyrics of Earth* appeared in 1895, the same year as his election as an F.R.S.C.; his third book *Alcyone* was ready for the press when he died on February 10, 1899. Lampman's themes continued to be the delights of nature with her striking march of seasons and unsuspected and sudden displays of beauty, her harmony and fulfilment in contrast with commercial society's discordant futility. Although metrically versatile, Lampman expresses many of his finest lyrics in the sonnet form. In one of his infrequent attempts at satire "The City of the End of Things," he represents his revulsion against the increasing mechanization of society. But he apparently did not find this genre sufficiently congenial to develop. Nor, with the exception of "At the Long Sault: May, 1660," which tells dramatically the story of Daulac's desperately gallant defence of Montreal against attacking Iroquois, does Lampman excel in narrative poetry.

His observant yet brooding spirit is best represented in his descriptive poetry, which imaginatively evokes the exciting sounds and sights of nature, and in his sonnets declarative of inner conflict and resentment against a system that fell far short of his utopian socialism. The unremitting craftsmanship of his work was appropriately described by his literary executor, Duncan Campbell Scott (who issued editions of Lampman's poems in 1900 and 1925), at the dedication of the Lampman memorial cairn near Morpeth in 1930, as "a symbol of moderation and poise in temper and style." Munro Beattie, "Archibald Lampman" in *Our Living Tradition* (Toronto, 1957); W. E. Collin, "Natural Landscape" in *The White Savannahs* (Toronto, 1936); Carl Y. Connor, *Archibald Lampman, Canadian Poet of Nature* (New York and Montreal, 1929); Louis Dudek, "Significance of Lampman," *Culture,* 18 (Sept., 1957); Desmond Pacey, *Ten Canadian Poets* (Toronto, 1958); F. W. Watt, "The Masks of Archibald Lampman," *UTQ,* XXVII (Jan. 1958).

GUSTAVE LANCTOT (1883-). Né à Saint-Constant (Laprairie), il étudia le droit à l'Université de Montréal, l'économie politique à l'Université d'Oxford dont il est docteur; et les lettres à l'Université de Paris. Archiviste et professeur, il fut directeur des Archives nationales à Ottawa de 1937 à 1948. Il a été en 1948 président de la Société royale du Canada qui lui a décerné aussi sa médaille Tyrrell. Archiviste, il a longtemps écrit surtout sur des questions controversées, et publié des biographies de François-Xavier Garneau (1926) et de Jacques Cartier (1947), et des ouvrages sur *L'administration de la Nouvelle-France* (1929), *Faussaires et faussetés en histoire canadienne* (1949), *Filles de joie ou filles du Roi* (1952), avant de faire la synthèse de ses travaux sur le régime français dans son *Histoire du Canada* en trois volumes (1960-1964). On lui doit aussi un ouvrage sur *Le Canada et la Révolution américaine* (1965), et plusieurs autres volumes.

ANDRE LANGEVIN (1927-). Né à Montréal, Langevin a été journaliste et est depuis plusieurs années à l'emploi de Radio-Canada comme réalisateur à la radio. Il est l'auteur de trois romans et de deux pièces de théâtre. Il n'a guère eu de succès au théâtre avec *Une nuit d'amour* (1954) et *L'Oeil du peuple* (1957), mais ses trois romans comptent parmi les meilleurs des années récentes.

Son premier roman, *Evadé de la nuit* (1951), lui mérita le Prix du Cercle du Livre de France et révélait un puissant tempérament de romancier. Le livre manque d'unité, le ton en est souvent forcé et l'auteur abuse avec un certain masochisme d'images qui donnent la nausée. Mais il est difficile de rester indifférent à ce drame de l'incommunicabilité des êtres qui empêche ses personnages de se rencontrer ailleurs que dans la mort. La vie est ici une marche aveugle dans un tunnel sans issue.

Poussière sur la ville (1953) est un des meilleurs romans canadiens. Avec une rare économie de moyens, Langevin y raconte la vie tragique d'un jeune médecin trompé qui voit sa femme se suicider parce que son amant décide d'épouser une autre femme. Le drame d'Alain Dubois est de vouloir vivre conscient et responsable dans un monde qui n'est ni l'un ni l'autre. Ce bref roman a la rigueur d'une tragédie classique et est écrit dans un style d'une belle simplicité.

Le troisième roman de Langevin, *Le temps des hommes* (1956) est moins réussi, mais cette histoire d'un prêtre défroqué qui cherche une raison de vivre et croit l'avoir trouvée lorsqu'il rencontre un meurtrier qui fuit la justice et qu'il cherche à sauver, est pathétique. Il y a ici un effort pour écrire un roman idéologique et Langevin a sans doute été influencé par les existentialistes; il est à son meilleur cependant quand il se contente de raconter une histoire comme il l'a fait dans *Poussière sur la ville*. Tout ce monde de Langevin est celui de déshérités qui sombrent dans le désespoir faute de pouvoir sortir de leur solitude perpétuelle et son oeuvre est un sorte de chant âpre et sévère inspiré par un sentiment de commisération à l'égard des hommes qui ne sont pas heureux.

Sur son oeuvre on peut consulter Gilles Marcotte, *Une littérature qui se fait*; W. E. Collin, *André Langevin and the problem of suffering* dans *Tamarack Review* (Winter 1959).

JACQUES LANGUIRAND (1930-   ). Né à Montréal, il est venu tôt au théâtre, a été comédien et est maintenant animateur à la télévision. Influencé par Beckett et Ionesco, il a le goût des situations cocasses ou sordides, des dialogues féroces ou loufoques et ses personnages insolites et invraisemblables soulignent le caractère absurde de l'existence. Ses principales pièces sont *Le Gibet* (1960) et *Les Insolites* (1962). Il a aussi publié un roman, *Tout compte fait* (1963) dans lequel un personnage appelé l'Eugène fait le bilan de sa vie dont il découvre la médiocrité en la comparant à ses rêves de jeunesse. On y retrouve l'atmosphère de son théâtre et ce thème, central chez lui, de l'incommunicabilité des êtres.

GEORGE THOMAS LANIGAN (1846-1886). Born at Three Rivers, Lower Canada, Lanigan was educated in Montreal. After a brief period as a telegrapher, he became sports editor of the Montreal *Gazette,* in 1869 founded the Montreal *Star,* and later served with the New York *World.* He wrote several good prose articles and pieces of literary criticism under the pseudonym Allid, and published translations of French-Canadian Folk songs entitled *National Ballads of Canada, Imitated and Translated from the Originals* (1865).

He is best known for his delightful absurdity "Threnody for the Ahkoond of Swat." His *Fables,* by G. Washington Aesop (1878), were quoted by Mark Twain in his "Library of American Humour."

GATIEN LAPOINTE (1931-   ). Né à Ste Justine (Dorchester), Lapointe a étudié au Séminaire de Québec, à l'Université de Montréal et à l'Université de Paris dont il est docteur ès lettres. Chargé de cours au Collège militaire de St-Jean et à l'Université de Montréal, il a obtenu en 1961 le prix du Club des poètes de Paris et, en 1963, le prix Du Maurier et le prix du Gouverneur général du Canada pour la poésie.

Tout jeune, il avait publié *Jour malaisé* (1953) et *Otages de la joie* (1955) et, depuis son séjour de six ans en Europe, son talent s'est affermi et ses deux derniers recueils comptent parmi les meilleurs des dernières années: *Le temps premier* (1962) et *Ode au St-Laurent* (1963). Cette poésie est simple, directe et dense. On y trouve des images justes et fortes et surtout des vers qui sont des apophtegmes par lesquels il définit le rôle du poète qui est de connaître, d'aimer et de nommer les choses. Cette poésie claire est un éloge de l'ordre et de la lumière, sources de joie. Le dernier recueil est plus *incarné,* il est l'affirmation de l'identification du poète avec son pays.

PAUL-MARIE LAPOINTE (1929-). Né à Saint-Félicien, Lapointe a étudié au Séminaire de Chicoutimi, au Collège de St-Laurent et à l'Ecole des Beaux-Arts de Montréal. Journaliste, il a collaboré à *L'Evénement-Journal,* à *La Presse* et au *Nouveau-Journal.* Il a été plus tard scenariste à la télévision et est depuis 1964 directeur du *Magazine Maclean.*

Fortement influencé par le surréalisme, il a d'abord publié des poèmes automatistes, manifestation ésotérique d'une révolte contre les valeurs bourgeoises *Le Vierge incendié* (1948). En 1960, il a publié *Arbres,* choix de poèmes inspirés par la misère des hommes, la puissance créatrice de la nature et le salut par l'amour: plus accessibles que les premiers, ces poèmes ont aussi une valeur polyphonique. On retrouve dans *Pour les âmes* (1965) ce mariage de l'amour charnel et de l'action sociale qui est une double défense contre le destin de l'homme d'ici sans cesse menacé par le froid des coeurs et celui du pays. C'est l'amour qui vaincra la mort: il y faut un supplément d'âme.

RINA LASNIER (1915-). Née à St-Grégoire (Iberville), Rina Lasnier a étudié au Collège Marguerite Bourgeoys de Montréal, au Palace Gate à Exeter (Angleterre) et à l'Université de Montréal. Elle fut journaliste et a occupé divers emplois de bibliothécaire, de secrétaire et de publiciste. Membre de l'Académie canadienne-française, elle a reçu le Prix Duvernay. Elle habite Joliette depuis 1955 et, en 1962, elle a été nommée membre du Conseil des Arts de la province de Québec.

Auteur d'oeuvres théâtrales inspirées par l'histoire religieuse du Canada: *Féerie indienne* (1939), *Le jeu de la voyagère* (1941) *Les fiançailles d'Anne de Nouë* (1943), *Notre-Dame du pain* (1947), Rina Lasnier est surtout un poète d'inspiration religieuse, mystique, dont l'oeuvre a une grande unité spirituelle et a atteint à une densité et à une profondeur toujours accrues. Ses premières *Images et proses* (1941) étaient des poèmes lyriques d'une forme très libre inspirés autant par l'amour de la nature que par la piété religieuse, et on y trouvait déjà le conflit intime de la poétesse divisée contre ellemême, assoiffée de possession et portée au renoncement. Son deuxième recueil *Madones canadiennes* (1944) réunit des pièces inspirées par des statues de la Vierge recueillies par Marius Barbeau; ce n'est pas son oeuvre la plus forte, mais on y trouve des réussites, surtout sur le ton mineur dans lequel sont écrites des pièces comme *Berceuse, La Dormition* ou *La Madone du prisonnier.*

Le Chant de la montée (1947) est un poème en quinze chants aux strophes amples et enveloppantes, entrecoupés d'interludes d'un ton léger, évoquant avec l'opulence et le charme des soiries et des parfums de l'Orient l'histoire de Rachel et de Jacob. Inspiré par l'Ecriture, ce poème n'en est ni une traduction, ni une paraphrase, mais une oeuvre originale et personnelle qui reprend, à propos de ces personnages bibliques, le thème essentiel de cette poésie qui est ce déchirement de la femme dont le ciel et la terre se disputent le coeur; l'auteur s'est proposé de montrer comment l'amour humain est une préfiguration de l'amour surnaturel mais les cris du coeur qui surgissent un peu partout dans cette oeuvre lui donnent une résonance profondément humaine et un accent tragique.

On retrouve les mêmes thèmes, et aussi le même sentiment de la nature, dans les derniers recueils, les plus dépouillés, les plus directs et les plus denses D'*Escales* (1950) à *Mémoire sans jours* (1960) en passant par *Présence de l'absence* (1956), Rina Lasnier n'a cessé de redire, sur un ton de plus en plus tendu, voire par moments presque crispé, ce mal d'être une femme en proie à la solitude, atteinte par la poignante douceur des choses et des hommes et rêvant toujours à son Dieu intangible. On y trouve des exercices peu convaincants, des pièces légères d'une tendresse qui tombe parfois dans la mièvrerie, et surtout des coulées de lave qui charrient tout sur leur passage, comme cette *Malemer* qui est une plongée dans la nuit profonde et agitée des tourments humains dont la poétesse aspire à sortir pour retrouver la lumière et la pureté d'un ciel sans nuages. Rina Lasnier reste une poétesse d'une profonde inspiration religieuse, mais les tentations de la terre occupent dans son oeuvre une place de plus en plus grande, de plus en plus dominante. En 1963 ont paru *Les Gisants*.

On peut consulter à son sujet Gilles Marcotte, *Une littérature qui se fait*; Victor Barbeau, *Images et proses de Rina Lasnier,* dans *L'Action Nationale,* Tome 17 (1941); Guy Sylvestre, *Le Chant de la Montée* dans *Le Droit* (10 avril 1948); Gérard Bessette, *Un grand poète,* dans *Canadian Literature* (Spring 1961) et le livre d'Eva Kushner (1964).

MARGARET LAURENCE (1926-   ). Born in Neepawa, Manitoba, Jean Margaret Laurence received her B.A. degree in 1947 from United College of the University of Manitoba. After graduation she married a civil engineer whose work took them to Somaliland, Ghana, and England where she now lives. Her early stories are primarily concerned with the West African concept of "Free-Dom." Her first published novel, *This Side Jordan* (1960), set in contemporary Ghana, is an imaginative depiction of the birth of that nation, of its contrapuntal influences of old and new, and its conflict of established white supremacy and emerging African intellectualism.

In 1963 a collection of ten stories appeared, *The To-Morrow Tamer and Other Stories,* which reveal a perceptive understanding of the response of individual West Africans in their struggle to achieve emancipation and human dignity. *The Prophets' Camel Bell* (1963, republished as *New Wind in a Dry Land,* 1964) is a sympathetically presented collection of historical and folk tales, poetry and even jokes of Somaliland.

The Stone Angel (1964), with its Manitoba prairie setting, illuminates by flashback technique the past of ninety-year-old Mrs. Hagar Currie Shipley as recalled a few days before her death. Her life, with its excesses of love, hate and meanness, is portrayed with intuitive insight in a style that is firm and convincing.

Another novel entitled *A Jest of God,* with a Canadian prairie setting, was published in 1966. Barry Callaghan, "The Writings of Margaret Laurence," *The Tamarack Review,* 36 (Summer, 1965); S. E. Read, "The Maze of Life: The Work of Margaret Laurence," *Can. Lit.,* 27 (Winter, 1966).

ANDRE LAURENDEAU (1912-   ). Né à Montréal, Laurendeau a étudié au Collège Sainte-Marie, à l'Université de Montréal et à l'Institut catholique de Paris. Avocat, il s'est surtout occupé des mouvements nationalistes du Québec et il a été directeur de *L'Action Nationale* avant d'entrer au *Devoir* dont il est le rédacteur-en-chef. Anti-conscriptioniste, il fut chef du parti du Bloc populaire provincial et député à l'Assemblée législative de 1944 à 1948. Il a aussi exprimé ses vues dans *Notre nationalisme* (1935) et *La crise de la conscription, 1942* (1962). Il est président conjoint de la Commission royale d'enquête sur le bilinguisme et le biculturalisme.

De plus en plus attiré par le théâtre et les belles-lettres, il a écrit une pièce psychologique qui a eu un certain succès.

Deux femmes terribles (Ecrits du Canada français, no 11), ainsi qu'un livre d'une grande sensibilité qui est un recueil de courts récits évoquant divers aspects du merveilleux de l'enfance *Voyages au pays de l'enfance* (1960). Dans un roman cruel, *Une vie d'enfer* (1965), il a peint un homme qui semble vouloir avilir et détruire les autres dans une sorte d'effort continu pour se purifier lui-même de ses propres démons. Le thème central du récit est peut-être celui de la haine des sexes; le heros, en tout cas, ne peut aimer personne et cette solitude absolue est son enfer. Il semble qu'après avoir été attiré par la politique, Laurendeau veuille consacrer une partie croissante de son attention à la littérature qui l'avait attiré un moment de sa jeunesse alors qu'il avait fait partie de l'équipe de *La Relève.* Il est membre de la Société royale du Canada.

AGNES CHRISTINA LAUT (1871-1936). Born at Stanley, Ontario, Miss Laut was educated at the University of Manitoba and was for a time an editorial writer for the Manitoba *Free Press.* Even after she moved to the United States her interest in Canada continued and was reflected in her works dealing with Canadian history, especially the opening up of the West. *Lords of the North* (1900), *Heralds of Empire* (1902), *The Pathfinders of the West* (1904) and others, based on the personalities and events of the adventurers of the early West, are presented in a lively journalistic style.

IRVING LAYTON (1912-   ) Born in Rumania, Layton was brought in 1913 by his family (Lazarovitch) to Montreal where he was educated in the local public school system and Macdonald College (B.Sc. in Agriculture in 1939). He served in the army during World War II and upon discharge in 1943 took his master's degree at McGill

University. After graduation he taught high school for a while and lectured part-time at Sir George Williams University, Montreal. Although he began writing in high school, it was not until 1942 that he started seriously experimenting with various poetical forms to express his protest against the established order and his feeling that poetry must be an intensely personal experience.

His first book of poetry *Here and Now* (1945) emphasized this attitude. A prolific writer, he followed this initial publication with such volumes as *Now Is the Place* (1948), *The Black Huntsman* (1951), *Love the Conqueror Worm* (1952), *Cerberus* (1952), *In the Midst of My Fever* (1954), *The Long Pea-Shooter* (1954), *The Cold Green Element* (1955), *The Blue Propellor* (1955), *The Bull Calf and Other Poems* (1956), as well as collections of his work, *The Improved Binoculars* (1956), *A Red Carpet for the Sun* (1959), and *The Swinging Flesh* (1961), which included several short stories.

Influenced by the American poet William Carlos Williams, Layton is an imagist. He attempts to represent objective facts stripped to their essentials in language which is blunt and often coarse. He makes penetrating and caustic observations on what he calls, in his foreword to *The Swinging Flesh,* "pompous fools, the frustrated busybodies, the money-loving acquisitive dull clods and lobotomized ideologues who make it difficult for the high-spirited to live joyously."

In 1962, Layton published an anthology of Canadian love songs in *Love Where the Nights Are Long,* with a provocative introduction entitled "What Canadians Don't Know About Love." His *Balls for a One-Armed Juggler* (1963) includes poems in a more sombre tone than earlier volumes and expresses deep concern for modern man's predicament. *The Laughing*

Rooster appeared in 1964 and *Collected Poems,* which represents more than twenty books of verse, in 1965. Layton's poetry reflects his own intense passion for experience: he feels that love and the imagination are the only ways to dominate reality. Along with his emphasis on the sensual, he displays in certain lyrics an originality and freshness of imagery, a telling irony and prophetic indignation, frequently coupled with surprising sympathy and tenderness, and a versatility of form and technique. In some of his stories, as in his poetry, Layton, while retaining his central quality of exuberance, demonstrates a remarkable subtlety and finesse. Louis Dudek, "Layton on the Carpet," *Delta* 9 (Oct.-Dec. 1959); Wynne Francis, "Montreal Poets of the Forties," *Can. Lit.,* 14 (Summer, 1962); Northrop Frye, "Letters in Canada: 1954," *UTQ,* XXIV (April, 1955); Barrie Hale, "Baggy-Pants Rhetoric: Review of *The Swinging Flesh,*" *Can. Lit.,* 9 (Summer, 1961); Miriam Waddington, "Bouncy Sermons on Comedy of Sex," *The Globe Magazine,* January 15, 1966; George Woodcock, "A Grab at Proteus: Notes on Irving Layton," *Can. Lit.,* 28 (Spring, 1966).

STEPHEN LEACOCK (1869-1944). Born in Hampshire, England, Stephen **Butler Leacock emigr**ated at an early age with his family to Canada where they settled on a farm near Lake Simcoe, Ontario, in 1876. Raised in a rural environment and a poor but cultured home atmosphere which influenced his later work, Leacock received his education at Upper Canada College where he served as a Master from 1889 to 1899, and at the University of Toronto (B.A. 1891). After taking his Ph.D. (1903) at the University of Chicago, he was appointed Lecturer in Economics and Political Science at McGill University. In 1908 he became head of the department and remained there until his retirement in 1936. He wrote some dozen books on history, economics and political history, including *Elements of Political Science* (1906), for several years a standard text. He was elected F.R.S.C. in 1910.

It was as a humorist, however, that Leacock achieved his greatest fame, and his works have been translated into several languages. A prolific writer and a great showman, he took pride in producing a humorous book every year for an eager and admiring public. *Literary Lapses* (1910, *Histoires humoristiques,* 1963) drawn from sketches written in his twenties, was the first to appear and established his reputation as a humorist. The tremendous reception of this delightful book of satire, published at his own expense, encouraged him to bring out his popular *Nonsense Novels* (1911), and to follow this with what is probably his best known work, *Sunshine Sketches of a Little Town* (1912). In this picture of Mariposa, partly based on his recollection of Orillia, Ontario, he created vital characters who in their complacency, gullibility and prejudices are representative of small town life in Canada.

Leacock satirized the foibles, hypocrisies and inconsistencies of society with humour and mockery that could be sharp but were rarely savage. Although on the surface he delighted in burlesque and flippant nonsense, there is a deep undercurrent running through his work indicative of his sometimes sombre disposition and mature awareness of life's complexity. By caricature, distortion, sarcasm and irony, he presented the comical incongruity between the real and the ideal, and the plight of the ordinary man who retains his individuality and even dignity under the complex pressures of modern society. In particular, Leacock depicted the spirit and attitude of the Canadian caught between the two great influences of England and America.

Behind the Beyond, and other Contributions to Human Knowledge appeared in 1913 and was followed by his famous *Arcadian Adventures with the Idle Rich* (1914), in which he ridicules various aspects of the contemporary plutocratic society. *Moonbeams from the Larger Lunacy* (1915) and *Further Foolishness* (1916) are more sketches and satires on the follies of the day. A student of Dickens and Twain, Leacock sought like them to recall for his readers the kindness and simplicity of an earlier less complicated age, and to restore the primitive virtues of honesty and generosity. In 1921 he embarked on a successful lecturing tour of Great Britain. Having noted how the Englishman was prone to publish impressions of America on first acquaintance, he decided "to restore the balance of trade" by writing *My Discovery of England* (1922), a comic survey of England with a series of ten humorous themes on a mixed variety of subjects.

As a literary critic he discussed the theory and technique of humour in several works such as *The Greatest Pages of American Humour* (1916), *Mark Twain* (1932), *Charles Dickens, His Life and Work* (1933), *Humour, Its Theory and Techniques* (1935) and *Humour and Humanity* (1937). He also contributed extensively to periodicals in both America and Great Britain. His autobiographical *The Boy I Left Behind Me* (1946) was posthumously published.

Uniquely Canadian, Leacock with his colourful personality and delight in being the "campus character" endeared himself to his students and his audiences. He was honoured many times for his contributions to Canadian literature, and a fund was established after his death to award annually a Leacock Medal for the best piece of humorous work produced in Canada. S. Ross Beharriell, Introduction to

Nonsense Novels (Toronto, 1963); Ralph L. Curry, Introduction to *Arcadian Adventures with the Idle Rich* (Toronto, 1959); David Dooley, Introduction to *Frenzied Fiction* (Toronto, 1965); Robertson Davies, "Stephen Leacock" in *Our Living Tradition,* 1st Series (Toronto, 1957); Desmond Pacey, "Stephen Leacock as a Satirist," *Queen's Quarterly,* 58 (Summer, 1961); F. W. Watt, "Critic or Entertainer," *Can. Lit.,* 5 (Summer, 1960); R. E. Watters, "Stephen Leacock's Canadian Humour," *Can Lit.,* 5 (Summer, 1960); George Whalley, Introduction to *My Discovery of England* (Toronto, 1961).

PAMPHILE LEMAY (1837-1918). Né à Lotbinière, Lemay étudia au Séminaire de Québec et à la faculté de théologie de l'Université d'Ottawa, puis opta pour le droit et fut admis au barreau en 1864. En 1867, il fut nommé bibliothécaire de la législature de Québec et il se retira en 1892. Il fut un des membres fondateurs de la Société royale du Canada.

Auteur de romans sans valeur et de contes (*Contes vrais,* 1899) pittoresques et didactiques, Lemay est surtout connu comme poète bien que son oeuvre considérable soit presque toute d'une grande médiocrité. Ses meilleurs poèmes sont les derniers, les sonnets intitulés *Les Gouttelettes* (1904). Les poésies antérieures inspirées par l'amour de la nature, l'originalité de nos coutumes ou le sentiment religieux sont mièvres et gauches. Il a aussi traduit en vers l'*Evangeline* de Longfellow et, en prose, *The Golden Dog* de Kirby.

ROGER LEMELIN (1919-). Né à Québec, Lemelin a étudié à l'Académie commerciale de Québec. Immobilisé par un accident de ski, il a découvert la littérature et s'est découvert une vocation d'écrivain. Employé par un oncle dans une exploitation forestière, il a publié des romans et a adapté le second pour la télévision où il a obtenu un immense succès populaire avec *Les Plouffe,* aussi télévisé en anglais: *The Plouffe Family.* Membre de la Société royale du Canada, il partage son temps entre sa carrière d'industriel et son oeuvre d'écrivain.

Au pied de la pente douce (1944, *The Town Below,* 1948), connut un succès considérable. Lemelin s'y révélait tout de suite un conteur né. Il y a dans ce roman une veine tragique et une veine satirique qui ne parviennent pas à se marier complètement; la veine tragique tient à la double faillite de deux jeunes hommes qui tentent en vain de s'élever au-dessus de leur milieu; la veine satirique a surtout retenu l'attention et donne au roman une saveur unique dans une littérature plutôt austère. Ses dons de satiriste se sont aussi exercés avec succès dans *Les Plouffe* (1948, *The Plouffe Family,* 1950), pittoresque évocation d'une humble famille de Québec. Lemelin s'y complait volontiers dans la scène décorative et recherche souvent le pittoresque pour lui-même, ce qui enlève à son oeuvre un certain poids de vérité. Il a néanmoins le sens du ridicule et sait animer ses personnages; aussi *Les Plouffe* est-il un des romans canadiens les plus vivants, quoique moins touchant que le premier.

Après un recueil de nouvelles assez réussies, *Fantaisies sur les péchés capitaux,* (1949) notamment une satire comme *Le chemin de croix,* Lemelin voulut renouveler sa manière, dépasser les descriptions de moeurs pour atteindre au roman d'analyse. Dans *Pierre le magnifique* (1952, *In Quest of Splendour,* 1955), nouveau roman de l'ambition, l'auteur n'a pas su unir en un tout cohérent l'aventure intérieure de Pierre Boisjoly, la caricature du milieu politique québécois et les développements sociaux et économiques. Cette oeuvre hybride est peut-être mieux écrite que les précédentes; elle

est moins vraie, moins humaine. L'avenir de Lemelin n'est pas de ce côté.

Sur Lemelin on peut consulter Clément Lockquell, *Au pied de la pente douce,* dans *Lectures* 1944; Roger Duhamel, *Courrier des lettres* dans *L'Action universitaire,* janvier 1949; Guy Sylvestre, *Pierre le magnifique* dans *La Nouvelle Revue canadienne,* janvier 1953; René Arthur, *Roger Lemelin* dans *Le Digeste français,* octobre 1950; W. E. Collin, *Roger Lemelin: The pursuit of grandeur, Queen's Quarterly* (Summer 1954).

JEAN LE MOYNE (1913-   ). Né à Montréal, Le Moyne a étudié au Collège Sainte-Marie. Il a participé à la fondation de *La Relève* (1934), a fait quatre voyages en Europe et fut journaliste à *La Presse* et au *Canada* avant de devenir rédacteur en chef de *La Revue Moderne* (1953-1959), puis scénariste à l'Office national du Film. Il a édité, avec Robert Elie, les *Poésies complètes* et le *Journal* de leur ami Saint-Denys-Garneau. En 1961, il a réuni en volume, *Convergences,* des essais parus dans les revues depuis vingt-cinq ans et qui constituent un des plus grands livres des lettres canadiennes. Il comprend des essais sur des problèmes généraux (la religion au Canada français, le rôle de la femme, etc.), sur des écrivains et penseurs (Teilhard, Henry James, Jouhandeau, Saint-Denys-Garneau) et sur des compositeurs. Ces textes constituent une sorte de journal d'une âme profondément religieuse à la recherche de la vérité et du bonheur; ils sont très personnels (et souvent discutables) et d'une élévation de pensée peu commune. En 1966, ils ont paru en traduction anglaise: *Convergence.*

DOUGLAS LEPAN (1914-   ). Born in Toronto, Ontario, LePan graduated from the University of Toronto and subsequently continued his studies at Oxford. Upon his return to North

America, he taught briefly at the University of Toronto and at Harvard (1939-1941). During the war he served in the artillery in the Italian campaign, and after discharge held various important positions in the Civil Service. He was granted a leave of absence in 1948 to study writing under a Guggenheim Scholarship.

His first volume of poetry was *The Wounded Prince and Other Poems* (1948). His work is primarily a reflection upon the enigma of war. With paradox and subtle irony, he superimposes the past and the future upon the present, creating an underlying sense of order in chaos. In his second collection, *The Net and the Sword* (1953), concerned with his war-time experiences in Italy, the predominant theme is the active response of creative individuals to the challenge of destruction.

After a distinguished career in the Department of External Affairs, LePan in 1959 was appointed Professor of English at Queen's University, and subsequently Principal of University College, University of Toronto. By temperament a perfectionist, in his writing he is a consummate artist. His style differs from that of other Canadian poets, particularly in its luxuriant whorl of sensuous, often visceral, imagery. His poetry is characterized by maturity and sophistication, by a precision of expression and subtlety of word association, and by a pervading Virgilian sense of the dignity of individual man. LePan's first novel, *The Deserter* (1964), won a Governor-General's Award. It describes a young soldier who deserts his unit after the war to enter a phase of searching for the meaning of life. Marilyn Davis, "The Bird of Heavenly Airs: Thematic Strains in Douglas LePan's Poetry," *Can. Lit.,* 15 (Winter, 1963); Elliott Gose, "Bright But Powdery," *Can. Lit.,* 24 (Spring, 1965).

ROSANNA ELEANOR LEPROHON (1832-1879). Born and educated in Montreal, Rosanna Eleanor Mullins Leprohon contributed fifteen poems, one sketch and five serial novels to *The Literary Garland*, a Montreal periodical, between 1846 and 1851. Thus, before she was twenty-two years of age, she had considerable experience as a sentimental romancer. After her marriage to Mr. J. L. Leprohon of Montreal, she moved in the social circles of the oldest French families and became uniquely qualified to write in English about their history and traditions. *Antoinette de Mirecourt: or Secret Marrying and Secret Sorrowing* (1864), set in Montreal in the earliest years of mingled French-English society after the defeat of Montcalm, was published in English, but was also popular in a French translation. *The Manor House of de Villerai*, a romance to which *Antoinette* was a sequel, was almost lost with the collapse of *The Family Herald*, in which it had been published in 1859; it reappeared largely as a French book in L. de Bellefeuille's translation (1861). Mrs. Leprohon's *Poetical Works* (posthumouly published in 1881) reflect the historical interests and the national spirit of the Montreal Irish-Canadians led by Thomas D'Arcy McGee. Brother Adrian (Henri Deneau), *Life and Works of Mrs. Leprohon* (M.A. thesis, University of Montreal, 1948).

KENNETH LESLIE (1892-   ). Born in Pictou, Nova Scotia, Kenneth Leslie attended university at Dalhousie (B.A., 1912, Nebraska (M.A., 1914), and Harvard. He has published four volumes of poetry: *Windward Rock* (1934); *Such a Din* (1935); Lowlands Low (1935); and *By Stubborn Stars* (1938), which won a Governor-General's Award.

Leslie's presentation of the power and mystery of the sea is particularly affecting. He is presently editor of *New*

Man, a leftist political pamphlet which is published every two months in Pictou.

country is a pale and vulgar expression of the Confederation ideal.

LIONEL LEVEILLE (1875-). Né à Saint-Gabriel de Brandon, Léveillé étudia au Séminaire Joliette et à la faculté de droit de l'Université de Montréal. Admis au barreau en 1907, il exerça sa profession et fut aussi journaliste à *La Presse.*

Il publia plusieurs recueils de poésies, d'abord sous le nom d'Englebert Gallèze:*Les chemins de l'âme* (1910), *La claire fontaine* (1913) puis, sous son nom; *Chante, rossignol, chante* (1925) et *Vers la lumière* (1931). Avec une tendresse souvent mélancolique, ou un humour attendri, il a chanté les petites gens de la campagne, leurs moeurs rustiques et les vieilles traditions paysanes dont, devenu citadin, il avait gardé la nostalgie.

NORMAN LEVINE (1924-). Born in Ottawa, Albert Norman Levine lived there until he joined the R.C.A.F. in 1942. He served in a bomber squadron in Europe, and after returning to Canada attended McGill University (B.A., 1948, M.A., 1949). During these years he wrote verse and prose which were published in various magazines.

From 1949 until 1965, except for brief visits home, Levine resided in England. There he produced the poems which appeared in *The Tightrope Walker* (1950, 1951) and three books, *The Angled Road* (1952), which attempts to record a wartime airman's search for values, *Canada Made Me* (1958), and *One Way Ticket* (1961, 1963), which is a collection of short stories with a carnival background. Virtually all of these writings reflect autobiographical influences and Levine's view, which is trenchantly developed in *Canada Made Me,* that his native

WILLIAM DOUW LIGHTHALL (1857-1954). Born in Hamilton, Upper Canada, Lighthall graduated with highest honours from McGill and in 1881 began practising law in Montreal. He collected and edited a popular anthology of verse *Songs of the Great Dominion* (1889). His first of several novels *The Young Seigneur* (1888) was a historical romance, as were *The False Chevalier* (1898), and *The Master of Life* (1908), a tale of Hiawatha and the Five Nations which is perhaps his best work. Elected F.R.S.C. in 1902, he later served as president not only of the Society but also of the Canadian Authors Association. Lighthall was a versatile writer in a variety of genres: philosophy, biography, fiction, travel and poetry. In much of his work he utilizes a wealth of Indian lore and French Canadian atmosphere in an engaging manner. His own collected poems, *Old Measures* (1922), indicate his continuing interest in indigenous traditions and Canadian nationalism.

DOROTHY LIVESAY (1909-). Born in Winnipeg, Dorothy Livesay was the daughter of Florence R. Livesay, writer of poems and short stories, and J. B. F. Livesay, the distinguished Canadian journalist who was largely responsible for the foundation of the Canadian Press. In 1920 she moved with her family to Clarkson, Ontario. Upon graduation from Toronto's Glen Mawr school for girls, she entered Trinity College, where in her first year she won the Jardine Memorial prize for poetry. A brochure of her poems entitled *Green Pitcher* appeared in 1928. The simple lyrics included in this small volume showed maturity and intensity of feeling, and were strongly influenced by her admiration for the Imagist poets. Her second chapbook

Signpost appeared in 1932 and treats the themes of love, death and nature.

During her third academic year she attended classes at the University of Aix-Marseilles and produced a number of short stories which were later printed in *Northern Review*. While in France, she became involved with Henry Barbusse's League of Revolutionary Writers, an association which had an important influence on her writing. After graduation from Trinity College (B.A. 1931), she spent a year at the Sorbonne (1931/32), and then returned to Canada to enter the School of Social Science at Toronto University. In 1933/34 she worked in the Family Welfare Agency in Montreal and subsequently travelled to the United States, where she was influenced by the writings of such left-wing poets as C. Day Lewis, Stephen Spender and W. H. Auden. In 1937 she was married to Duncan Cameron Macnair.

"The Outrider," an early revolutionary poem, appeared in 1935; and *Day and Night,* a collection of "social" verse which won a Governor General's Award, was published in 1944. *Poems for People,* published three years later, tends to personalize the earlier social themes, and the resulting humanism raises the book in excellence above its predecessor. The poetry retains the simplicity of the first two chapbooks, and reaffirms her interest in individual emotion and natural description. In 1947, Dorothy Livesay was awarded the Lorne Pierce Medal for her contribution to literature. Two further volumes *Call My People Home* (1950) and *New Poems* (1955) contain direct and passionate affirmations of the value of love, joy and art. *Selected Poems, 1926-1956,* published in 1957, includes a judiciously chosen collection of her best work, which is musical and compassionate without being sentimental. *The Colour of God's Face* (1965) is a pamphlet of poems inspired by a tour of teaching English in Northern Rhodesia. In addition to writing poetry, Dorothy Livesay has served as a reporter on various newspapers, worked as Director of Adult Education for the Y.M.C.A. in Vancouver, and taught creative writing at the University of British Columbia. She has recently been appointed as Poet-in-Residence at the University of New Brunswick. W. E. Collin, "My New Found Land" in *The White Savannahs* (Toronto, 1936); Desmond Pacey, Introduction to *Selected Poems* (Toronto, 1957); E. J. Pratt, "Dorothy Livesay," *Gants du Ciel,* 11 (Spring, 1946); M. W. Steinberg, "Dorothy Livesay; poet of affirmation," *British Columbia Library Quarterly,* 24 (October, 1960); Robert Weaver, "The Poetry of Dorothy Livesay," *Contemporary Verse,* 26 (Fall, 1948).

CLEMENT LOCKQUELL (1908-   ). Le frère Clément Lockquell est né à Québec et a étudié aux universités de Montréal et Laval. Docteur en philosophie, il a enseigné la philosophie et les lettres à l'Université Laval dont il fut doyen de la faculté de commerce de 1954 à 1962. Chroniqueur littéraire vigoureux, il est aussi l'auteur d'un roman, *Les élus que vous êtes* (1950), qui peint la vie communautaire, les conflits de personnalité et les aspirations spirituelles de quelques religieux canadiens. Il est membre de la Société royale du Canada.

JEAN AUBERT LORANGER (1896-1942). Né à Montréal, Loranger reçut une éducation privée. Il fut d'abord à l'emploi de la Régie des alcools de la province de Québec à Paris, puis journaliste à *La Patrie, La Presse* et *Montréal-Matin.* Il a publié une plaquette renfermant des contes et les premières poésies unanimistes au Canada, *Les Atmosphères* (1920), ainsi qu'un volume de *Poèmes* (1922) et un recueil de contes ruraux, *Le Village*

(1925). Marcel Dugas lui a consacré quelques pages (95-103) dans *Littérature canadienne* (1929).

A. R. M. LOWER (1889-   ). Born in Barrie, Ontario, Arthur Reginald Marsden Lower graduated from the University of Toronto in 1914. After teaching briefly, he joined the R.N.V.R. during World War I. After the war he took his doctorate at Harvard and then taught in both the United States and Canada. During these years he contributed many articles to learned journals and wrote several brilliant and provocative books, including *Documents Illustrative of Canadian Economic History* (1933), *Colony to Nation: A History of Canada* (1946), *Canada, Nation and Neighbour* (1952) and *Canadians in the Making, a Social History of Canada* (1958). His emphasis is upon the sociological aspects of Canadian history within a framework of friendly relationships with the United States. Elected F.R.S.C. (1941), he was appointed to the Douglas Chair of Canadian History at Queen's University (1947).

MALCOLM LOWRY (1909-1957). Born in Cheshire, England, Malcolm Boden Lowry received his early education at a private school in Cambridge. At the age of seventeen, influenced by reading O'Neill's *The Moon of the Caribbees,* he shipped to the Far East as a deckhand. On his return to England in 1929, he entered St. Catherine's College, Cambridge, where he studied English and Classics and graduated in 1932. At college he wrote his first novel from the vivid memories of his voyage, *Ultramarine* (1933, partially revised and republished in 1962), the hero of which—like Lowry himself—was already a heavy drinker.

After leaving Cambridge, he holidayed in Spain with the American writer Conrad Aiken, who had become

a close friend, lived in France and travelled to the United States. He spent some time in Hollywood writing movie scripts, stayed for a while in New York and then moved to Cuernavaca, Mexico. There with his first wife, Jan, from whom he was later divorced, he began work on his second novel *Under the Volcano* which was not completed until 1947. In 1939 he moved north to a beach colony of squatters at Dollarton, near Vancouver, British Columbia. In 1940 he married a Hollywood starlet and mystery writer, Margerie Bonner. Their experiences while living under primitive conditions, and their happy communion with nature, are described in such short stories as "The Forest Path to the Spring" in *Hear Us O Lord from Heaven Thy Dwelling Place* (1961, *Ecoute Notre voix O Seigneur,* 1962), which won a Governor-General's Award. Rejected by the army because of an old knee injury, Lowry lived at Dollarton, with the exception of brief trips to Mexico, Europe and Eastern Canada, until 1954. In that year, after spending the most productive years of his life in Canada, he left for Sicily and thence to England where he died "by misadventure."

His masterpiece, *Under the Volcano* (*Au dessous du volcan,* 1949), is the epic of a former British consul in Mexico who because of his alcoholism loses his wife, his self-respect and eventually his life. Lowry describes the theme as "the migraine of alienation," and in the Preface to the French edition of 1949 says that his purpose in part was "to create a pioneer work in its own class, and to write at last an authentic drunkard's story." The action takes place on the Day of the Dead, All Soul's Day (November 2), 1938, and is recalled one year later. Although the narrative element is slight, the metaphorical action, symbolism and allegory are complex and intense. The fall of man, his remorse and the paradox of his strength and weakness are depicted in language that is richly allusive. With tremendous organization, Lowry introduces symbols drawn from the Bible, classical mythology, oriental religion and modern literature. Displaying poetic skill in imagery and rhythm, he varies the style from Joycean internal monologue through incantations to powerfully descriptive passages. The novel has been translated into several European languages.

In his poetry, as in his fiction, there is a haunting note of loneliness, doubt and desire for love; his later work reveals the anguish and despair of a tortured soul. His poem "Sunrise," as Professor Birney notes, "is the fable of his life, an 'eloquence' that cries to us from his sinking, from his descent into that doom from which no friend or force was strong enough to save him." And yet Lowry was deeply spiritual and looked forward to happier hours in "God's snug little bar."

In addition to the two novels published during his lifetime, one volume of seven related stories entitled *Hear Us O Lord from Heaven Thy Dwelling Place* (1961), *Selected Poems* (1962), *Selected Letters of Malcolm Lowry* (1966), and various individual poems have appeared since his death. His collected poems *The Lighthouse Invites the Storm* and other works are to come. Under the editorship of his wife, there will be published two novels in incomplete draft form set in Mexico, *Dark as the Grave Wherein My Friend Is Laid* and *La Mordida,* one almost complete work entitled *October Ferry to Gabriola* with its setting in British Columbia, and a novella *Lunar Caustic* set in the psychiatric wards of New York City's Bellevue Hospital. From all this evidence of literary production, Lowry emerges as a highly gifted novelist, a distinguished short story writer, a poet of merit, and in his personal correspondence a sensitive critic of literature, music and art. Earle Birney, Foreword to "Twelve Poems by Malcolm Lowry," *Northwest Review,* V, 1 (Winter, 1962);

Earle Birney, "Glimpses into the Life of Malcolm Lowry," *Tamarack Review,* 19 (Spring, 1961); *Canadian Literature,* 8 (Spring, 1961), Special Malcolm Lowry Issue; *Les Lettres Nouvelles,* 5 (July-August, 1960), Special Malcolm Lowry Issue; George Woodcock, "Malcolm Lowry as a Novelist," *British Columbia Library Quarterly,* 24 (April, 1961).

ALBERT LOZEAU (1878-1924). Né à Montréal, Lozeau fréquenta l'école primaire, mais dès l'âge de quinze ans fut atteint du mal de Pott qui allait le terrasser complètement en 1896. Incapable de marcher, il resta alité plusieurs années jusqu'à ce que diverses interventions chirurgicales améliorent son sort et lui permettent de s'asseoir. Il passa les vingt dernières années de sa vie dans un fauteuil à lire et à recevoir des amis dont quelques poètes de l'Ecole littéraire de Montréal dont il devint membre. Autodidacte, il a beaucoup lu les poètes français et le goût lui est venu d'écrire des vers; en 1907, il publia un premier recueil de poésies, *L'Ame solitaire.* Elu membre de la Société royale du Canada en 1911, il publia *Le Miroir des Jours* en 1912 et *Lauriers et Feuilles d'érable* en 1916. Il a préparé une édition de ses *Poésies complètes* qui a paru en trois volumes en 1925. Il a aussi publié trois volumes de *Billets du soir* parus dans *Le Devoir.* Il a aussi écrit la préface du *Cap Eternité* de Charles Gill.

Lozeau a beaucoup fréquenté les poètes de la Pléiade et les romantiques, mais sa poésie est d'un ton personnel et sincère. Les pièces de circonstances, surtout les dernières inspirées par la grande guerre, sont médiocres, mais presque toute son oeuvre est la confession simple, directe et pudique d'une âme solitaire prisonnière d'un corps perclus. On retrouve la douleur partout dans cette oeuvre—douleur physique et souffrance morale—mais le poète parvint presque toujours à une sérénité résignée et son oeuvre est sans amertume. Il a chanté la nature entrevue par la fenêtre avec des accents d'une grande délicatesse, mais il a surtout chanté ses rêves, ses amours déçues, ses amitiés fidèles qui venaient rompre un moment la monotonie d'une vie tout entière paralysée par un mal incurable. Lozeau fut un des meilleurs poètes intimistes du Canada français; il n'a chanté que des sentiments simples et des sujets humbles, mais il l'a fait avec une tendresse, une sincérité, une discrétion qui sont touchantes. Poète mineur, il a laissé une oeuvre qui, dans son ordre, est nettement supérieure aux entreprises ambitieuses et manquées de certains de ses confrères. Yves de Margerie a publié le *Lozeau* de la collection Classiques canadiens (1958).

JACK LUDWIG (1922-   ). Born in Winnipeg, Manitoba, Ludwig graduated from the University of Manitoba (B.A. 1944) and took his Ph.D. at the University of California in English Literature. After lecturing at several American colleges, he became professor of English (Graduate Division) in 1961 at New York State University, Long Island. He has published short stories in various Canadian and American journals and his work is included in Weaver's *Ten for Wednesday Night* (1961), Foley's *The Best American Short Stories* (1961), *The O. Henry Prize Stories* (1961) and Pacey's *A Book of Canadian Stories* (1962). His stories are lively and colourful, and they often deal with Jewish life in small towns. He was co-editor of *The Noble Savage,* a twice yearly review. *Confusions* (1963), a satiric novel of academic life, in a small California university, is concerned with the clash of cultures and ideals of a young Jewish professor and his fellow intellectuals. Articles by

Ludwig appear frequently in *Holiday*. Another novel, *Above Ground,* is forthcoming.

PETER MCARTHUR (1866-1924). Born on a farm in Western Ontario, McArthur attended the University of Toronto for a year in 1888 and then taught school for a short time. Augmenting his funds with the proceeds from jokes, epigrams and humorous verse sold to Toronto's *Grip,* he discovered that these were being reprinted in American periodicals and henceforth submitted his pieces directly to them. After only five months at the University of Toronto, he left because of lack of money and began reporting for the Toronto *Mail and Empire.* The reception given his works encouraged him to go in 1890 as a free lance writer to New York where he sold articles to such magazines as *Harper's, Scribner's, Atlantic Monthly* and *Life.* His humorous essays on Canadian life, short stories and verses were very popular, and in 1895 he was appointed assistant and later editor of *Truth,* for which he obtained contributions from such talented Canadians as Stephen Leacock, Duncan Campbell Scott, Bliss Carman and Charles G. D. Roberts. McArthur moved to England in 1902 and was a regular contributor to *Punch* and *Review of Reviews.* While in London, he wrote *To Be Taken with Salt: An Essay on Teaching One's Grandmother to Suck Eggs* (1903) dealing with the decision of a young "colonial" who attempted to teach his "grandmother" England and discovered that Grandmother knew much more than her grandson cared to admit.

McArthur joined an advertising firm in New York in 1904. While there he brought out a collection of his verse, most of it previously published, *The Prodigal and Other Poems* (1907). In 1908 he returned to his father's farm, where he employed his wit in delightful portrayals of country life. He began

[98]

a series of articles which ran like a diary for fifteen years twice weekly in the Toronto *Globe* and for a time also in *The Farmer's Advocate*. The Red Cow and her granddaughter, Fenceviewer II, Bildad the pup, Houdini the heifer and Socrates the ram were only a few of the rollicking characters whose latest antics excited his readers. The columns in the *Globe* were revised and reproduced beginning with *In Pastures Green* (1915), including *The Red Cow and Her Friends* (1919), and ending with the two posthumous volumes *Around Home* (1925) and *Friendly Acres* (1927). These essays brought to his urban and rural readers alike an appealing homely philosophy with a happy comment on life's little events, pictured and enhanced by humour and imagination. *The Affable Stranger* (1920) is a fresh approach to a plea for better understanding between Canada and the United States. While his poems of seasons and seasonal events and his humorous *vers de société* were popular in their day, it is in his role as a humorous and unpretentious recorder of the events of pastoral life that he excels. W. A. Deacon, *Peter McArthur* (Toronto, 1923).

NELLIE MCCLUNG (1873-1951). Born in Chatsworth, Ontario, Nellie Letitia Mooney McClung moved out West when she was seven. After graduation from the Winnipeg Normal School, she taught in prairie schools until her marriage in 1896. Her first book *Sowing Seeds in Danny* (1908), which ran to a score of editions, and *The Second Chance* (1910) were drawn from her own experiences of the early West. Her active support of the suffragette movement is reflected in *Purple Springs* (1921). From 1921 to 1925 she served in the Alberta Legislature. Among her many works, her autobiographical *Clearing in the West* (1935) and *The Stream Runs Fast* (1945) are full of reminiscences which give a panorama of prairie life. Throughout her lifetime, Mrs. McClung was in demand as a lecturer both in the United States and Canada.

EDWARD MCCOURT (1907-   ). Born in Ireland, Edward Alexander McCourt emigrated to Canada with his family in 1909. He graduated from the University of Alberta in 1932 and was awarded a Rhodes Scholarship. After finishing his studies at Oxford in 1937, he returned to Canada to teach at various Canadian colleges and universities. Since 1944 he has been Professor of English at the University of Saskatchewan.

Beginning his career as a writer with the publication of short stories, he turned to novels of the Canadian West. *The Flaming Hour* (1947) is concerned with the Indian problem of Riel's day. *Music at the Close* (1947), as Claude Bissell notes, "becomes at times a careful piece of social documentation." It covers a period of twenty-six years, including the crash of the stock market in 1929 and the plight of the prairie farmers during the thirties, and ends with the escape of such a farmer from possible future frustration by death on D-Day.

Turning briefly from creative to scholarly writing, he published *The Canadian West in Fiction* (1949), an important survey and evaluation of Western regional literature. He reverted to fiction in 1950 with *Home Is the Stranger,* which treats the basic theme of man's struggle with the cold impersonality of nature.

The Wooden Sword (1956) is a psychological study of the intellectual, noteworthy for its representation of the academic community. *Walk through the Valley* (1960), a record of a boy's growth to maturity, illustrates McCourt's realistic and accurate approach to regionalism and his practical application of the methods of description which he himself advocates in *The Canadian West in Fiction. Fasting Friar* (also entitled *The Ettinger Affair*, 1963) is set in the academic world and deals with the problem of the individual and liberal values. *The Road Across Canada* (1965) presents the author's personal impressions of a trip across the Trans-Canada Highway from St. John's to Victoria. R. G. Baldwin, "The Novels of Edward McCourt," *Queen's Quarterly*, LXVIII, no. 4 (Winter, 1962); Claude T. Bissell, "Letters in Canada: 1950," *UTQ*, XX (April, 1951); Wilfrid Eggleston, *The Frontier and Canadian Letters* (Toronto, 1957).

JOHN MCCRAE (1872-1918). Born in Guelph, Ontario, McCrae graduated from Toronto University in science and medicine in 1898. He served in South Africa from 1899 to 1900 in the artillery, and on his return was appointed to the medical staff at McGill University and the Montreal General Hospital. He enlisted in the army in 1914 and served with distinction in France until his death. For some years his poems, many of which were in the form of the French *rondeau*, appeared in periodicals. His most famous poem "In Flanders Fields" was published anonymously in *Punch* (1915). John McCrae, *In Flanders Fields and Other Poems*, "With An Essay in Character" by Sir Andrew MacPhail (Toronto, 1919).

THOMAS MCCULLOCH (1777-1843). Born in Scotland, McCulloch was educated at the University of Glasgow. In 1803 he came to Nova Scotia as a missionary and became a leading preacher, philosopher and educator. He founded Pictou Academy, and when it amalgamated with Dalhousie College in 1838 became its president. His literary reputation today rests on *The Stepsure Letters*, first published in the *Acadian Recorder* (1821-1823). This satirical

social commentary, which still retains much of its original appeal, is a forerunner of the vein of humour of Haliburton and Leacock. Thomas McCulloch, *The Stepsure Letters* (Toronto, 1960), Introduction by Northrop Frye, Notes by John A. Irving and Douglas G. Lockhead.

MRS. EWEN MACDONALD. *See* Montgomery, L. M.

WILSON MACDONALD (1880-1967). Born in Cheapside, Ontario, Wilson Pugsley MacDonald received his early education at Woodstock College, and was an undergraduate at McMaster University when his first poem was published by the Toronto *Globe* in 1899. After graduation in 1902 and travel in England, he returned to work as a bank clerk in Canada, and then as an advertising copywriter in the United States. His first published volume *The Song of the Prairie Land* appeared in 1918.

One of the last members of the Canadian school of romantic poetry, MacDonald reflects in his work the influence of Lampman and others of the Confederation group. The poems included in *The Miracle Songs of Jesus* (1921) and *Out of the Wilderness* (1926) reveal a fine sense of lyrical description. Yet the outburst of attention and praise which greeted his first three publications of verse, and particularly *Out of the Wilderness*, was destined to be short-lived. Subsequent volumes of lyrics, religious poems and verse satire showed a lack of stylistic discrimination, a refusal to recognize modern trends and a clinging to the romantic quest for beauty which, as the title of his *A Flagon of Beauty* (1931) suggests, forms the theme of much of his poetry. The best of his satire, indeed, proclaims permanent human values and expresses contempt for the materialism of the twentieth

[100]

century as well as for its approach to art. Another volume of poems *The Lyric Year* appeared in 1952.

MacDonald steadfastly refused to be other than a full-time poet, and effectively made his work known by delivering lectures and readings throughout Canada. He visited Russia in 1957 and wrote a humorous booklet on his experiences there. A Wilson MacDonald Poetry Society exists in Canada and the United States. He died on April 8, 1967.

FRANKLIN MCDOWELL (1888-1965). Born in Bowmanville, Ontario, Franklin Davey McDowell began his career as a journalist, joining the staff of the Toronto *World* in 1909, and later the Manitoba *Free Press* and the Toronto *Mail and Empire*. In 1923 he became a Public Relations representative for the Canadian National Railway.

His first novel *The Champlain Road* (1939) won a Governor General's Award. Choosing his material from Canadian history, McDowell developed his thesis that the fall of Huronia affected the subsequent history of Canada. *Forges of Freedom* (1943), his second novel, drew on British history, and dealt with the Peasant's Revolt of the fourteenth century.

For some years after his retirement from the CNR in 1953, McDowell continued to write short stories and articles for Canadian and American magazines.

GWENDOLYN MACEWEN (1941-   ). Born in Toronto, Gwendolyn Margaret MacEwen attended primary school in Winnipeg and secondary school in Toronto. She started producing poetry when she was twelve years old and left school at eighteen to devote her full time to writing.

Her volumes of poetry include *Selah* (1960), *The Drunken Clock* (1961), *The Rising Fire* (1963) and *A Break-*

fast for Barbarians (1966). Her verse varies from a wide-ranging but undisciplined treatment of traditional Jewish themes and imagery to powerfully suggestive and energetic presentations of the human struggle for generation and fulfillment.

In the novel, *Julian, The Magician* (1963), the central figure is a Polish magician who comes to believe that his power is really supernatural and subsequently suffers Christ-like disgrace, trial and crucifixion. Miss MacEwen, who was married to poet Milton Acorn, now lives on Ward's Island of Toronto. E. B. Gose, "They Shall Have Arcana," *Can. Lit.*, 21 (Summer, 1964); Milton Wilson, "Letters in Canada: 1963," UTQ, XXXIII (July, 1964).

THOMAS D'ARCY MCGEE (1825-1868). Born in County Louth, Ireland, McGee received a cursory education and at seventeen emigrated to the United States where he joined the staff and was later editor of the Boston *Pilot*. Returning to England in 1845, he did journalistic work for the *Dublin Freeman's Journal,* and in 1846 became editor in Dublin of the *Nation,* the organ of the "Young Ireland" movement, which attempted to stimulate and direct the aspirations of the Irish people. His inspirational verses, often in ballad form, were written with sincerity and national spirit. Like his *Historical Sketches of O'Connell and His Friends* (1845) and *Gallery of Irish Writers* (1846), they did much to inform, educate and arouse his countrymen.

As one of the leaders of the abortive rebellion of 1848, McGee was forced to flee the country with a price on his head. He escaped to New York, where he founded the short-lived *New York Nation;* he then moved to Boston, where in 1850 he established the *American Celt* which he published for seven years. During this period he wrote *A History of the Irish Settlers in North America* (1850), *The Part Taken by Catholics in the American Revolution* (1852) *The Political Causes and Consequences of the Protestant "Reformation"* (1853), *A History of the Attempts to Establish a Protestant Reformation in Ireland* (1853) and *The Catholic History of North America* (1853). Disillusioned with the American political scene, he accepted the invitation of some Irish Roman Catholics to emigrate to Montreal where he founded *The New Era* (1857/58). In Canada, McGee found the civil and religious liberty of which he had dreamed, and henceforth became a great champion of the cause of national unity. In 1858, in *Canadian Ballads and Occasional Verses*, he recounted some of the country's legends in the manner of his Irish poems. The same year he turned to the political arena as representative for Montreal West in the Lower Canada Legislative Assembly. He became a member of the Reform Government in 1862, but when he was dropped from its executive council in 1863, he joined the Conservative party in which he served with Macdonald as Minister of Agriculture (1864-1867). Although busy in politics, he continued his literary work and in 1863 brought out *A Popular History of Ireland*.

A brilliant orator and an ardent advocate of Canadian union, McGee went as a delegate to the Charlottetown-Quebec Conference in 1864, where he did much to ensure the success of Confederation. Although one of the fathers of Confederation, he stood aside in the formation of the first cabinet for Edward Kenny, who McGee felt could best serve the people of Nova Scotia and the Irish Roman Catholics. His support of Confederation was eloquently expressed in *The Crown and the Confederation* (1864), and his addresses on the subject were published under the title *Speeches and Addresses Chiefly on British American Union*

(1865). In 1867 he again represented Montreal West, but this time in the newly formed House of Commons. Incurring the wrath of the Fenian Organization in the United States by his bitter condemnation of their politics and raids on Canada, McGee was assassinated by one of their members in 1868. After his death his works were collected and edited by Mrs. J. Sadlier in *The Poems of Thomas D'Arcy McGee* (1869), and by Charles Murphy in *D'Arcy McGee: A Collection of Speeches and Addresses* (1937). A. Brady, *D'Arcy McGee* (Toronto, 1925); Kathleen O'Donnell, *Thomas D'Arcy McGee's Irish and Canadian Ballads* (U.W.O. M.A. Thesis, 1956), J. Phelan, *The Ardent Exile* (Toronto, 1951); Isabel Skelton, *The Life of Thomas D'Arcy McGee* (Quebec, 1925).

TOM MACINNES (1867-1951). Born in Dresden, Ontario, and educated at the University of Toronto and Osgoode Hall, Thomas Robert Edward MacInnes was called to the British Columbia bar in 1893. He was in government service for some time, witnessed the Yukon gold rush, and spent some years in China, where he became interested in Chinese philosophy.

His first volume of verse *A Romance of the Lost* (1908) was incorporated in his next collection *Lonesome Bar, A Romance of the Lost, and Other Poems* (1909). Based on his experiences in the Yukon, these pieces are exuberant in mood, vigorous in rhythm and often coarse and slangy in language. His later publications *In Amber Lands* (1910) and *The Rhymes of a Rounder* (1913) illustrate his continuing interest in French verse forms, such as the ballade and villanelle, and in Chinese philosophy. In 1923 his *Complete Poems* were published.

Chinook Days (1926), a fictional account of his memories, is full of

MacInnes' typical boldness, zest and optimism. In 1927 he produced *The Teaching of the Old Boy,* a treatise on the philosophy of the Chinese sage Laô Tse, and *Oriental Occupation of British Columbia,* a social history. His last poems appeared in a volume entitled *In the Old of My Age* (1947).

L. A. MACKAY (1901-   ). Born in Hensall, Ontario, Louis Alexander MacKay graduated in Classics from the University of Toronto, was a Rhodes Scholar at Oxford and returned to join the faculty of The University of Toronto. During this period he was a contributor to *Saturday Night* and *Canadian Poetry Magazine.* He did a fine series of critical articles on Canadian literature in *The Canadian Forum* (1932/33). He published a small volume of verse under the pseudonym "John Smalacombe," *Viper's Bugloss* (1938), and submitted poems to several magazines. After some years at the University of British Columbia (1941-1948), during which he was awarded a Guggenheim Fellowship (1945), he became Professor of Latin at the University of California. His chief book of poems is *The Ill-tempered Lover and Other Poems* (1948), which was a reissue of the earlier volume along with pieces which had been published in magazines during the intervening years. MacKay's best verse, written with clarity and ordered simplicity, reflects in its satire and disillusionment a classicist's commentary on topical events. His *The Wrath of Homer* (1948) is an academic study.

ALEXANDER MCLACHLAN (1818-1896). Born of poor parents in Renfrewshire, Scotland, McLachlan received a meagre education before being apprenticed to a tailor. In 1840 he emigrated to a small clearing in Peel County, Upper Canada, and attempted over the next

few years to farm in various parts of Ontario. During this period he wrote verse which was published in *The Spirit of Love and Other Poems* (1846). In 1850 he settled in Wellington County and brought out his second book, *Poems* (1856), which was followed by *Lyrics* (1858). A disciple of Robert Burns, MacLachlan expressed the sentiments of the Scottish settlers in Canada and their gradual transition from colonial emigrants to Canadian nationals. In *The Emigrant and Other Poems* (1861) his intention in the title poem was to create a history of a backwoods settlement. He completed only the first of several proposed parts of this long narrative which was to recount the story of the settler's departure from home, of his arrival in the New World, of clearing the land and building his log cabin.

Although McLachlan's poetry was lacking in polish and urbanity and frequently descended to doggerel, he constantly expressed his own independent strength of character, his belief in human equality and rejection of sham in politics as well as in religion. The note of homesickness of the Scottish settlers voiced in the earlier poems was replaced in later verse by an enthusiastic acceptance of Canada as their true native country. Often called the "Burns of Canada," McLachlan was engaged by the Canadian government in 1863 to lecture in Scotland on the advantages in Canada for immigrants. In 1874 he made a second tour of Scotland. That same year he produced his fifth volume of verse *Poems and Songs. The Poetical Works of Alexander McLachlan* (1900) was published posthumously by a group of his admirers.

HUGH MACLENNAN (1907-   ). Born at Glace Bay, Cape Breton Island, MacLennan graduated in Classics from Dalhousie University (B.A. 1929), received a Rhodes Scholarship to Oriel College, Oxford (B.A., M.A. 1932), and took his Ph.D. in 1935 at Princeton University. His doctoral thesis, *Oxyrhynchus, An Economic and Social Study* of the ancient religious centre of the Roman Empire, was later published in 1940. After graduation he taught Latin and history (1935-1945) at Lower Canada College, Montreal.

His first novel, *Barometer Rising* (1941, *Le Temps tournera au beau*, 1966), is the description of eight days which are climaxed by the devastating Halifax explosion of 1917. MacLennan was living there at the time as a youth, and the scenes which he recreates are vivid and realistic, sustaining the excitement and drama of the events up to the instant of the explosion. While the structure is weakened by too many coincidences and complications, the novel combines a powerful narrative with an allegorical interpretation of Canada that exhibits perception and understanding of the national character. MacLennan skilfully blends these two aims by a technique which utilizes the Joycean internal monologue and cinematic close-up and fade-out to attain an authentic and powerful climax. In 1943, MacLennan was awarded a Guggenheim fellowship to study and write in New York. His second novel, *Two Solitudes* (1945, *Les deux solitudes*, 1963), which won a Governor General's Award, is concerned with the theme of Canadian unity, particularly of the two dominant cultural groups in Canada. The book treats with sensitiveness and understanding the Anglo-French relations in Canada as exhibited in Montreal. In the first half of the novel, the characterization is sure and the realism convincing, but the second half of the story is more contrived and less powerful than the first. *The Precipice* (1948), set in a narrow-minded Ontario town, attempts to illustrate differences between Canadians and Americans.

Although the essays of MacLennan will probably take second place to his fiction, he formulates in many of them definitions and ideas later incorporated in his novels. *Cross Country* (1949), a collection of ten essays which won the Governor General's Award for non-fiction, discusses one of his favourite themes, the Canadian character. As in his later similar volumes, *Thirty and Three* (1954), which also won the Governor General's Award, and *Scotchman's Return and Other Essays* (1960), he seeks to understand the transition taking place in Canada, and loads his essays with reminiscences and personal revelations which present him in the role of a "man who lives a life of quiet and surprisingly cheerful desperation, reconciled to the facts of existence."

In 1951 he was appointed to the English Department of McGill University. The same year in *Each Man's Son*, a regional novel set in a rugged coal-mining town in his native Cape Breton, MacLennan treated sympathetically and unpretentiously the paternal interest of a doctor in a young boy. In 1952 he was awarded the Lorne Pierce Medal for his contributions to Canadian literature, and was elected F.R.S.C. in 1953.

The Watch that Ends the Night (1959), which won another Governor General's Award, is an exciting and provocative novel which, like *Barometer Rising,* deals with a returning Odysseus long considered dead. Embracing a variety of social situations and contemporary political ideologies, the story skilfully relates memories of the past to urgent personal crises. *Seven Rivers of Canada* (1961) relates something of the history, geography and geology of such rivers as the Saskatchewan and Mackenzie. These facts are illuminated by anecdote, travelogue and literary allusion which bring out admirably the vastness and challenge of Canada. Honoured with many university degrees and literary awards, MacLennan ranks high among contemporary Canadian writers. Hugo McPherson, "The Novels of Hugh MacLennan," *Queen's Quarterly*, 60 (Summer, 1953); Hugh MacLennan, "The Story of a Novel" in *Masks of Fiction* (Toronto, 1961); R. E. Watters, "Hugh MacLennan and the Canadian Character" in *As a Man Thinks* (Toronto, 1935); George Woodcock, "A Nation's Odyssey" in *Masks of Fiction* (Toronto, 1961).

MARSHALL MCLUHAN (1911-). Born in Edmonton, Alberta, Herbert Marshall McLuhan graduated from the University of Manitoba (B.A. 1933, M.A. 1934) and went on to do postgraduate work at Cambridge University (B.A. 1936, M.A. 1940 and Ph.D. 1943). After holding positions in American universities from 1936 to 1944, he returned to Canada to teach at Assumption College, Windsor, and after 1946, at St. Michael's College, Toronto, He was elected F.R.S.C. in 1964, and is Director of the University of Toronto's Centre for Culture and Technology.

He contributed to various Canadian and American scholarly journals. In *The Mechanical Bride: Folklore of Industrial Man* (1951), he explored in a provocative and original fashion the semantic and kinetic aspects of language, and in particular the impact of advertising, movies and journalism on the North American public. McLuhan was co-editor with anthropologist Edmund S. Carpenter of *Explorations* (1953-1959), a series of studies in culture and communication. *The Gutenberg Galaxy: The Making of Typographic Man* (1962), which won a Governor General's Award, "is concerned with that association of cultural and political events which, from the origins of phonetic literacy to the development of typography, have shaped the Western individual and society." In this controversial study, which concludes with the new electronic influences on communication, and in *Understanding Media*

(1964), McLuhan presents his sweeping theories in a mosaic rather than a linear manner. Tony Emery, Revolutions in Communications," *Can. Lit.*, 14 (Autumn, 1962); Harold Rosenberg, "Philosophy in a Pop Key," *The New Yorker* (February 27, 1965).

ARCHIBALD MACMECHAN (1862-1933). Born in Berlin (Kitchener), Ontario, Archibald McKellar MacMechan graduated with honours from the University of Toronto and took his doctorate at Johns Hopkins in 1889. From that year until his death, he was Professor of English at Dalhousie University, Nova Scotia. He won popular recognition with his whimsical essays of *The Porter of Bagdad and other Fantasies* (1901) and of *The Life of a Little College* (1914). In addition to his scholarly publications, MacMechan wrote literary articles and book reviews for the Montreal *Standard* for twenty years. He produced a book of poems *Three Sea Songs* (1919) and was elected F.R.S.C. in 1920. His *Old Province Tales* (1924) and *Sagas of the Sea* (1924) are notable for their description of Nova Scotia's scenery and history as well as for their stirring adventures. His *Headwaters of Canadian Literature* (1924) was a valuable critical work on Canadian literature. He published in *Book of Ultima Thule* (1927) and *Red Snow on the Grand Pré* (1931) further lively descriptions of his adopted Maritime province. In 1932 he was awarded the Lorne Pierce medal. A versatile editor, poet, novelist, scholar and a competent essayist during his lifetime, he left a book of verse *Late Harvest* (1934) which was published posthumously.

SIR ANDREW MACPHAIL (1864-1938). Born in Orwell, Prince Edward Island, MacPhail graduated in medicine from McGill and received his L.R.C.P. from

London in 1893. Serving as a medical officer during World War I, he returned to Montreal to practise, and from 1907 to 1937 was Professor of Medicine at McGill. He edited *The University Magazine* from 1907 until 1920. He wrote numerous essays and critical and biographical works. *Essays in Puritanism* (1905), *Essays in Politics* (1909) and *Essays in Fallacy* (1910) have a genial vigour of style and reveal his mastery of the clipped phrase and pungent statement. For a time he served as editor to the *Journal of the Canadian Medical Association.* In 1918 he was made a Knight Bachelor, and in 1919 received an O.B.E. He published a translation of the French Canadian novel *Maria Chapdelaine* (1921). Of his numerous works, probably the best known is the biography *Three Persons* (1929). In 1930 he received the Lorne Pierce Medal.

JAY MACPHERSON (1931-). Born in England, Miss Macpherson came to Canada at the age of nine. She received her B.A. in 1951 from Carleton College, and completed her Ph.D. in English at the University of Toronto. Her first publication was *Nineteen Poems* (1952). *O Earth Return* appeared in 1954, but her reputation as a poet was established by the publication in 1957 of *The Boatman,* for which she received a Governor General's Award.

A member of the faculty of Victoria College, Miss Macpherson is one of the chief exponents of what has recently been called the mythopoeic school of poetry. In her technique she has been strongly influenced by Robert Graves and Northrop Frye. A professed gnostic in her symbolism, she combines echoes of Greek mythology, Elizabethan and Blakean lyric, Anglo-Saxon riddles and nursery rhymes, and all forms of balladry. Although she employs an abundance of traditional material, her work nonetheless retains an intensely personal quality, is finely articulated and skilfully controlled.

In *The Boatman,* a series of eighty poems, arranged in six sections, the title poem represents the poet as boatman, the reader as the ark and the animals as the pieces of information that must go into the mind of the reader. This complex image is delicately handled; the poems range in mood from quiet irony to witty humour. The reader discovers in Miss Macpherson's poetry "The Third Eye" which she herself defines as the insight "to concentrate, refine and rarify/And make a Cosmos of miscellany."

Her *Four Ages of Man* (1962), a delightfully written and illustrated account of classical myths, was produced for older children. Arnold Edinborough, "High Cockalorum in Verse," *Saturday Night,* LXXII (July 20, 1957); Northrop Frye, "Letters in Canada: 1957," *UTQ,* XXVII (July, 1958); James Reaney, "The Third Eye: Jay Macpherson's *The Boatman,*" *Can. Lit.,* 3 (Winter, 1960).

ALBERT MAILLE. *Voir* Dreux, Albert.

ANDREE MAILLET (1921-). Née à Montréal, fille du journaliste Roger Maillet, madame Lloyd Hamelyn Hobden a longtemps dirigé la revue *Amérique française* et, après avoir écrit des livres pour la jeunesse, dont *Profil de l'orignal* (1952), elle a publié coup sur coup un roman, *Les Remparts de Québec* (1964) et trois recueils de nouvelles: *Les Montréalais* (1963), *Le lendemain n'est pas sans amour* (1963), *Nouvelles montréalaises* (1965), sans compter les poèmes et les pièces de théâtre. Elle donne le meilleur d'elle-même dans la nouvelle où elle allie le réalisme à la fantaisie, le trait bien observé au rêve le plus insolite et crée ainsi une image diverse, très animée, parfois pathétique, parfois désopilante de cet univers cosmopolite et plein d'imprévu qu'est devenu Montréal.

CHARLES MAIR (1838-1927). Born in Lanark, Upper Canada, Mair entered Queen's University as a medical student in 1868. His first book of poetry *Dreamland and Other Poems* appeared in the same year. He subsequently gave up his medical studies, took employment with the government, and became involved with the "Canada First" movement. Appointed paymaster to a party which was to construct an emigration route from the Red River to Lake of the Woods, he was in the Red River district at the outbreak of the first Riel Rebellion. He escaped with Dr. Shultz to Portage la Prairie, where for five years he was in the fur trade and general business. In 1877 he took up residence at Prince Albert. For many years he acted as an Immigration officer at various points in the West.

Tecumseh, a verse drama, was written in 1882, but not published until four years later. Composed as a patriotic exercise, it represents one of the few attempts to dramatize Canadian history in verse. Most successful are the passages in which Mair employs his gift for accurate observation and description of landscape. For the most part, however, his work is heavily rhetorical, and often artificial in style and diction. He demanded for the new Dominion "an original and distinctive literature," and stressed the need to realize and exploit the vast potential which Canada affords to the writer. Considered a forerunner of Lampman, Roberts and Carman, Mair was the first Canadian poet to take an interest in the West.

The Last Bison appeared in 1890, one year following its author's election as F.R.S.C. The earlier stiffness and ponderous rhetoric are even more evident here than in *Tecumseh*. *Through the Mackenzie Basin* (1908), an account of the Laird treaty expedition into the Athabaska and Peace River country in 1899, is his only prose book. Although characteristically heavy, it contains many of the virtues and few of the faults of his poetry. In 1921, Mair retired to Victoria, British Columbia. A collection of his poems had appeared in 1901 and a volume of his complete works was published by the Radisson Society a few months before his death. A. E. Fraser, "A Poet Pioneer of Canada," *Queen's Quarterly,* XXXVI (1928); John Matthews, "Charles Mair" in *Our Living Tradition,* 5th Series (Toronto, 1965); Frank Norman Shrive, *Charles Mair: Literary Nationalist* (Toronto, 1965).

ELI MANDEL (1922-). Born in Saskatchewan, Mandel lived there until he joined the Army Medical Corps in 1943. After serving in England and Europe, he returned to Canada, completed his doctorate at the University of Toronto and joined the English Department of the University of Alberta. A contributor to Canadian and American literary magazines, he first collected his poems for publication in *Trio,* which also included work by Gael Turnbull and Phyllis Webb. His poetry reflects the influence of the mythopoeic school of Canadian poetry. The "Minotaur Poems" printed in *Trio* are characterized by an application of mythological and anthropological data to contemporary themes.

His first independent publication appeared in 1960. *Fuseli Poems* takes its title from the Swiss-British painter Henry Fuseli, the spirit of whose paintings Mandel has translated into poetic form. Fuseli was a friend of William Blake, whom Mandel greatly admires. Like the earlier "Minotaur Poems," these verses have a labyrinthine quality, which is supported by a solid stylistic texture and a tortured use of imagery which finds suffering, violence and melodrama inherent in the commonplace.

With Jean-Guy Pilon, Mandel edited *Poetry 62* (1961), an anthology of contemporary Canadian poets that sought to establish the existence of a dramatic strain in Canadian poetry. He is a Professor of English at the University of Alberta in Edmonton and the author of *Black and Secret Man* (1964), a second book of poems. Louis Dudek, "Two Canadian Poets: Ralph Gustafson and Eli Mandel," *Culture,* XXII (June, 1961); James Reaney, Review of *Fuseli Poems, Queen's Quarterly,* LXVII, 4 (Winter, 1961).

CLEMENT MARCHAND (1912-   ). Né à Sainte-Geneviève de Batiscan, Marchand fut orphelin dès l'âge de sept ans et élevé par un oncle; il a étudié au Séminaire de Trois-Rivières et est devenu journaliste et imprimeur. Il dirige à Trois-Rivières l'hebdomadaire *Le Bien public* et l'imprimerie du même nom. Il a fondé et dirigé une revue mensuelle éphémère, *Le Mauricien* devenu ensuite *Horizons.*

Il a débuté par des contes réalistes d'inspiration rurale, *Courriers des villages* (1939) et il a réuni en volume sous le titre *Les Soirs rouges* (1947) des poèmes inspirés par la nostalgie de la campagne et par l'étouffement qu'éprouve l'homme contemporain dans les villes tentaculaires. Il fut un des premiers à introduire le thème du prolétariat dans la poésie canadienne et il l'a fait avec force; il a aussi écrit des pièces courtes d'un ton plus fantaisiste. Membre de la Société royale du Canada depuis 1947, il a aussi édité le *Choix de poésies* de Nérée Beauchemin (1950).

GILLES MARCOTTE (1925-   ). Né à Sherbrooke, Marcotte a étudié au Séminaire St Charles Borromée et à la faculté des lettres de l'Université de Montréal. Journaliste, il a été critique littéraire du *Devoir,* réalisateur à la télévision et chargé de recherches à l'Office national du Film, directeur littéraire de *La Press* de 1961 à 1966, il est professeur à la faculté des lettres de l'Université de Montréal. En 1960, il a séjourné en France comme boursier du Conseil des Arts du Canada.

En 1962 il a publié un recueil de ses principaux articles de critique, *Une littérature qui se fait,* qui donne une idée incomplète de la littérature canadienne mais qui renferme quelques essais qui comptent parmi les plus pénétrants et les mieux écrits sur quelques poètes. Plus qu'à leur valeur esthétique, Marcotte s'intéresse au sens profond des oeuvres et à l'expérience humaine qu'elles traduisent.

Il a aussi publié deux romans, *Le Poids de Dieu* (1962) et *Retour à Coolbrook* (1965). Le premier est l'histoire grave d'un jeune prêtre qui s'interroge sur le sens de sa vocation et qui est heurté par certains de ses confrères comme par les événements auxquels il est mêlé. C'est un récit austère inspiré par une haute conception du sacerdoce.

Dans le second, il peint le portrait d'un médiocre qui ne réussit ni sa vie professionnelle (il est journaliste) ni sa vie sentimentale. Ce double échec est vécu dans la petite ville de province (Sherbrooke) où il est revenu après avoir vainement essayé de réussir à Montréal et dont il nous donne une image assez triste. Cette vie provinciale dégage un profond ennui, et l'auteur l'a bien fait sentir dans ce roman plutôt gris. Ces deux romans sont des romans de l'échec.

MARIE-VICTORIN (1895-1944). Né à Kingsey Falls, Joseph Louis Conrad Kirouac entra chez les frères des Ecoles chrétiennes et, sous le nom de frère Marie-Victorin, s'est acquis un réputation internationale comme botaniste. Docteur ès sciences, fondateur de l'Institut botanique de Montréal, membre de la Société royale du Canada et de nombreuses sociétés savantes, il est surtout connu comme l'auteur de la monumentale *Flore laurentienne* (1935), mais il s'était aussi intéressé aux lettres et au théâtre et il a écrit des récits, d'un style malheureusement trop recherché, pour chanter les beautés de la nature et les moeurs des habitants: *Récits laurentiens* (1919) et *Croquis laurentiens* (1920). Sa biographie a été écrite par Louis-Philippe Audet (1942) et par Robert Rumilly (1949).

JOSEPH MARMETTE (1844-1895). Né à Saint-Thomas (Montmagny), petit fils de Sir Etienne Pascal Taché, il étudia à l'Université Laval, fut à l'emploi du gouvernement de Québec, attaché à l'Agent général du Canada à Paris, puis à l'emploi des Archives du Canada. Il est l'auteur de plusieurs romans historiques: *Charles et Eva* (1867), *François de Bienville* (1870), *Le chevalier de Mornac* (1873), etc. Ses qualités d'écrivain n'étaient pas très grandes, mais il fut un des premiers au Canada à vouloir faire une carrière d'écrivain et ses récits abondent en scènes romantiques dans le goût du temps. Il fut un des membres fondateurs de la Société royale du Canada.

ANNE MARRIOTT (1913-   ). Born in Victoria, British Columbia, Joyce Anne Marriott was educated there in private schools. Many of her early poems had appeared in various periodicals when, in 1939, she produced *The Wind Our Enemy*, expressing with vivid and moving imagistic pictures the disheartening effect of continuous drought on the Canadian prairie. *Calling Adventurers* (1941), consisting of the verse choruses of *Payload,* a documentary radio drama of the Canadian North, won for Miss Marriott the Governor General's Award for Poetry. The same year she brought out another book of verse, *Salt Marsh and Other Poems* (1942). *Sandstone and Other Poems* (1945), a selection, illustrates Miss Marriott's realism and ironic socialistic criticism.

CLAIRE MARTIN (1914-   ). Pseudonyme de madame Roland Faucher, née à Québec, qui a étudié chez les Ursulines et chez les Soeurs de la Congrégation de Notre-Dame. Elle a été speakerine à la radio et, de 1962 à 1965, présidente de la Société des Ecrivains canadiens. Elle a débuté par un volume de nouvelles, *Avec ou sans amour* (1958) qui lui mérita le Prix du Cercle du Livre de France. Ces récits brefs révélaient un don d'observation cruel et soulignaient en raccourcis heureux les tares de ses personnages. *Doux-amer* (1960) est le roman d'une liaison entre une romancière et son éditeur qui se transforme en amitié amoureuse. Elle y analyse les ressorts secrets de l'amour humain avec une pénétration qu'on retrouve dans *Quand j'aurai payé ton visage* (1962), autre roman d'une liaison, d'une rupture et d'une réconciliation entre une femme et son jeune beau-frère. Chez Claire Martin, l'amour est toujours précaire, menacé, mais il est l'aventure essentielle de ses personnages qui ne trouvent leur vérité que dans et par lui. Elle a démontré une fois de plus, dans les souvenirs d'enfance parus sous le titre *Dans un gant de fer* (1965), qu'elle est un de nos plus parfaits prosateurs.

VINCENT MASSEY (1887-   ). Born in Toronto, Ontario, Massey received a thorough education at St. Andrew's College, the University of Toronto and Oxford University. On returning to Canada in 1913, he lectured in Modern History at the University of Toronto and was Dean of Residence of Victoria College. That year as Chairman of the Massey Foundation he supervised the planning and construction of Hart House. During the war years he served in the army and later worked with the government on War and Repatriation

Committees in Ottawa. Massey returned to Toronto in 1919 to the family firm of Massey-Harris, of which he became president in 1921. In 1925 he began his active political career as Minister without Portfolio in the Liberal government, and in 1926 he brought out his first book, *Canadian Plays from Hart House Theatre* (1926), a collection of plays by promising Canadian authors. The following year, he edited a second volume of plays under the same title.

During his career as a Canadian diplomat in England and the United States, Massey produced *Good Neighbourhood and Other Addresses* (1930) and *The Sword of Lionheart* (1942). On his return to Canada, after serving as High Commissioner to England, he published *On Being Canadian* (1948). In 1949, he headed a Royal Commission whose subsequent "Massey Report" was the inspiration for the formation of the Canada Council. *Speaking of Canada* (1959) is a collection of speeches which he gave while touring Canada as Governor General. The memoirs of his public career are recorded in *What's Past Is Prologue* (1963). *Canadians and Their Commonwealth*, lectures delivered in 1961 at Oxford University, and *Confederation on the March*, a collection of recent addresses, were published in 1965.

JOSEPH MELANCON. *Voir* Rainier, Lucien.

JAMES DE MILLE. *See* de Mille, James.

W. O. MITCHELL (1914-   ). Born in Saskatchewan, William Ormond Mitchell graduated from the University of Alberta in 1942. He began his career as a salesman and then taught school for three years before settling in High River, Alberta. A frequent contributor to *Maclean's, Liberty* and other Canadian magazines, he published his first novel *Who Has Seen the Wind* in 1947. A study in alienation, it describes life in a small prairie town as seen through the eyes of a boy between the ages of four and eleven; it makes no attempt to dramatize the effects of drought and dust. The development of the boy from the childhood world of imagination to early maturity is portrayed in prose which rises to an almost lyric eloquence. Mitchell's understanding of the mind of the child, with its curious involutions and images, is acute and sensitive without being sentimental. He portrays his characters with an affectionately comic note in a style that is appropriately unpretentious.

Since the publication of this first novel, Mitchell has devoted much of his time to the writing of radio serials and television scripts. He is well known to CBC listeners and viewers through his classic serial "Jake and the Kid," which was published and won the Leacock medal for humour in 1962. Mitchell's novel *The Kite* (1962) is concerned with a columnist who interviews a resident of the foothills, Daddy Sherry, reputedly the oldest and wisest man in the world. Patricia Barclay, "Regionalism and the Writer: A Talk with W. O. Mitchell," *Can. Lit.*, 14 (Autumn, 1962); Claude T. Bissell, "Letters in Canada: 1947," *UTQ*, XVII (April, 1948); Warren Tallman, "Wolf in the Snow," *Can. Lit.*, 5 (Summer, 1960).

NICHOLAS MONSARRAT (1910-   ). Born in Liverpool, Nicholas Monsarrat attended Winchester College (1923-1928) and Cambridge (1928-1931). He then became a writer and broadcaster. From 1948 to 1953 he was Director of the United Kingdom Information Office at Johannesburg, South Africa. He moved to Ottawa to hold a similar position (1953-1956).

His experience in the Royal Navy as a Lieut.-Cmdr. during World War II gave him material for his sea stories.

The Cruel Sea (1951), a novel which depicts vividly the problems of command of a naval vessel in the Battle of the Atlantic, made Monsarrat famous. Since that time he has published *The Story of Esther Costello* (1953), *The Tribe That Lost Its Head* (1956), *The Ship That Died of Shame, and Other Stories* (1959), *The Nylon Pirates* (1960), *The White Rajah* (1961), *The Time Before This* (1962), *Smith and Jones* (1963), *Something to Hide* (1965), and *The Pillow Fight* (1965).

Monsarrat is a member of the Board of Governors of the Stratford (Ontario) Festival; *To Stratford with Love* appeared in 1964. His home is now in England, and he publishes most of his books abroad.

L. M. MONTGOMERY (1874-1942). Born at Clifton, Prince Edward Island, Lucy Maude Montgomery was of Canadian-Scots descent. Her mother died when she was very young and her father moved to the West, leaving his daughter with her grandparents at Cavendish, P.E.I. She attended Prince of Wales College at Charlottetown, graduating at seventeen with a teacher's license.

For a year she lived in Prince Albert with her father, but she returned to the Maritimes to attend Dalhousie University and to work for a time on the Halifax *Chronicle.* For several years she taught in P.E.I. villages and then lived with her widowed grandmother, helping her in the Cavendish post office.

L. M. Montgomery had been an inveterate scribbler from childhood. At the age of twelve, she won a short story contest sponsored by the *Family Herald and Weekly Star,* and later wrote for various children's publications. The climax of this long apprenticeship was the publication of *Anne of Green Gables* (1908), a book which quickly achieved and maintained an international readership.

Anne of Green Gables, a story for girls in early adolescence, tells how Anne Shirley, an orphan and often a rebel, finds a home with an elderly brother and sister, the strong-willed, upright and rather fearsome Marilla and her kind, wise and tolerant brother Matthew. Anne's triumphs and disappointments are set against the rural Cavendish background which L. M. Montgomery knew well and which she describes in careful detail. The element of whimsy in Anne's nature, evidenced by her naming of such local landmarks as "The Lake of Shining Waters," reflects the daydreams of a young girl with a fine balance of common sense, both in the authoress and her heroine, which helped to make the book popular with an adult as well as a young reading public. Mark Twain called it "The sweetest creation of child life yet written."

The "Anne" series was continued through a number of volumes from *Anne of Avonlea* (1909) to *Anne of Ingleside* (1939). In 1911, L. M. Montgomery married the Reverend Ewen Macdonald, a Presbyterian clergyman. Henceforth she combined the roles of minister's wife, mother of two sons and very productive novelist. She wrote *Emily of New Moon* (1923), whose heroine is an aspiring teenage authoress, and its two sequels, *Emily Climbs* (1925) and *Emily's Quest* (1927). In *The Blue Castle* (1926) and *A Tangled Web* (1931) she tried her hand at adult novels. These were less successful, however, than her girls' series, to which she returned in *Pat of Silver Bush* (1933) and *Mistress Pat* (1935). She was honoured by an O.B.E. in 1935. Wilfrid Eggleston, editor, *The Green Gables Letters from L. M. Montgomery to Ephraim Weber* (Toronto, 1960); Hilda M. Ridley, *The Story of L. M. Montgomery* (Toronto, 1956).

LOUVIGNY DE MONTIGNY (1876-1955). Né à Saint-Jérôme, Louvigny Testard de Montigny étudia au Collège Sainte-Marie et à la faculté de droit de l'Université de Montréal. Encore étudiant, il participa à la fondation de l'Ecole littéraire de Montréal. Il fut quelque temps journaliste, puis entra au Sénat comme traducteur. En 1915, il devenait directeur du service de traduction du Sénat. De 1906 à 1954, il fut le représentant au Canada de la Société des Gens de lettres et il joua un rôle actif dans la fondation de la Canadian Authors Association et de la Société des écrivains canadiens. Il publia *Maria Chapdelaine* en 1916 et écrivit la préface de cette première édition. Il a plus tard écrit une thèse sur *La revanche de Maria Chapdelaine* (1937). Il est l'auteur de pièces de théâtre d'inspiration folklorique et de contes pittoresques inspirés par les moeurs canadiennes, *Au pays de Québec* (1945). Il a aussi publié un ouvrage important sur *La langue française au Canada* (1915).

EDOUARD MONTPETIT (1881-1954). Né à Montmagny, Monpetit a étudié au Collège de Montréal et à la faculté de droit de l'Université de Montréal. Admis au barreau en 1904, il pratiqua sa profession sans enthousiasme et accepta bientôt de devenir professeur d'économie politique à l'Université de Montréal. Il se rendit alors en France où il étudia à l'Ecole libre des sciences politiques et au collège des sciences sociales. En 1910, il devint professeur à l'Ecole des Hautes Etudes commerciales, directeur de l'Ecole des sciences sociales et professeur à la faculté de droit. En 1920, il devint secrétaire général de l'Université de Montréal et continua à exercer une influence étendue par ses cours et conférences. Son prestige était immense et il a été chargé de nombreuses missions universitaires à l'étranger; il fit aussi partie de la délégation canadienne à des conférences internationales et à la Société des Nations en 1935. Il fut un des premiers à éveiller l'attention des Canadiens français sur l'importance de l'économique et, sans être un technicien très poussé, il a publié plusieurs ouvrages d'économie qui sont aussi ceux d'un humaniste préoccupé par les questions de style.

Il est l'auteur d'ouvrages d'économie comme *Pour une doctrine* (1931), *Les Cordons de la bourse* (1935) et *La Conquête économique* (1938, 1940, 1942), mais aussi de recueils d'essais et de conférences qui sont des modèles du genre comme *Au service de la tradition française* (1920) ou *D'azur à trois lys d'or* (1937). Il a aussi laissé des *Souvenirs,* décevants parce que trop discrets, sur les personnages qu'il a connus et les événements auxquels il a été mêlé (*Vers la vie,* 1944; *Vous avez la parole,* 1949 et *Aller et retour,* 1954).

SUSANNA MOODIE (1803-1885). Born in Suffolk, England, a sister of Catharine Parr Traill, Susanna Strickland Moodie emigrated to Canada in 1832 with her husband. They first settled on a farm near Coburg, Upper Canada, and then moved to the backwoods north of Peterborough where they spent several years clearing the land granted to her husband as a former British officer, and carving out their homestead from the wild terrain and bush. After participating in suppressing the Rebellion of 1837, Captain Moodie was appointed Sheriff of Hastings County, and in 1840 moved his family to Belleville, Upper Canada, where Mrs. Moodie continued a literary career already begun in England. Although her extensive contributions to the *Literary Garland* (1838-1851) included lyrics on nature, historical romances, novels and short stories, it was her accurate and detailed presentation of the hardships and adventures of the pioneers in Canada that later won her literary fame.

In 1852 she published her masterpiece *Roughing It in the Bush,* parts of which had previously appeared in sketch form in the *Literary Garland.* In this autobiographical work, Mrs. Moodie included personal anecdotes and graphic accounts of such daily occurrences as a logging bee. The pioneer characters, often rough and eccentric, who surrounded her in the bush were described in a style characterized by economy, vividness and dry humour.

Life in the Clearings Versus the Bush (1853) was a group of autobiographical sketches of the folk in towns and villages. Mrs. Moodie also published in book form stories from the *Literary Garland* such as *Mark Hurdlestone* (1853), *Flora Lindsay* (1853), *Matrimonial Speculations* (1854) and *Geoffrey Moncton* (1856). These were conventionally sentimental novels with settings outside Canada. In 1871 she republished *Roughing It in the Bush* with a modified introduction designed to please the readers of the New Dominion. Carl F. Klinck, Introduction to *Roughing It in the Bush* (Toronto, 1962); Edward A. McCourt, "Roughing It with the Moodies," *Queen's Quarterly,* 52 (Spring, 1945); George H. Needler, *Otonabee Pioneers* (Toronto, 1953).

BRIAN MOORE (1921-   ). Born in Belfast, Ireland, Moore served with the British Ministry of War Transport in North Africa, Italy and France during the closing years of World War II. Shortly after the war he came to Canada, where he took a position as a newspaperman in Montreal. His first novel *The Lonely Passion of Judith Hearne,* set in Belfast, appeared in 1956, and earned for him the Great Britain Best First Novel Award and the Province of Quebec Literary Award. Like all Moore's central characters, Judith Hearne, an older woman who finds the only succour for her wasted years in alcohol, is a misfit in society, lonely, friendless and tortured by constant and humbling self-appraisal. The general theme is developed further in *The Feast of Lupercal* (1957), the story of Diarmuid Devine, a bachelor school-teacher of Belfast who is timid toward life and passes inhibited years in quiet misery. Devine is thoroughly unheroic, frustrated in his development toward a full, happy life, and a victim of his own ineptitude. Moore treats him with a compassion and a gentle irony which relieve the atmosphere of futility that surrounds him.

The Luck of Ginger Coffey (1960) received a Governor General's Award. Although this novel is also the record of a failure, Moore's sense of the comic comes through more clearly than in the earlier novels. Ginger Coffey is himself a comic character, and Moore misses no opportunity to play upon the ludicrous and absurd, as well as the pathetic elements of his story. The book has been adapted for a movie as well as an opera.

Moore's short stories and articles have appeared frequently in the *Atlantic Monthly, Northern Review, The Tamarack Review* and other publications. In 1961 he was granted a Canada Council award to aid in the writing of a further novel, *An Answer from Limbo* (1962). Set in New York, where Moore has spent most of his time since 1958, this work portrays the struggle of an Irish expatriate, Brendan Tierney, to become a successful writer. The *Emperor of Ice Cream* (1965) is also concerned with a rebellious literary youth, Gavin Burke, who finds in a Belfast air raid a reconciliation with life—"the only emperor" in Wallace Stevens' poem from which the novel's title is taken. Jack Ludwig, "A Mirror of Moore," *Can. Lit.,* 7 (Winter, 1961); F. W. Watt, "Letters in Canada: 1960," *UTQ,* XXX, 4 (July, 1961).

PAUL MORIN (1889-1963). Né à
Montréal, Morin a étudié au Collège
Sainte-Marie, au lycée Saint-Louis de
Gonzague à Paris, à la faculté de droit
de l'Université de Montréal, dont il était
licencié, et à l'Université de Paris, dont
il était docteur ès lettres. Il a enseigné
la littérature française à McGill University et à la University of Minnesota.
Il s'occupa ensuite de traduction et de
linguistique. Il a beaucoup voyagé en
Europe et, en 1923, il était élu à la
Société royale du Canada. Il vivait
retiré de tout depuis plusieurs années
lorsqu'il est décédé en 1963. Il a publié
sa thèse sur *Les sources de l'oeuvre de
Henry Wadsworth Longfellow* (1913),
et trois recueils de poésies, *Le Paon
d'émail* (1911), *Poèmes de cendre et
d'or* (1922) et *Géronte et son miroir*
(1960). Seuls les deux premiers ont été
reproduits dans l'édition définitive de
ses *Oeuvres poétiques* (1961), le
troisième ne comprenant pratiquement
que de vains exercices de virtuosité.

La publication du *Paon d'émail* en
1911 fut une sorte de scandale. Le
poète tournait résolument le dos à
toutes les traditions canadiennes et
publiait des poèmes d'une perfection de
forme qui n'avait pas encore été
atteinte au Canada français et d'une
inspiration purement "artiste": la
plupart de ses poésies étaient des
tableaux aux formes nettes et aux
couleurs vives inspirés par des paysages
français, italiens, grecs, turcs, voire
chinois. Le ton en était parfaitement
païen comme chez les poètes de la
Grèce antique, comme aussi chez
Heredia, Henri de Régnier et la
comtesse de Noailles. Toute son oeuvre
lui était inspirée par ses voyages et
par ses lectures et n'était qu'un effort
pour fixer par les mots, comme fait le
peintre sur la toile, des visions de bonheur menacées par le temps qui finit
par tout détruire. L'impassibilité est
moins grande dans les *Poèmes de cendre
et d'or,* la forme plus souple et plus
variée, mais l'inspiration reste exotique,

le vocabulaire recherché, la technique
souveraine et l'esprit sophistiqué. Cet
art savant d'un érudit sceptique et
cynique est un produit de civilisation
décadente en même temps qu'une
réussite indéniable sur la plan de la
virtuosité. On pourra lire le chapitre
de Marcel Dugas dans *Littérature
canadienne* (1929), celui de Louis
Dantin dans *Poètes de l'Amérique
française* (tome I, 1928), l'article de
Jean-Ethier Blais dans *L'Action universitaire* (juillet 1948). Jean-Paul Plante
a préfacé le *Paul Morin* des Classiques
canadiens (1958).

FARLEY MOWAT (1921-   ). Born in
Belleville, Ontario, Mowat received his
elementary education in various schools
in the Eastern and Western parts of
Canada. From 1940 to 1946, he served
as an infantry officer in Sicily and North
West Europe. After returning to Canada
he continued his studies, spent two years
(1947/48) in the Arctic, and received
his B.A. in 1949 from the University of
Toronto. As a freelance writer, he
contributed articles and short stories to
various Canadian and American
periodicals.

Mowat's first work *People of the
Deer* (1952) is about the Eskimos and
is critical of their treatment by government officials. His writings for juvenile
readers have been particularly successful: *Lost in the Barrens* (1956) won a
Governor General's Award and *The
Dog Who Wouldn't Be* (1957) has
been an even greater favourite. In 1958,
Mowat produced a popular edition of
Samuel Hearne's *Coppermine Journey,*
as well as *The Grey Seas Under,* a story
of the rescue work done by a salvage
tug and her men in the Atlantic. His
book *The Desperate People* (1959) returns to the theme of the Eskimos and
their problems. *Ordeal by Ice* (1960)
presents an imaginary journey in the
Arctic Sea, and combines incidents compiled from the voyages of early

explorers in search of the North West passage. *The Serpent's Coil* (1961) depicts the epic struggle of men and ships against a North Atlantic hurricane in the late summer of 1948. This novel, like many of his other stories of the sea and the north, is based on actual incidents. *The Black Joke* (1962), an adventure story about the rum-running days around St. Pierre and Miquelon, and *Owls in the Family* (1963), personal reminiscences of the author's own fascinatingly amusing pets, are appealing juvenile novels. His *Never Cry Wolf,* which explodes some myths about that animal's rapacity, also appeared in 1963. *Westviking: the Ancient Norse in Greenland and North America* (1965) is a dramatic account of early excursions into this continent. Mowat now lives in Burgeo, Newfoundland.

ROSANNA ELEANOR MULLINS. *See* Leprohon, Rosanna Eleanor (Mullins).

EMILY GOWAN MURPHY (1868-1933). Born in Cookstown, Ontario, Emily Gowan (Ferguson) Murphy was educated at Bishop Strachan School, Toronto. In 1904 she moved to Alberta where she actively engaged in social welfare and campaigned successfully for women's rights. Although she wrote some fiction, she achieved popular fame by the original and vivacious manner in which she employed the essay form in her descriptive etchings of the Canadian mid-west, *Janey Canuck in the West* (1910), *Open Trails* (1912) and *Seeds of Pine* (1914).

SINCLAIR MURRAY. *See* Sullivan, Alan.

JEAN NARRACHE. *Voir* Coderre, Emile.

EMILE NELLIGAN (1879-1941). Né à Montréal d'un père irlandais et d'une mère canadienne française, Nelligan fut mauvais écolier et dut interrompre ses études à dix-huit ans. Dès ses années de collège, il fut attiré vers la poésie et il écrivit des vers. Des amis l'encouragèrent et en 1897 il devint membre de l'Ecole littéraire de Montréal. Presque toute son oeuvre fut écrite de 1897 à 1899; il manifesta alors des signes d'égarement mental et fut interné à Saint-Jean-de-Dieu où il mourut en 1941. Toute son oeuvre avait été écrite avant l'âge de vingt ans et il fut le plus précoce des meilleurs poètes canadiens.

Nelligan est le grand nom de l'Ecole littéraire de Montréal et sa gloire. Il n'y a passé que deux ans, mais cela lui a suffi pour produire une oeuvre poétique qui est la plus haute de sa génération au Canada français. Ses poésies ont paru d'abord dans *Le Monde illustré* et dans *La Patrie* et elles furent réunies en volume dès 1903 par son ami Louis Dantin qui les a fait précéder d'une importante préface. Elles furent rééditées en 1925, 1932, 1945 et, en 1952 Luc Lacourcière donna la première édition critique des *Poésies complètes* dans la collection du Nénuphar. Peu d'oeuvres poétiques canadiennes ont été l'objet d'aussi nombreuses études et le nom de Nelligan a toujours été considéré comme prestigieux.

Le poète du *Vaisseau d'or* a tourné le dos aux traditions patriotiques et romantiques du dix-neuvième siècle. Très tôt, il a lu Baudelaire et les symbolistes français et il a été nettement influencé par Rollinat, Rimbaud, Rodenbach et Verlaine. Il a su cependant dominer ces influences et atteindre à un style personnel. Naturellement porté au rêve et à la mélancolie, il a écrit plusieurs poèmes élégiaques d'une tendresse et d'une tristesse émouvantes. Les souvenirs de son enfance rêveuse lui ont fourni une partie considérable de son inspiration. Puis, peu à peu, le thème de la mort est apparu et a donné à ses derniers poèmes un accent parfois macabre. Là où il est supérieur à tous ses prédécesseurs canadiens—et d'ailleurs à presque tous ses successeurs —c'est non seulement dans la maîtrise des techniques les plus diverses, mais aussi et surtout dans l'art de marier les images et les symboles pour créer une atmosphère poétique intense et communicative.

Il y a dans cette oeuvre des exercices de virtuosité—le jeune homme dut se faire la main—mais il y a aussi des pages qui sont une plaintive musique et d'autres qui sont des éclats lyriques irrésistibles. Avec lui, le *moi* a pris la première place dans la poésie canadienne et Nelligan a ouvert des voies nouvelles et marqué la fin d'une époque. La poésie n'est plus ici un moyen, elle est désormais un art qui n'obéit qu'à ses lois propres.

En plus des préfaces de Louis Dantin et de Luc Lacourcière aux éditions de 1903 et de 1952 on consultera principalement sur Nelligan la thèse de Paul Wyczynski (1960).

ERIC NICOL (1919-   ). Born in Kingston, Ontario, Eric Patrick Nicol was educated in Vancouver. He graduated with an M.A. from the University of British Columbia, where he returned to lecture in English following postgraduate work at the Sorbonne. Since 1950 he has been a radio script writer for the B.B.C. and freelance writer for Canadian magazines and the CBC. He is a syndicated columnist with the Vancouver *Daily Province.*

Several of his humorous books, *The Roving I* (1950), *Shall We Join the Ladies?* (1955) and *Girdle Me a Globe* (1957) won the Leacock Medal for Humour. *An Uninhibited History of Canada* (1959), *Say, Uncle: A Completely Uncalled for History of the U.S.* (1962) and *Russia, Anyone?* (1963)—published with cartoons by Peter Whalley—are typical of Nicol's clever manipulation of amusing incidents and remarks but lack the sustained wit that made earlier volumes

so successful. *A Herd of Yaks* (1962) selected "the best of Nicol." *Space Age, Go Home!* (1964) is a collection of short pieces contributed to newspapers or other publications on a great variety of subjects concerned with modern living. Nicol has also written several plays: *The Bathroom* was produced on television. *The Bear Went over the Mountain* (1964) is an anthology of tall animal stories. His Confederation satire, called *100 Years of What?*, appeared in 1966.

FREDERICK NIVEN (1878-1944). Born in Chile, Frederick John Niven was educated in Glasgow, Scotland. Here he spent some time as an assistant librarian before paying a visit in 1899 to British Columbia where he worked in railway and lumber camps. The experience gained was used on his return in several sketches written for the Glasgow *Weekly Herald. The Lost Cabin Mine* (1909) was the first of his more than thirty novels.

In 1912, Niven toured the Canadian West and did another series of articles. After the war he returned from England to Kootenay Lake, British Columbia, where his fraternization with the district Indians gave him the authentic material to write *The Flying Years* (1935), which deals with two generations in the changing West, and *Mine Inheritance* (1940), a stirring history of the Red River Settlement. In *The Transplanted* (1942), published posthumously, he skilfully reconstructs a mining town in which every character has come from a different place. In all his works Niven took great care to ensure verisimilitude of facts and atmosphere, and presented a vivid description of the West. In addition to some poems, he also published an autobiography, *Coloured Spectacles* (1938).

ALDEN A. NOWLAN (1933-   ). Born in Windsor, Nova Scotia, Nowlan left school while still a youngster. In 1962 he settled in Saint John, New Brunswick, as news editor of *The Telegraph Journal*. He began producing poems which appeared in numerous periodicals in Canada and the United States and were published in *The Rose and the Puritan* (1958) and *A Darkness in the Earth* (1958). His later verse is collected in *Under the Ice* (1961), *Wind in a Rocky Country* (1961), and *The Things Which Are* (1962). His work is included in *Five New Brunswick Poets* (1962). He is particularly successful in his realistic but sympathetic treatment of rural life in the Maritimes. His short stories have been published in Canadian journals and are represented in Pacey's *A Book of Canadian Stories* (1962).

JONATHAN ODELL (1737-1818). Born and educated in Newark, New Jersey, Odell became a surgeon in the British Army. He resigned his commission to study for the priesthood in England, and subsequently served as a rector in Burlington, New Jersey. During the American Revolution he was a chaplain with a Loyalist regiment and contributed to *Rivington's New York Gazetteer* virulently invective essays and verses attacking the revolutionists and their leaders. After the war he returned for a brief stay in England, and in 1784 settled in New Brunswick. His poetry was published along with that of a fellow Loyalist writer in *The Loyal Verses of Joseph Stansbury and Doctor Jonathan Odell* (1860). This volume is interesting as one of the few remaining publications of original Loyalist sentiment.

MARTHA OSTENSO (1900-1963). Born in Norway, Miss Ostenso emigrated in 1902 with her family to America. She grew up in Manitoba and was educated at the University of Manitoba and Columbia University. Author of numerous short stories, she has produced a book of verse *In a Far Land* (1924) and some ten novels. The best known of these is *Wild Geese* (1925), which won a $13,500 prize and depicts, with an uncompromising realism unusual in Canadian novels of that time, the loneliness and hardships of life for new settlers in Manitoba.

Miss Ostenso (Mrs. Douglas Durken) lived in the United States for many years. In addition to writing fiction and verse, she collaborated with Sister Elizabeth Kenny in a biography *And They Shall Walk* (1943), which was also a popular film.

FERNAND OUELLETTE (1930-). Né à Montréal, il a étudié au Collège Séraphique d'Ottawa et à la faculté des Sciences sociales de l'Université de Montréal dont il est licencié. Il a été libraire et est maintenant réalisateur au service des émissions culturelles de Radio-Canada. Il a publié trois recueils de poèmes: *Ces anges de sang* (1954), *Séquences de l'aile* (1958) et *Le soleil sous la mort* (1964). Cette poésie sévère, hautement spiritualiste et parfois un peu trop cérébrale, allie aux thèmes tragiques de la cruauté de ce monde le thème de l'évasion vers les espaces interstellaires, antinomie résolue surtout dans le dernier recueil par l'amour de la femme et de la patrie qui rendent ce monde encore habitable pour le poète. Cette poésie a un accent nettement contemporain tant par son caractère souvent angoissé et violent que par son langage qui emprunte volontiers à la science son vocabulaire et ses images. Mais on y trouve aussi parfois des notes de tendresse. Ouellette a aussi publié des essais dans *Liberté*, notamment sur le compositeur Edgar Varèse pour qu'il a un véritable culte.

DESMOND PACEY (1917-). Born in Dunedin, New Zealand, William Cyril Desmond Pacey received his preliminary education at Magnus School, England, and after emigrating to Canada in 1931 at Caledonia High

School. He graduated with his B.A. from Victoria College, Toronto, in 1938, and after receiving a Massey Travelling Fellowship, studied at Trinity College, Cambridge, where he received his Ph.D. in 1941. Returning to Canada, he taught English at Brandon College, Manitoba, from 1940 to 1944, and then moved to the University of New Brunswick as Professor and Head of the English Department, and Dean of Graduate Studies.

In 1945 he published *Frederick Philip Grove,* a critical examination based on correspondence with Grove. *A Book of Canadian Stories* (1947), an anthology with biographical sketches of the authors, was followed in 1952 by *Creative Writing in Canada,* which became the standard reference work on English-Canadian literature for a decade and was revised in 1961. He was elected F.R.S.C. in 1955. *Ten Canadian Poets* (1958)—including Sangster, Roberts, Carman, Lampman, D. C. Scott, Pratt, Smith, F. R. Scott, Klein, Birney—not only contained new biographical material but also a critical evaluation of the older poets.

In addition to numerous scholarly articles, Pacey has produced both poetry and short stories. He is the author of a whimsical verse fantasy for children, *The Cow with the Musical Moo* (1952). His short stories, which have appeared in magazines in Canada and abroad, were collected in *The Picnic and Other Stories* (1958). He was one of the editors of the *Literary History of Canada* (1965).

FRANK L. PACKARD (1877-1942). Born in Montreal, Frank Lucius Packard graduated from McGill and later did postgraduate work at the University of Liége, Belgium. He practised engineering for several years before turning to writing for a profitable livelihood. In 1906 he began contributing to popular magazines and subsequently produced a novel *On the Iron at Big Cloud*

(1911). He published some thirty-one novels, specializing with great success in the mystery and adventure thriller. His series about a wealthy playboy detective, which began with *The Adventures of Jimmy Dale* (1917), was particularly popular.

P. K. PAGE (1916-   ). Born in England, Patricia K. Page emigrated to Canada in 1919 and received her early education in Calgary, Alberta. Following her graduation from school, she went to England for one year. Upon her return to Canada she lived in Maritime cities where she met Alan Crawley, editor of *Contemporary Verse,* whose influence on her work she acknowledges. During World War II she became associated with a group of Montreal poets, including Patrick Anderson and F. R. Scott, who produced *Preview.*

Her early poems, which appeared in various literary journals including the London *Observer,* were first collected in *Unit of Five* (1944), edited by Ronald Hambleton. In the same year, under the pseudonym of Judith Cape, Miss Page published a novel *The Sun and the Moon.* Her first complete volume of poetry *As Ten As Twenty* appeared in 1946. Her verse reflects to some extent the imagery and socialistic attitudes of Anderson. Interested in psychology, Miss Page is adept at drawing sketches of types. Her understanding of people is essentially feminine, and her interpretations are couched in rich, sensuous imagery which is consistently apt and distinctive. The predominant theme of this volume is the love of humanity.

Her second volume *The Metal and the Flower* (1954) received a Governor General's Award. The poems included represent a development from her earlier work, in that she has employed a symbolic language that operates on various levels of instinct, sense and intellect. There is improvement also in the attainment of a freer, less mannered style, although some of these later poems lack the vitality and individuality of the best of her earlier work. Miss Page is married to William Arthur Irwin, who has held various foreign appointments in the Department of External Affairs as Head of Mission. In the late 1950's, while she was in Brazil, she turned to drawing instead of writing. She has had one-man shows in Toronto and Mexico City, and has works in the National Gallery, the Toronto Gallery, and elsewhere. Her signature for drawings is "P. K. Irwin." Her home is in Victoria, B.C. Northrop Frye, "Letters in Canada: 1954," *UTQ,* XXIV (April, 1955); John Sutherland, "The Poetry of P. K. Page," *Northern Review,* 1 (Dec.-Jan., 1946-47).

PHILIPPE PANNETON. *Voir* Ringuet.

SUZANNE PARADIS (1936-   ). Neé à Québec, Suzanne Paradis y a étudié à l'Ecole Normale. Elle a épousé le poète Louis-Paul Hamel. Ecrivain très abondant, elle a publié en quatre ans trois romans, qui sont d'un irréalisme trop grand pour s'imposer, cinq volumes de poésies d'un souffle rare, d'un enthousiasme sain et d'une écriture ferme: *A temps le bonheur* (1960), *La Chasse aux autres* (1961) *La Malebête* (1962), *Pour les enfants des morts* (1964) et *Le Visage offensé* (1966). La pensée de l'auteur n'est pas toujours claire et son abondance lui nuit, mais elle atteint souvent à un lyrisme émouvant pour célébrer la beauté de la vie et la joie de l'amour.

ETIENNE PARENT (1802-1874). Né à Beauport, Parent étudia aux séminaires de Nicolet et de Québec. Il collabora au *Canadien* de 1822 à 1825 puis, après avoir étudié le droit, il ressuscita le journal en 1831 et le dirigea jusqu'en 1842. Il fut emprisonné pour cinq mois

lors de la rébellion de 1837 bien qu'il eût retiré son appui à Papineau quand ce dernier prêcha le recours aux armes. Il fut ensuite député à la législature (1841/42), greffier du conseil exécutif (1842-1847), puis sous-secrétaire d'état (1847-1872).

Avec Papineau, Lafontaine et Garneau, Parent fut un des maîtres à penser des Canadiens de son temps. Il fut le premier journaliste de sa génération et il prolongea l'action qu'il exerça par *Le Canadien* en donnant de nombreuses conférences dont plusieurs ont été publiées. Sa langue était lourde et souvent incorrecte, mais ses écrits ont néanmoins eu une grande influence grâce à la force de ses convictions et à la solidité de son argumentation. Il lutta pour la défense des intérêts des Canadiens français à une époque particulièrement troublée, et il fut un des premiers à attirer leur attention sur l'importance de l'économie dans la vie de la colonie. On ne saurait le tenir pour un écrivain de qualité, mais son oeuvre de journaliste est un des documents majeurs pour l'étude de son temps.

GILBERT PARKER (1862-1932). Born near Napanee, Ontario, Horatio Gilbert Parker graduated from the Ottawa Normal School and taught school for a while. After attending Trinity College, Toronto, he served briefly as a curate at Trenton, Ontario. Desiring a warmer climate for his health, he sailed in 1885 to Australia where he worked as associate editor on the Sydney *Morning Herald.* Although he had already published a privately printed collection of poems, *Embers* (1885), several of which were later set to music, it was in Australia that he attracted literary notice with the moderately successful *Adaptation of Faust* (1888) and two other plays which were also produced in Sydney. While his dramatic achievement was negligible, it did give him valuable experience for his later fictional treatment of character and plot.

After further extensive travels, he spent a few years in London, England, and published his first book of tales of the Canadian Northland *Pierre and His People* (1892) and its sequel *An Adventurer of the North* (1895). A second book of verse *A Lover's Diary* appeared in 1894 and *When Valmond Came to Pontiac* in 1895. This novel, published in the year of his marriage to a wealthy American woman, is about "a Lost Napoleon" who came to a small Quebec village. *The Seats of the Mighty* (1896) is a romance set in Quebec city in the period familiar to Canadian readers through William Kirby's *The Golden Dog* (1877). Prints and maps accompanying the text gave evidence of Parker's research to "give more vividness to the atmosphere of the time, and to strengthen the veri-similitude of a piece of fiction which is not [he believed] out of harmony with fact." His best contribution to Canadian letters, however, was in the early short stories, in which fancy and poetry create a myth of the North.

By 1900, Parker had returned to England and become a member of Parliament. For eighteen years he was Conservative M.P. for Gravesend. He was the author of about thirty other books, including such romances as *The Battle of the Strong* (1898), set in the Channel Islands, *The Weavers* (1907), a novel of Egypt, and *The Judgement House* (1913), against the background of London and South Africa. Parker was a very popular author, winning readers by striking incidents, robust or mysterious characters, glamorous settings, touches of the poetic and the biblical, and by obvious ethical stability.

Among the many honours awarded him, Parker was created a Knight (1902), a Baronet (1915), a member of the Privy Council (1916) and elected a F.R.S.C. After his death in England

his body was buried at his own request in the Bay of Quinte region in which he had grown up as a boy. John C. Adams, "Sir Gilbert Parker as a Dramatist," *Canadian Author and Bookman*, XL (Winter, 1965); John W. Garvin, "Sir Gilbert Parker and Canadian Literature," *Canadian Bookman,* 14 (Sept., 1932).

AIME PELLETIER. *Voir* Vac, Bertrand.

ALBERT PELLETIER (1895-   ). Né à St-Pascal (Kamouraska), Pelletier a étudié au Collège Ste-Anne de la Pocatière et aux universités Laval et de Montréal. Notaire, il a exercé quelques années à St-Jovite puis a été de 1925 à 1958 au service du Procureur général de la province de Québec. Il a collaboré à divers journaux et réuni ses meilleurs articles de critique dans *Carquois* (1931) et *Egrappages* (1933). Il a fondé les éditions du Totem et dirigé la revue *Les Idées* (1931-1939).

Esprit fortement cartésien, il recherchait avant tout la clarté et la logique dans les oeuvres dont il a étudié plus volontiers le contenu intellectuel que les caractères littéraires. Fermé à tout ce qui est mystère, il n'a pas saisi la beauté de certaines oeuvres poétiques, mais il a apporté à l'étude de plusieurs oeuvres un sens critique d'une rigueur implacable à une époque où l'on se contentait souvent d'idées vagues et de style imprécis. Il s'est exprimé souvent avec violence et ses jugements étaient parfois trop sévères, mais il a contribué à rendre maints esprits plus exigeants envers eux-mêmes et envers les autres.

GEORGES PELLETIER (1882-1947). Né à Rivière du Loup, Pelletier étudia au collège de Sainte-Anne de la Pocatière, à l'Université Laval dont il était licencié en droit, et à l'Université de Montréal dont il était docteur en science politique. Disciple de Bourassa, il passa toute sa vie au *Devoir* dont il fut le directeur de 1932 à 1947. Il fut un des principaux porte-paroles du nationalisme et il serait souhaitable de recueillir en volume ses meilleurs articles, surtout ceux où il maniait l'ironie avec beaucoup de finesse. Il a publié des portraits savoureux, *Silhouettes d'aujourd'hui* (1927). Il était membre de la Société royale du Canada.

LEN PETERSON (1917-   ). Born in Regina, Saskatchewan, Leonard Byron Peterson attended Luther College in Regina and graduated from Northwestern University in 1938. He moved to Toronto where he wrote radio scripts and short stories. During World War II he served in the Canadian Army.

The best known of his many excellent radio and television plays is "Burlap Bags," a comic contemporary satire. His novel *Chipmunk* (1949) is the bleak story of a Toronto baker who rejoins the army in his frustration and loneliness, and whose last gesture is an impulsively rebellious outcry against the folly of war. Peterson's play *Look Ahead* (1962) satirizes religion, education, and society in general.

ALPHONSE PICHE (1917-   ). Né à Chicoutimi, Piché a étudié au Séminaire de Trois-Rivières et est employé comme comptable par une maison d'affaires. Il occupe une partie de ses loisirs à écrire et il a publié trois recueils de poèmes: *Ballades de la petite extrace* (1946), d'un humour tendre inspiré par les joies et les misères des petites gens; *Remous* (s.d) et *Voie d'eau* (1950), ce dernier fait de petites pièces opposant la terre et l'eau, symboles de la laideur et de la pureté respectivement. Tous trois ont été réédités dans Poèmes (1966).

MARJORIE PICKTHALL (1883-1922). Born in Middlesex, England, the daughter of the half-brother of authoress Marmaduke Pickthall, Marjorie Lowry Christie Pickthall moved with her family to Southwater, Sussex. Here as a little girl she played in the English countryside with the imaginary playmates of her writings. When the family emigrated to Toronto in 1889, Marjorie continued her interest in music, drawing and writing. She was still a student at Bishop Strachan School when she sold her first story "Two-Ears" to the Toronto *Globe*. In 1899 her poem "Song of the Nixies" won for her a *Mail and Empire* prize. Within the next ten years she published fictitious melodrama of pioneer life for children, and her poems and short stories began to appear in such literary journals as the *University Monthly, Atlantic Monthly, Scribner's* and *Harper's*.

At Victoria College, Toronto, where she worked for a time in the library, she was encouraged by Professor Pelham Edgar and Sir Andrew MacPhail to publish in 1913 her first book of poems, *The Drift of Pinions*. This work contains much of her best verse, including "The Bridegroom of Cana," "Père Lalemant" and "Duna." Strongly influenced both by the pre-Raphaelite and the Irish renaissance poets, she is a careful craftsman. With little experience of life, she drew upon a sensitive imagination to create poetic beauty within the narrow range of natural scenes, Biblical stories, Indian legends and Celtic lore. She is particularly effective in evoking by the use of ornate diction and imagery a dreamy unearthly atmosphere in which the mood of sadness prevails.

Miss Pickthall returned to England before the war, took a cottage near Salisbury and there attempted two novels, *Little Hearts* (1916), dealing with the period of the Jacobite Rebellions in England, and *The Bridge* (1922), a psychological tale of the Great Lakes, which were neither as good nor as successful as her poetry.

She also produced *Lamp of Poor Souls and Other Poems* (1915) and wrote many poems which later appeared along with a short blank verse drama in *The Woodcarver's Wife and Other Poems* (1922). After the war she returned to Toronto and thence to Vancouver where she lived two years before her untimely death. A collection of her short stories *Angel Shoes and Other Stories* (1923) and a book of verse *Little Songs* (1923) were published after her death. A complete edition of her poems was brought out in 1936. W. E. Collin, "Dream-Gardens" in *The White Savannahs* (Toronto, 1936); Lorne Pierce, *Marjorie Pickthall, A Book of Remembrance* (Toronto, 1925).

LORNE PIERCE (1890-1961). Born at Delta, in Eastern Ontario, Pierce received his B.A. from Queen's University in 1912. Upon graduation he entered the Methodist ministry, enrolling in Union Theological Seminary, New York. In 1917 he received his B.D., and his M.A. in ethics and metaphysics from New York University.

During World War I he became a sergeant in the Queen's Field Ambulance. In 1920 he completed his Th.D. at Montreal Theological College and became editor of The Ryerson Press in Toronto.

As editor, Pierce had an incalculable influence on Canadian letters. He devoted himself to the cause of fostering a distinctive national culture, encouraging Canadians to take a stronger interest in their own history and literature. *Marjorie Pickthall: A Book of Remembrance* (1925) was the first of his biographical works on Canadian writers. Elected F.R.S.C. in 1926, he founded a medal which is now awarded yearly in his name by the Royal Society to those who have made outstanding contributions to letters in Canada. In 1925 he initiated the Ryerson Poetry Chapbooks for established and little-known poets. "The Makers of Canadian Literature Series," begun during the early years of his career as editor, reached thirteen volumes and included important studies of Canadian writers in English and French. Pierce's own *An Outline of Canadian Literature* (1927) was the first historical joint survey of English-French literature in Canada. His *Beverley Papers,* a series of ten brochures containing reflections on such matters as Canadian racial duality and present-day Christianity and its relations to culture, began to appear in 1929.

Meanwhile he was attempting in a more personal way to promote the welfare of the Canadian author. Frederick Philip Grove, Pratt, Carman, Roberts and Knister among others profited from Pierce's interest and encouragement. His influence in education has also been important. In such books as *New History for Old* (1931) and *Education in a Democracy* (1933), as well as many school readers, he sought to stimulate research and inquiry into Canadian history.

Pierce's own style is characterized by ease, fluency and simplicity. He addressed his essays "to the world of kindred spirits at large." During his thirty-five years of direct participation in Canadian letters, Pierce built up a personal Canadian library consisting of more than 4,000 books, manuscripts and pictures now housed in the Lorne Pierce Room at Queen's University. Recipient of many honorary degrees, he retired from the editorship in 1960, and in the same year he published his last work *A Canadian Nation* in which he sums up his knowledge and philosophy of Canada. C. H. Dickinson, *Lorne Pierce: A Profile* (Toronto, 1965); "Persona Grata: Romantic Puritan," *Saturday Night* (Nov. 26, 1955).

JEAN-GUY PILON (1930-   ). Né à Saint-Polycarpe, Pilon a étudié à la faculté de droit de l'Université de Montréal dont il est licencié (1954). Superviseur des émissions littéraires à Radio-Canada, il est aussi directeur littéraire des éditions de l'Hexagone; il a fondé les Rencontres des Poètes canadiens et la revue *Liberté*; il a toujours été un membre actif des sociétés d'écrivains et a voyagé en Europe et en Amérique du sud.

Après avoir débuté par des poèmes d'un romantisme assez usé, *La Fiancée du matin* (1953), Pilon n'a cessé de tendre à un dépouillement et à une pureté sans cesse accrus. Dans *Les Cloîtres de l'été* (1955) et surtout dans *L'Homme et le Jour* (1957) et *La Mouette et le large* (1960), il a atteint à un ascétisme verbal qui exclut toute coquetterie et qui réduit la parole à l'essentiel. Cette poésie virile et saine n'est faite que de temps forts et elle a quelque chose de dur et de rigoureux; elle est l'affirmation de plus en plus consciente de l'acceptation de la condition canadienne et contemporaine du poète qui a surmonté les tentations du voyage, de l'exil et de la trahison. Avec une grande simplicité Pilon écrit une poésie directe, intime, courte de souffle, qui est une déclaration d'espoir dans l'homme et dans l'avenir. *Recours au pays* (1961), repris dans *Pour saluer une ville* (1963), réitère la réconciliation du poète avec son pays et son peuple.

JEAN-PAUL PINSONNEAULT (1923-   ). Né à Waterloo, il a étudié au Collège de Saint-Laurent. Journaliste et éditeur, il est devenu, après un séjour en France, directeur littéraire des éditions Fides. Il est l'auteur de trois pièces inédites et de quatre romans de facture traditionnelle qui nous donnent de la vie une image sombre et presque désespérante. Il est le romancier de l'échec de l'amour qui se heurte à l'égoïsme; la solitude de ses personnages victimes de leurs vices ou de ceux des autres, n'est jamais plus grande que dans son meil-

leur roman, le dernier: *Les terres sèches* (1964) qui est le roman tragique de la grandeur et de la misère du sacerdoce.

DAMASE POTVIN (1881-1964). Né à Bagotville, Potvin a étudié au Séminaire de Chicoutimi et fut journaliste pendant près de quarante ans; depuis 1945, il fut employé au département de l'Instruction publique de la province de Québec. Il a écrit de nombreux contes et romans inspirés par l'amour de la nature et tous prêchent le retour à la terre avec plus de sincérité que d'art. Ses meilleurs sont *Le Français* (1923), *La Robe noire* (1932) et *La Rivière à Mars* (1934).

E. J. PRATT (1883-1964). Born at Western Bay, Newfoundland, the son of a Methodist minister, Edwin John Pratt was brought up in various coastal villages. Educated at St. John's Methodist College, he trained for the ministry and as a young man preached and taught at Moreton's Harbour, Clarke's Beach, Belle Island and Portugal Cove. These were the settings of many of the poems included in his first books of verse. In 1907 he enrolled at Victoria College, Toronto, where he gradually added to his interest in theology the study of psychology and literature. After completing his academic work (B.A. 1911, B.D. 1913, Ph.D. 1916), Pratt lectured in psychology before joining the Department of English at Victoria College, with which he continued to be associated until his retirement as professor in 1953.

Pratt's first volumes of verse—*Rachel* (1917) and *Newfoundland Verse* (1923)—are concerned with the sea and the rugged life of the Newfoundland coast. They reflect his admiration for physical courage and energy, as well as his warm sympathy with human suffering. *The Witches' Brew* (1925), a delightfully whimsical description of an under-sea Saturnalian orgy attended by all the hosts of Hell, is a Hudibrastic satire on the era of prohibition. His third book *Titans* (1926), consisting of "The Cachalot" and "The Great Feud" with their memorable passages of sustained intensity and verbal brilliance, established Pratt as a major Canadian poet. *The Iron Door* (1927) is an ode which examines the mystery of death.

With *The Roosevelt and the Antinoe* (1930), Pratt turned again to the sea as his setting. For this narrative of heroic rescue, as for many of his later works, he investigated carefully all the available facts concerning the actual exploit. The poem begins quietly, picks up speed as the storm breaks, and rises to a peak of excitement as the natural elements seem to frustrate the courageous attempts of the sailors on the *Roosevelt* to rescue the perishing crew of the *Antinoe;* but human endurance and selfless daring finally triumph.

In 1930, Pratt was elected F.R.S.C. Two more volumes of short poems— *Verses of the Sea* (1930) and *Many Moods* (1932)—were followed by an even more powerful narrative of the sea, *The Titanic* (1935). In this complex and moving poem, Pratt is concerned with the struggle of forces not only of nature against man but within man himself. The irony of *hubris* (a tragically false sense of security and pride), the primitive superstitions of old sailors, the contrast between the iceberg's surface beauty and its submerged menace, and the conflict of human nobility and barbaric self-preservation are dramatically depicted. The unity of the work is faultless as every detail focuses upon the single climactic moment of action when the ship and the iceberg collide.

In *The Fable of the Goats and Other Poems* (1937), the title poem is a beast fable which satirizes militarism and totalitarianism and portrays love as superior to force. *Brébeuf and His Brethren* (1940) tells the story of the efforts of the Jesuit missionaries in Canada to win the Indians to the Christian way of life. Divided like an epic into twelve books, the narrative describes the difficult and heroic beginnings of the mission, its success in winning converts, its tragic destruction and the martyrdom of Lalemant and Brébeuf. In language and rhythm marked by excitement and dignity, Pratt explores the depths and complexity of human passion. The Indians are barbarously cruel and cunning, but they sometimes display courage, loyalty, endurance and even tenderness.

During the war Pratt published verse which reflects his concern for the victory of democratic principles. *Dunkirk* (1941) presents a realistic picture of the heroism and suffering of the 1940 evacuation of allied forces from France. *Still Life and Other Verse* (1943) contains "The Truant," which in asserting the unique creativity, defiant will and splendid capabilities of man expresses Pratt's concept of human life. Several of the poems depict war as a retrogression to primitive barbarism. His *Collected Poems* appeared in 1944, and in the following year he was created C.M.G. Other volumes about the war and its end were published in *They Are Returning* (1945) and *Behind the Log* (1947).

Pratt's next publication *Towards the Last Spike* (1952) is a narrative of the Canadian Pacific Railway. The conflict of politically opposing forces and of man against nature, which ended with the hammering of the last spike in Eagle Pass in 1885, are presented with power and imagination in this patriotic "verse panorama." A second edition of *The Collected Poems of E. J. Pratt* appeared in 1958. His poem "Landfall Ahead" was composed in 1957, in honour of the Queen's visit to Canada to open the St. Lawrence Seaway.

In all his work, Pratt sees human life in the heroic terms of a Christian humanist: despite the destructive mechanistic forces arrayed against him, and the conflict within himself, man has the capacity to triumph. Generous, compassionate and modest, Ned Pratt had a rollicking zest for life. Loved and respected as a teacher and friend, he won international recognition not only as Canada's foremost writer but also as a major contemporary poet. "A Garland for E. J. Pratt on his seventy-fifth birthday," *Tamarack Review*, 1 (Winter, 1957); Munro Beattie, "E. J. Pratt" in *Literary History of Canada* (1965); Earle Birney, "E. J. Pratt and His Critics" in *Our Living Tradition*, 2nd series (Toronto, 1959); W. E. Collin, "Pleiocene Heroics" in *The White Savannahs* (Toronto, 1936); Northrop Frye, Introduction to *The Collected Poems of E. J. Pratt* (2nd edition, Toronto, 1958); Northrop Frye and Roy Daniells, "Recollections of E. J. Pratt," *Can. Lit.*, 21 (Summer, 1964); Desmond Pacey, *Ten Canadian Poets* (Toronto, 1958); "Salute to E. J. Pratt," *Can. Lit.*, 19 (Winter, 1964); John Sutherland, "E. J. Pratt: A Major Contemporary Poet," *Northern Review*, V, 2 and 3, April and May, 1952); Henry W. Wells and Carl F. Klinck, *Edwin John Pratt: The Man and His Poetry* (Toronto, 1947).

ALFRED W. PURDY (1918-   ). Born near Wooler, Ontario, Purdy was educated at Albert College. During World War II he served in the R.C.A.F. He published his first book of verse *The Enchanted Echo* in 1944. As its title suggests, this volume contains echoes of the poetry of earlier romantics like Roberts and Carman. Purdy's later collections exhibit a more modern approach. *Pressed on Sand* (1955) and *Emu, Remember* (1956) are written in a casual lyric verse which makes skilful use of slant rhyme. *The Crafte So Longe To Lerne* (1959) and especially *Poems for all the Annettes* (1962) and *The Blur in Between* (1963) reveal his ability to present trivial subjects with imaginative insight. Although his style is also occasionally commonplace, it has a very personal intensity, and is

effectively satirical. The poems of *The Cariboo Horses* (1965) powerfully express such themes as the impact of Canada's limitless landscape, the contemporary sense of human failure and social dissolution. Purdy, who has travelled widely, now lives in Toronto. Peter Stevens, "In the Raw: The Poetry of A. W. Purdy," *Can. Lit.*, 28 (Spring, 1966); Phyllis Webb, "Magnetic Field. Review of *Poems for All the Annettes*" in *Can. Lit.*, 15 (Winter, 1963).

THOMAS H. RADDALL (1903-   ). Born in Kent, England, Thomas Head Raddall moved with his family to Halifax in 1913. He attended the Halifax Academy until his father's death in 1918, when he left school and took a position as wireless operator aboard vessels in the Canadian Merchant Marine and at various East Coast stations. His intimate knowledge of naval operations provided him with background material for his later works. In 1922 he became bookkeeper for a small pulp mill, and accountant in 1923 for a newsprint mill in Nova Scotia where he began writing short stories and historical articles which appeared in *Blackwood's Magazine*. He remained with the mill until 1938, when he devoted himself full-time to his literary career.

In 1939 he began to contribute frequently to *Maclean's, Saturday Evening Post, Blue Book, Collier's* and *The Dalhousie Review*. He published a collection of short stories *Pied Piper of Dipper Creek* (1939) with an introduction by John Buchan, who linked Raddall with the school of Sir Walter Scott, Stevenson, Kipling and Conrad, complimenting him for his "rare gift of clean spare-limbed narrative." A story-teller who insisted on accurate and authentic detail, Raddall published his first historical romance, *His Majesty's Yankees* (1942), which depicts Nova Scotia during the American revolution. Although swarming with characters and filled with violent action, the novel gives a vivid comprehensive picture of life at the time.

Raddall continued his literary career with a second historical novel, *Roger Sudden* (1944), based on the struggle between the English and French for supremacy in Canada and notable for its understanding and sympathetic treatment of the Micmac Indians. Then followed *Tambour and Other Stories* (1945), a collection of short stories, *Pride's Fancy* (1946), a romantic tale of colonial privateering, and *Halifax, Warden of the North* (1948, rev. 1965), a history of Halifax, which won a Governor General's Award.

With *The Nymph and the Lamp* (1950, *La Nymphe et la lampe,* 1952), *Tidefall* (1953) and *The Wings of Night* (1956), Raddall turned from a historical to a modern setting and drew upon his earlier experiences of the East Coast to describe convincingly his favourite themes of struggle and passion. In *The Governor's Lady* (1960) and *Hangman's Beach* (1966) he returned to the historical novel.

Raddall belongs to the Romantic tradition of novelists. His characters, although drawn with little psychological subtlety, face exciting situations and have to take decisive action. Painstakingly accurate in his historical detail, he spins vivid and suspenseful tales of an age when the heroic virtues of courage and magnanimity had full play. Winner of three Governor General's Awards, Raddall was elected F.R.S.C. in 1949 and presented with the Lorne Pierce Medal in 1956. J. R. MacGillivray, "Letters in Canada: 1942," *UTQ,* XII (April, 1943); Claude Bissell, "Letters in Canada: 1950," *UTQ,* XX (April, 1951); Claude Bissell, "Letters in Canada: 1956," *UTQ,* XXVI (April, 1957); John Matthews, Introduction to *The Nymph and the Lamp* (Toronto, 1963).

LUCIEN RAINIER (1877-1956). Né à Montréal, Joseph Melançon étudia au Collège Sainte-Marie et, après avoir fréquenté deux ans l'Ecole littéraire de Montréal, décida de devenir prêtre et fut ordonné en 1900. Il fut vicaire, curé et, longtemps, aumônier de religieuses à Montréal. En 1931, il a recueilli une partie de ses poésies dans *Avec ma vie.* Paul Wyczynski a étudié *Les débuts poétiques de Joseph Melançon* (*Revue de l'Université d'Ottawa,* 1956) et on trouve quelques pièces inédites et des pages de son journal dans l'édition des Classiques canadiens préparée par le Père Lavergne (1961).

Lucien Rainier a écrit des pièces de circonstances qui sont sans intérêt et des poèmes d'inspiration historique qui ne manquent pas d'originalité, mais ses meilleures pages sont d'inspiration spirituelle et établissent des correspondances mystérieuses entre la nature et l'âme. Romain légaré lui a consacré une étude dans le tome II des *Archives des lettres canadiennes.* On consultera aussi la monumentale thèse de Soeur Marie Henriette-de-Jésus (1966).

JAMES REANEY (1926-). Born near Stratford, Ontario, Reaney received his early education there. In 1944 he entered the University of Toronto, where, as an undergraduate, he began writing the collection of poems published in 1949 under the title of *The Red Heart.* In its forty-two poems Reaney often deals with social themes, but is inclined to treat them much more fancifully than did his colleagues of the forties. His poetry is marked by a peculiar combination of childlike gaiety and intellectual sophistication, and he employs highly developed systems of imagery which are often teasingly obscure.

After receiving his M.A. (1949) in English literature, Reaney joined the faculty of the University of Manitoba, and received his Ph.D. (1958) from the University of Toronto. During this period he came under the influence of Northrop Frye. Reaney subsequently made an intensive study of the Elizabethans, and in particular of Spenser, whose *Shepherd's Calendar* is emulated in Reaney's second volume of poetry, *A Suit of Nettles* (1958). For this book he draws upon his early experience of Ontario farm life to depict allegorically a community of geese throughout the successive months of the year. Reaney's oddly sophisticated naïveté and capacity for erudite satire lend an unmistakable distinction to poems which are at once earthy, intellectual and sparkling. *A Suit of Nettles,* like its predecessor *The Red Heart,* won a Governor General's Award.

Since 1960, Reaney has been Professor of English at the University of Western Ontario. He edits the significant little magazine *Alphabet,* a semi-annual "devoted to the Iconography of the Imagination." Recently he has turned his attention to drama, and has produced a number of stage plays. *The Kildeer and Other Plays* (1962) includes two comedies, *The Kildeer* and *The Sun and the Moon,* a chamber opera libretto *Night Blooming Cereus* (for which John Beckwith wrote the music) and *One-Man Masque,* an amusing presentation of man's progress from birth to eternity. This volume shared a Governor General's award for drama with *Twelve Letters to a Small Town* (1962), in which Reaney paid poetic tribute to his birthplace Stratford.

In *The Dance of Death at London, Ontario* (1963), with drawings by Jack Chambers, Reaney satirizes a cross-section of that town. A versatile writer, he has published several short stories and a juvenile novel about York entitled *The Boy with an R in His Hand* (1965), has produced some unpublished plays (*The Easter Egg* and *Listen to the Wind*), and is working on a novel set in Perth County. Alvin

Lee, "A Turn to the Stage: Reaney's Dramatic Verse," *Can. Lit.,* 15 (Winter, 1963) and *Can. Lit.,* 16 (Spring, 1963); Milton Wilson, Review of *A Suit of Nettles* in *Canadian Forum,* 38 (October, 1958).

JEAN-JULES RICHARD (1911-). Né à Saint Raphaël (Bellechasse), autodidacte, journaliste à la pige, il a publié trois romans et un recueil de nouvelles. Son premier roman, *Neuf jours de haine* (1948) est le roman canadien français le plus remarquable qu'ait inspiré la deuxième guerre mondiale. Les misères physiques et morales des soldats y sont décrites avec un réalisme troublant; l'écriture n'est malheureusement pas souvent à la hauteur de l'inspiration. Après un recueil de nouvelles, *Ville rouge* (1950), un second roman peu réussi, *Le feu dans l'amiante* (1956) inspiré par les conflits qui opposent les syndicats aux capitalistes américains à Asbestos, il a publié *Journal d'un hobo* (1965) qui raconte les pérégrinations sans but d'un clochard hermaphrodite qui fréquente surtout des milieux mal famés et parle leur langue. Cette oeuvre sans finesse ne manque pas toujours d'une certaine force un peu brutale qui lui donne une valeur de choc.

JOHN RICHARDSON (1796-1852). Born in Queenston, Ontario, the son of a Scottish surgeon attached to Simcoe's Queen's Rangers and of a mother whose maternal ancestors were Indian, Major John Richardson was educated at Detroit and Amherstburg. At fifteen he enlisted and fought for more than a year in the War of 1812, until he was captured at Moraviantown in 1813 and spent the rest of the War in a prison camp in Kentucky. After his release he was commissioned in the British Army. In 1815 he went to England on half-pay, served briefly in the West Indies and on his return spent many years in London or Paris, devoting part of his time to literary work. In London he produced his first book, a narrative poem in four cantos, *Tecumseh or The Warrior of the West* (1828), based on his combat experiences. From this poorly received verse he turned to fiction with *Ecarté, or The Salons of Paris* (1829), a novel of life in Paris published anonymously, which although vivid in its description of French vice lacked depth of characterization and unity of plot. *Wacousta or The Prophecy: A Tale of the Canadas* (1832), the story of Pontiac which Richardson had heard as a boy and with which he was very familiar, was more successful, ran through many editions and is considered his masterpiece. Although melodramatic, and stilted in dialogue, the story is carefully constructed and filled with rapid action and vivid suspenseful scenes. It won for its author international fame.

Restless and seeking adventure, he joined the British Legion in Spain, served from 1834 to 1837 and gathered the material to write his *Journal of The Movements of the British Legion* (1836). He returned to Canada in 1838 as correspondent of the *Times*, but after irritating his editor by supporting Lord Durham's progressive views was dropped from the staff. In 1840 he settled in Brockville, Upper Canada, where he edited *The New Era or Canadian Chronicle* in 1841/42, while he prepared for the press his principal historical work *War of 1812* (1842). *The Canadian Brothers* (1840), written as a sequel to *Wacousta* and set in the period of the War of 1812, emphasized the Canadian achievements in the war and the national patriotism that was arising. In 1843/44, he edited in Kingston *The Canadian Loyalist or Spirit of 1812*, a pro-Tory paper. When the Tories succeeded to office, Richardson was rewarded by being appointed Superintendent of Police on the Welland Canal in 1845. He soon lost this post, however, because of his arrogance and belligerence. More pleasing insights into the man and his times are provided in his excellent autobiography *Eight Years in Canada* (1847). His failure to receive further preferment or adequate income from his continuing publications, and the lack of interest in his works, caused him in 1849 to seek fame in New York. There, during the next three years, he adapted his fiction of Indian warfare to the cheap paperback market and added an erotic Gothic tale *The Monk Knight of St. John* (1850). Popular for a time, he eventually alienated his new friends and died in lonely poverty. William F. E. Morley, compiler, "A Bibliographical Study of John Richardson," *Papers of the Bibliographical Society of Canada*, IV (1965); Desmond Pacey, "A Colonial Romantic: Major John Richardson, Soldier and Novelist," *Can. Lit.*, 2 (Autumn, 1959), and 3 (Winter, 1960); John Richardson, *Richardson's War of 1812*, edited with a biography and bibliography by A. C. Casselman (Toronto, 1902); R. P. Baker, *A History of English-Canadian Literature to the Confederation* (Cambridge, 1920).

MORDECAI RICHLER (1931-   ). Born and educated in the Jewish section of Montreal, Richler decided at the age of fifteen to become a writer. After attending Sir George Williams College, he went abroad for two years, spending eight months in Spain, the setting for his first novel *The Acrobats* (1954). This book concerns a young Canadian artist who feels one of a lost generation, and who is ultimately destroyed by his inability to commit himself to any purpose. Richler's presentation is lively, often ironical and adolescently frank.

Returning to Canada in 1952, he worked as a news editor for the CBC in Montreal. In 1955 he published his second book, *Son of a Smaller Hero*, set in the "ghetto" district in Montreal. A great deal of Richler's writing is concerned with Jews, not for purposes of interpretation, but because Jews are the people of his *milieu*.

Richler has spent a good deal of time in England and Europe, writing film scripts and working on his novels. *A Choice of Enemies* appeared in 1957, and deals with the question of the loyalty investigations in America. These first three novels are similar in their portrayal of lives ruined by conflict, and in their terse, satiro-comic style. Richler's writing is distinguished by its honesty, realism and colloquial exuberance. These qualities are particularly evident in *The Apprenticeship of Duddy Kravitz* (1959, *L'apprentissage de Duddy Kravitz*, 1960). Its setting, as in *Son of a Smaller Hero*, is Montreal, and again the principal characters are Jewish. Duddy Kravitz is a tough, ambitious, St. Urbain Street boy who, through a fascinating series of episodes, becomes a "big-time operator." The story is told in a loose, fast-moving manner, with liberal use of the comic distortions by which Richler achieves his humour. He has a facility for conveying sense perceptions with evocative power, for sketching characters quickly and accurately and depicting their search for values in a changing society. *The Incomparable Atuk* (1963), a satire on Toronto as seen through the eyes of an untutored Eskimo, is in the same vein.

In addition to his novels, Richler has published articles and stories in English, American and Canadian magazines, and worked on the film script for John Osborne's *Room at the Top* and *Life at the Top*. He is finishing another novel to be entitled *St. Urbain's Horseman*, to be set in Montreal and London, England, where he resides.

P. D. Scott, "Choice of Certainties," *Tamarack Review* 8 (Summer, 1958); Warren Tallman, "Wolf in the Snow, Part II," *Can.Lit.*, 6 (Autumn, 1960); Ruth McKenzie, "Life in a New Land," *Can.Lit.*, 7 (Winter, 1961).

RINGUET (1895-1960). Né à Trois-Rivières, Philippe Panneton étudia dans divers collèges et aux universités Laval, de Montréal et de Paris. Médecin, il pratiqua à Montréal, Joliette et Trois-Rivières et fit de nombreux voyages en Europe, au Mexique et en Amérique du sud. Il s'intéressa aussi aux lettres et participa à de nombreux programmes à la radio et à la télévision avant de devenir ambassadeur au Portugal en 1957. Il est décédé en 1960.

Après avoir publié en 1924, en collaboration avec Louis Francoeur, des pastiches d'écrivains canadiens, *Littérature . . . à la manière de*, il s'est classé au premier rang des romanciers canadiens dès son premier roman *30 arpents* (1938, *Thirty Acres*, 1940) qui lui valut le prix des Vikings. Ce roman naturaliste, écrit avec vigueur, construit avec art, est le tableau réaliste, dur et sombre de la misère d'une famille de cultivateurs qui, devant les malheurs répétés, finit par renoncer à la terre pour sombrer dans le prolétariat d'une ville industrielle de la Nouvelle-Angleterre. On y trouve, comme chez Zola, l'observation froide et précise des tares humaines. Le roman a une grandeur tragique peu commune dans les lettres canadiennes.

Un recueil de nouvelles, *L'Héritage* (1946), et un deuxième roman, *Fausse Monnaie* (1947), tous deux superficiels, d'un ton pessimiste et d'une écriture banale, déçurent après *30 arpents*. Un dernier roman, un des plus considérables de nos lettres, *Le poids du jour* (1949), sans atteindre à la force du premier, a néanmoins de bonnes parties et, aussi, une valeur documentaire très nette. Cette longue chronique, qui semble autobiographique jusqu'à un certain point, évoque le drame individuel et collectif qu'est la migration des ruraux vers la grande ville. Mal préparé à faire face au monde complexe et nouveau où il a pénétré, le campagnard perd l'unité intérieure qu'il avait pu maintenir dans la petite société plus simple du village et il est écrasé par son destin. Le roman est d'une écriture plutôt banale et d'une psychologie sommaire, mais juste.

Ringuet a aussi publié un ouvrage sur les découvertes des Amériques par les Européens et sur les Amérindiens, *Un monde était leur empire* (1943) et un double portrait de Colomb et de Vespucci, *L'Amiral et le Facteur* (1954). On a publié en 1965 ses *Confidences* qui nous éclairent sur l'homme, ses idées et ses goûts.

On peut lire à son sujet les articles de Claude-Henri Grignon: *Les 30 arpents d'un Canayen* dans *Les Pamphlets de Valdombre* (février 1939); de Gilles Marcotte dans *L'Action Nationale* (janvier 1950); de Jean-Paul Pinsonnault dans *Lectures* (mai 1953), ainsi que son auto-portrait: *Ringuet* par Louis-Philippe Panneton dans *Le Digeste français* (1950).

ADJUTOR RIVARD (1868-1945). Né à Saint Grégoire (Nicolet), Rivard étudia au Séminaire de Nicolet et à l'Université Laval. Admis au barreau, il pratiqua le droit à Chicoutimi et en 1896 il devint professeur de diction à l'Université Laval. En 1919, il fut élu bâtonnier de la province de Québec et en 1921, il fut nommé juge à la Cour d'Appel. Il était membre de la Société royale du Canada.

Toute sa vie, il fut préoccupé par la question linguistique au Canada français et il fut ici le meilleur philologue de sa génération. Ses *Etudes sur les parlers de France au Canada* (1914) restent encore un des meilleurs livres sur le sujet. Son *Manuel de la parole* (1901) est un manuel utile qui trahit les mêmes préoccupations. Pour étendre son action et la prolonger, il fonda la Société du parler français en 1902 dont il fut l'âme dirigeante pendant un quart de siècle, collaborant régulièrement au *Bulletin* de cette Société (1902-1918) auquel il donna, en plus d'études philologiques, des chroniques littéraires qui sont parmi les meilleures de l'époque. Il a aussi écrit des récits brefs inspirés par nos moeurs rurales qu'il a réunis dans *Chez nous* (1914) et dans *Chez nos gens* (1918) et qui sont parmi les meilleurs des écrivains de l'école du terroir.

CHARLES G. D. ROBERTS (1860-1943). Born at Douglas near Fredericton, New Brunswick, Charles George Douglas Roberts spent his boyhood at Westcock overlooking the Tantramar marshes. He was the son of a scholarly Anglican clergyman and a mother who came of a distinguished United Empire Loyalist family that traced its lineage back to the grandfather of Ralph Waldo Emerson. When Charles was fourteen, his family moved to the Rectory at Fredericton where he attended the Collegiate School and the University of New Brunswick. During these years Roberts read widely, especially in the Greek and Latin classics and in the English poets of the nineteenth century.

After graduating in 1879, he taught for two years as Headmaster of the Grammar School at Chatham, N.B. Here he published in 1880 his first book of verse *Orion and Other Poems*. For a few months in 1883/84, he edited Goldwin Smith's periodical *The Week* in Toronto, but he resigned because he disagreed with Smith's Annexationist sympathies. After a period of free-lancing, he was appointed, in 1885, Professor of English and French, later English and Economics, to the faculty of King's College of Windsor, Nova Scotia.

During the next decade, Roberts did his best work as a poet and developed his skill as a short story and novel writer. In February, 1897, he went to live with his cousin Bliss Carman in New York where, until 1907, he worked industriously turning out not only poems but adventure tales, romances and animal stories. Then he left America for seventeen years abroad in England and on the continent. In 1914 he enlisted as a private in the British Army, was commissioned, and in 1916 transferred to the Canadian Forces Overseas from which he was discharged at war's end as a major.

Even though his animal stories were immensely popular in their day and brought him international fame, Roberts will be remembered primarily as a poet. Aroused in his youth by the growing spirit of Canadian nationalism, he gave his feeling enduring expression not only in verses like "Canada" but indirectly in his poems of nature and the Acadian countryside. Of some ten volumes of poems, the three early ones contain his best works. *Orion and Other Poems* (1880), although imitative of Shelley, Keats, and Tennyson in its language and imagery, reveals Roberts' ability to depict with beauty and particularity his native landscape as well as to express with genuine feeling his own varying moods. *In Divers Tones* (1886), which contains his masterpiece of nostalgic remembrance "Tantramar Revisited," and *Songs of the Common Day* (1893) display a matter and manner ideally suited to his genius. His sonnets of country life at various seasons are characterized by a sincerity of tone, a simplicity of diction and an exactness of detail. *The Book of the Native* (1896), divided like the previous publications into lyrical and narrative poems, yet marred by Roberts' increasing tendency to philosophize, marks a decline in his poetic art.

In prose, Roberts turned out such diverse productions as a translation (1890) of Phillipe Aubert de Gaspé's historical romance of 1863 *Les Anciens Canadiens, A History of Canada* (1897), *The Canadian Guide Book* (1899), several romances and—most noteworthy of all—his animal stories. The romances, set in a skilfully portrayed national background, are for the most part poor in both structural unity and character delineation and generally lack reality. His stories of nature and wild life, however, like *Earth's Enigmas* (1896), *The Kindred and the Wild* (1902), *The Watchers of the Trails* (1904) and *Red Fox* (1905) in their appealing depiction of animal psychology remain classics in this genre which Roberts virtually invented.

In 1925, after some years of travel in Europe and Africa and residence in England, Roberts returned to Canada. A series of lectures and recitals took him across the country. He was hailed everywhere as a great national poet and awarded the first Lorne Pierce Medal for his outstanding contribution to literature. In the title piece of *The Iceberg and Other Poems* (1934), portraying with occasional vivid imagery the gradual dissolution of a once mighty and deadly iceberg, he demonstrated his ability to respond with considerable success to the newer school of poetry represented by writers like Pratt. In 1936, *Selected Poems,* the best single edition of Roberts' verse, appeared. Honoured on June 3, 1935, by a Knighthood, he remained a leading spirit in Canadian letters until his death in Toronto. James Cappon, *Charles G. D. Roberts* (Toronto, 1925); Joseph Gold, "The Precious Speck of Life," *Can. Lit.*, 26 (Autumn, 1965); Alec Lucas, "Nature Writers," *Literary History of Canada*, (1965); William H. Magee, "The Animal Story: a Challenge in Technique," *Dalhousie Review*, XLIV (Summer, 1964). Desmond Pacey, "Sir Charles G. D. Roberts" in *Our Living Tradition,* 4th Series (Toronto, 1962); Desmond Pacey, *Ten Canadian Poets* (Toronto, 1958); E. M. Pomeroy, *Sir Charles G. D. Roberts. A Biography* (Toronto, 1943).

THEODORE GOODRIDGE ROBERTS (1877-1953). Born in Fredericton, New Brunswick, Roberts, the youngest brother of the noted Charles G. D. Roberts, at the age of twelve began contributing verse to American magazines. After attending briefly the University of New Brunswick, he was in 1897/98 sub-editor and Spanish-American war correspodent for the New York *Independent*. He spent several months in Florida and Cuba and returned to Canada in 1899 to edit for two years *The Newfoundland Magazine*. With *The House of Isstens* (1900), Roberts began his career as a prolific writer of popular adventure stories and historical novels. Of these, *The Red Feathers* (1907), a book for boys, and *The Wasp* (1914) can be regarded as his finest. Their romantic characters and dramatic events reflect the influence of the Arthurian legend.

As a poet, he was associated with the Fredericton group—Roberts, Carman and Sherman—and like them he showed the strong influence of the New Brunswick landscape. His verse, published in *Seven Poems* (1925), *The Lost Shipmate* (1926) and collected in *The Leather Bottle* (1934), is characterized by its appropriate imagery and narrative interest.

JOHN D. ROBINS (1884-1952). Born in Windsor, Ontario, John Daniel Robins was educated at the University of Toronto (B.A. 1913, M.A. 1922) and at Marburg and Chicago (Ph.D. 1927). In 1919 he joined the staff of Victoria College in the German Department where, except for leave of absence during World War I, he remained until 1925. He then moved to the English Department in which he eventually became professor and head.

In 1943, he published his amusing *The Incomplete Anglers*. The appearance of his *Pocketful of Canada* (1946), a very popular paperback anthology of Canadian prose and verse, coincided with a renewed interest in Canada. *Cottage Cheese* (1951) is another entertaining account of the outdoors. He collaborated with Margaret V. Ray in editing *A Book of Canadian Humour* (1951).

MAZO DE LA ROCHE. *See* de la Roche, Mazo

ROBERT DE ROQUEBRUNE (1889-   ). Né à L'Assomption, Robert Laroque grandit à Montréal où il étudia au Mont Saint-Louis. Après un voyage en France, il s'intéressa aux lettres et, avec des amis, fonda *Le Nigog*, journal d'avant-garde qui eut une courte vie. Employé au bureau des Archives canadiennes à Paris, il passa sa vie à dépouiller les archives françaises pour y découvrir les sources se rapportant à l'histoire canadienne. Rentré à Ottawa durant la guerre (1940-1945), il retourna à Paris où il fut directeur du bureau des Archives canadiennes. Retraité, il habite la France.

Robert de Roquebrune a signé des articles sur des sujets historiques qu'ils a réunis dans *Les Canadiens d'autrefois* (1962). Il est plus connu comme romancier, tant par ses romans historiques: *Les Habits rouges* (1923), *D'un océan à l'autre* (1924), *La Seigneuresse* (1961) que par son roman d'analyse: *Les dames Le Marchand* (1927). Tous ces romans sont médiocres. Le livre qui lui assurera la survie littéraire, c'est *Testament de mon enfance* (1951 *Testament of My Childhood*, 1964) récit autobiographique qui évoque avec nostalgie les jours heureux et faciles passés dans son enfance au manoir ancestral. Roquebrune avait toujours écrit une langue claire et facile dans les romans qui sont tous des histoires romancées de ses ancêtres; dans *Testament de mon enfance*, sa prose a une chaleur et une poésie qu'on ne trouve pas ailleurs dans son oeuvre et ce document d'une époque qui a pris fin est un des meilleurs livres de la littérature canadienne française récente.

MALCOLM ROSS (1911-   ). Born in Fredericton, New Brunswick, Malcolm Mackenzie Ross was educated at the Universities of New Brunswick,

Toronto and Cornell. After receiving his Ph.D. (1941) from Cornell, he served with the National Film Board at Ottawa from 1942 to 1945. His first book, *Milton's Royalism* (1943), "a study in the conflict and symbol and idea in the poems," explores the effect of a poet's experience and environment upon his imagery. A member of the English Department of the University of Manitoba from 1945 until 1950, when he joined the faculty of Queen's, Ross has produced a number of scholarly books and articles which have established him as a distinguished Canadian literary critic. From 1953 to 1956, he was editor of *Queen's Quarterly*.

In 1954 he produced *Poetry and Dogma,* a study of symbolism in seventeenth century English poetry and of the impact which the Reformation had on religious imagery of the time. In the same year, Ross edited *Our Sense of Identity: A Book of Canadian Essays* which attempts to present the vision of Canada to her citizens. Inspired by this same desire, he became in 1957 general editor of "The New Canadian Library," a reprint series which makes a large selection of English- and French-Canadian classics available in paperbacks. Ross himself wrote the Introduction to Grove's *Over Prairie Trails,* Callaghan's *Such Is My Beloved* and *Poets of the Confederation.*

He edited, in 1959, *The Arts in Canada,* "a stock-taking at mid-century" by fourteen independent contributors, which attempts to discover patterns of significance that have emerged in Canadian arts, from painting to handicrafts, since World War II. In 1961 he edited, in collaboration with John Stevens, *Man and His World.* Ross was elected F.R.S.C. in 1955, and from 1956 to 1958 was President of the Humanities Association of Canada. In 1962 he resigned from the position of Head of the English Department, Queen's University, to become Professor of English at Trinity College, Toronto, where he is now Dean of Arts.

SINCLAIR ROSS (1908-   ). Born near Prince Albert, Saskatchewan, Ross began his career as a bank clerk in Winnipeg. One of a group of Western realistic novelists which appeared in the forties, he first gained recognition in Canadian literary circles by a number of short stories published in the *Queen's Quarterly*. Among these "The Painted Door" and "A Lamp at Noon" show this author's considerable talent. His first novel, *As for Me and My House,* appeared in 1941. It attracted very little attention at the time, but has since received widespread acclaim. Firmly placed in a Puritan frame of reference, the story is concerned with a prairie minister and his wife during the years of drought, and with their struggle to maintain their integrity and marriage despite a suffocating atmosphere of hypocrisy and tension. The general tone of monotony and reiteration, which is the author's intention, greatly increases the novel's effectiveness. The style, consistently fresh and clear, is characterized by an economy of expression and a restriction of scope unusual in Canadian fiction.

Ross' ability to evoke tense brooding atmosphere is apparent again in his second and less successful novel *The Well* (1958). Although his characters here tend to be static and lacking in that careful delineation found in the earlier work, his power to analyse and portray convincingly the prairie atmosphere is still evident. Both novels are to some extent studies in alienation: Philip Bentley and Chris Rowe, the two central characters respectively, are misfits in society, and Ross' treatment of the problems which they both face is warmly sympathetic and psychologically sound. Roy Daniels, Introduction to *As for Me and My House* (Toronto, 1957); Donald Stephens,

"Wind, Sun and Dust," *Can. Lit.*, 23 (Winter, 1965); Warren Tallman, "Wolf in the Snow," *Can. Lit.*, 5 (Summer, 1960).

---

w. w. e. ross (1894-1966). Born in Peterborough, Ontario, W. W. Eustace Ross graduated in science from the University of Toronto and joined the staff of the Dominion Weather Bureau, later going to the Agincourt Magnetic Observatory as a geophysicist. *Experiment 1923-29,* his first book of poems, and two subsequent volumes, *Laconics* (1930) and *Sonnets* (1932), were privately printed. Many of his poems have appeared in such magazines as *Dial* and *Poetry* with favourable criticisms from the American poet Marianne Moore. Influenced by his classical and medieval reading, he created imagistic lyrics that are simple, fresh and appealing with their direct-ness and disciplined, unconventional use of metrics.

SIMONE ROUTIER (1901-). Née à Québec, Simone Routier étudia au Couvent des Ursulines et à l'Université Laval. Artiste—elle dessine et joue le violon—elle a écrit aussi des poésies qu'elle publia en 1928, *L'Immortel Adolescent,* qui lui valurent le prix David. Employée aux Archives canadiennes de 1930 à 1950, d'abord à Paris puis à Ottawa, elle entra ensuite au ministère des Affaires extérieures et fut attachée de presse à l'ambassade du Canada à Bruxelles. Membre de l'Académie canadienne française, elle a épousé M. Fortunat Drouin en 1958. Après la guerre, elle avait fait un stage chez les Dominicaines.

Simone Routier a publié des réflexions inspirées par son séjour en Europe, *Paris-Amour-Deauville* (1932), et le récit de son retour de France au moment de l'occupation allemande, *Adieu Paris* (1940). Mais c'est son oeuvre poétique qui est la plus importante. Partie d'un romantisme sentimental atténué par une fine ironie, elle s'est éloignée graduellement de la technique traditionelle et a évolué vers une strophe qui rappelle celle d'Henriette Charasson après avoir pratiqué le vers libre. *Ceux qui seront aimés* (1931) et *Les Tentations* (1934) dénotaient une maturation progressive du sentiment et de l'intelligence, et son aventure spirituelle lui a inspiré ses *Psaumes du jardin clos* (1947) et son *Long Voyage* (1947). Elle est une des meilleures poétesses du Canada français.

CAMILLE ROY (1870-1943). Né à Berthier-en-bas (Saint-Valier), Camille Roy étudia au Séminaire de Québec et, ordonné prêtre en 1896, poursuivit ses études littéraires à l'Institut catholique de Paris et à la Sorbonne dont il était licencié ès lettres (1900). Toute sa vie fut consacrée à l'éducation et, après avoir enseigné la philosophie quelque temps, fut professeur de littérature française et de littérature canadienne au Séminaire de Québec et à l'Université Laval dont il fut recteur de 1924 à 1927 et de 1932 à 1943. Membre de la Société royale dès 1904, il en fut président en 1928. L'année suivante, il recevait la médaille Lorne Pierce.

Prédicateur et orateur recherché, Mgr Camille Roy a aussi écrit des essais sur l'éducation. Il a participé à la fondation de la Société du parler français et a joué un rôle de premier plan dans les Congrès de la langue française. Là où il a innové toutefois, c'est surtout en entreprenant dès le début du siècle et en poursuivant toute sa vie l'étude de la littérature canadienne française. Porté à la bien-veillance, il n'a pas toujours été assez sévère pour les écrivains médiocres, mais il estimait qu'il était nécessaire d'encourager les écrivains qui cher-chaient à produire une oeuvre sans l'appui d'une forte tradition littéraire

ni l'encouragement d'une société peu
intéressée aux lettres. Il a laissé un
manuel dépassé mais qui fut utile en
son temps et une étude sur *Nos origines
littéraires* (1909). Il a aussi réuni en
volumes de nombreux essais sur presque tous les écrivains canadiens de son
temps: *Essais sur la littérature
canadienne* (1907), *Nouveaux essais
sur la littérature canadienne* (1914),
Erables en fleurs (1923), *A l'ombre des
érables* (1924), *Etudes et croquis*
(1928), *Regards sur nos lettres* (1931).
De 1934 à 1938, il a regroupé ses essais
par genres et publié *Poètes de chez
nous, Romanciers de chez nous* et
Historiens de chez nous.

Mgr Roy fut le fondateur de la
critique et de l'histoire littéraire au
Canada français. Beaucoup de ses
jugements sont à reviser et, faute de
documents, il n'a pas pu établir tous
les faits importants concernant l'histoire
de la littérature canadienne. Il a fait
oeuvre de pionnier et personne n'a
travaillé autant que lui à attirer l'attention des lecteurs sur les oeuvres
canadiennes et à faire connaître
l'évolution de la littérature canadienne
française. Il a évidemment accordé une
grande importance à la valeur morale
des oeuvres et il était fermé aux
mouvements d'avant-garde; ses meilleures pages sont celles où il analyse
le sens et la valeur des oeuvres les plus
représentatives des traditions anciennes.

GABRIELLE ROY (1909-   ). Née à Saint
Boniface en Manitoba, Gabrielle Roy
fut institutrice au Manitoba et s'occupa
activement de théâtre à Winnipeg. Au
retour d'un voyage en France et en
Angleterre (1937/38), elle s'installa à
Montréal et consacra tout son temps à
la littérature. En 1947, elle épousa le
Dr Marcel Carbotte et elle vit à Québec
depuis lors. Elle est membre de la
Société royale du Canada et lauréate
de plusieurs prix, dont le Fémina en
1947. Tous ses livres ont été traduits
en anglais.

Après s'être fait la main par des
reportages et nouvelles publiés dans
quelques journaux et revues du Québec,
Gabrielle Roy connut un succès
retentissant avec son premier roman,
Bonheur d'occasion (1945), réédité à
Paris où il lui valut le prix Femina
(1947) et traduit à New York où le
tirage a atteint les 700,000 exemplaires
(*The Tin Flute*). Depuis, elle n'a cessé
de produire une oeuvre qui est certes
une des plus importantes de la littérature canadienne.

Bonheur d'occasion est une sorte de
grand reportage sur la misère d'une
famille pauvre de la banlieue de
Montréal durant les années de la crise
et de la guerre; c'est un reportage si
émouvant que c'en est simultanément
un roman de qualité. Cette triste histoire
d'un amour humble et frustré est en
même temps une fresque sociale d'un
réalisme touchant; l'auteur a un sens de
l'observation aigu, un don de sympathie
qui ne détruit pas la lucidité et une
langue sobre et familière.

Un deuxième roman *Alexandre
Chenevert* (1954, *The Cashier*, 1955)
est la simple histoire d'un caissier de
banque dont la vie n'a rien que de banal,
d'un homme qui est lui-même banal,
mais l'auteur a réussi à écrire à propos
d'un médiocre un roman qui ne l'est
pas. Cette espèce de Salavin canadien
parvient à nous intéresser parce qu'il
est le portrait fidèle et ému de ce
Canadien français moyen qui, derrière
une existence qui n'a rien de spectacu-
laire, cache une âme sensible à ses
propres malheurs, à ceux de son
entourage et même à ceux du monde
entier qui lui sont révélés chaque
jour par le journal. Ce roman, c'est
tout le mal du siècle vu dans le miroir
d'une âme simple.

Son dernier roman, *La Montagne
secrète* (1961, *The Hidden Mountain*,
1962) est moins réussi; cette biographie
romancée d'un peintre qui, dans les solitudes du grand nord canadien, puis à
Paris, cherche dans l'évocation de la

nature à atteindre à une beauté platonique, est l'oeuvre la plus appliquée de l'auteur, mais aussi la moins naturelle. Trois de ses livres sont largement autobiographiques et sont peut-être ses meilleurs.

Les récits réunis dans *La petite poule d'eau* (1950, *Where Nests the Water Hen*, 1961) constituent une chronique romancée de la vie des pionniers au nord du Manitoba; ses récits plaisent par le pittoresque des situations, et par la tendresse avec laquelle l'auteur évoque le souvenir de personnages simples et attachants.

On trouve la même tendresse dans *Rue Deschambault* (1955, *Street of Riches*, 1957) et dans *La Route d'Altamont* (1966, *The Road Past Altamont*), deux autres recueils de nouvelles qui révèlent une profonde nostalgie de son enfance et des vastes paysages de son Manitoba natal. Ecrits avec autant d'amour que de goût, ces récits simples, d'une émotion retenue, sont faits de personnages aimés et de charmantes anecdotes. Il y a là des pages de prose comme on en écrit peu ici.

On pourra consulter sur Gabrielle Roy la présentation de Gustave Lanctôt à la Société royale du Canada (no 5); Francis Ambrière, *Gabrielle Roy, écrivain canadien,* dans *Revue de Paris* (déc. 1947); Guy Sylvestre, *La Petite Poule d'eau,* dans *La Nouvelle Revue canadienne* (avril-mai 1951); Guy Sylvestre, *Alexandre Chenevert,* dans *La Nouvelle Revue canadienne* (avril-mai 1954); Firmin Roz, *Témoignage d'un roman canadien,* dans *Revue française de l'élite européenne* (août 1954); Alan Brown, *Gabrielle Roy and the temporary provincial* dans *Tamarack Review* (Autumn 1956); Hugo McPherson, *The Garden and the Cage* dans *Canadian Literature* (Summer 1959).

LAURA SALVERSON (1890-   ). Born of distinguished Icelandic descent in Winnipeg, Laura Goodman Salverson was educated there and in the western United States. Since her marriage in 1913 to an American of Norwegian descent, she has lived in Winnipeg and Toronto.

Mrs. Salverson started writing stories when she was still a child. Her first novel *The Viking Heart* (1923) began the exploration of what was to become the dominant recurring theme of all her work, the adaptation of Scandinavian settlers to Canadian life. *Wayside Gleams* (1925), a short collection of poems, appeared in the same year as *When Sparrows Fall* (1925), the experiences of second-generation settlers in the northern United States. In *Lord of the Silver Dragon* (1927) and *The Dove of El-Djezaire* (1933), realism of setting and detail were subordinated to a colourful and romantic plot. *The Dark Weaver* (1937), which won a Governor General's Award, depicts again a Scandinavian settlement on the Canadian prairies.

Confessions of an Immigrant's Daughter (1939), an autobiography which also won a Governor General's Award, displays Mrs. Salverson's pride in her Icelandic background and her ability to describe with vivid realism the privations and the triumphs of pioneer life in Western Canada. *Immortal Rock* (1954), tells the romantic story of the visit of the Norsemen to Minnesota in the fourteenth century and their struggle to survive. Edward A. McCourt, *The Canadian West in Fiction* (Toronto, 1949).

B. K. SANDWELL (1876-1954). Born in England, Bernard Keble Sandwell emigrated to Canada and received his education at Upper Canada College and the University of Toronto. After graduating in 1897, he became a journalist with the Toronto *News,* and in 1905 went as dramatic editor to the Montreal *Herald.* In 1907 he edited and published *The Musical Red Book of Montreal,* a record of music in that city from 1895 to 1907. In 1911 he became associate editor and later editor of the Montreal *Financial Times*. From 1919 to 1923, he taught economics at McGill Universtiy, and from 1923 to 1925 was head of the English Department at Queen's University.

His first book, *The Privacity Agent and Other Modest Proposals* (1928), a collection of essays, is marked by a highly individual and ironical tone. His aim is to improve the Canadian social and political world, and his norm is not just "the good old days" but that utopia where reason, common sense and justice prevail. To shock his readers into "thinking solemnly about solemn things," Sandwell employs a polished style characterized by provocative wit.

Although he produced other works, such as *The Canadian Peoples* (1941), a social history, and a further book of essays and addresses, *The Gods in Twilight* (1948), he is best known for his work in encouraging and sponsoring literary achievement in Canada as Editor of *Saturday Night* from 1932 to 1951. One of the original founders of the Canadian Authors Association, Sandwell was elected F.R.S.C. in 1925.

CHARLES SANGSTER (1822-1893). Born at Kingston, Ontario, the son of a Royal Navy shipbuilder and grandson of a United Empire Loyalist, Sangster left school at the age of fifteen in order to support a widowed mother, and took employment making cartridges at Fort Henry. Two years later he was transferred to the ordnance office there as a clerk, a position he retained for ten years. After a brief stay in Amherstburg in 1849, as editor of the *Courier*, he returned to Kingston to join the *British Whig* (1850-1861) as bookkeeper and proofreader, and finally the *Daily News* (1864-1868) as a reporter. During this journalistic period, Sangster wrote almost all his published poetry. Besides contributing to the *Literary Garland* and the *Anglo-American* magazines, he published at his own expense *The St.*

Lawrence and the Saguenay and other Poems (1856). Strongly influenced by Byron and Wordsworth, the pre-Confederation poet treats the themes of love and nature in this volume. His religious propensity and his conception of "art" encouraged him to write poems which were reverent, idealistic, sentimental and conventionally ornamental; his genuine responses to Canadian landscape and country life found little outlet in fresh diction.

In 1860, Sangster published *Hesperus and Other Poems and Lyrics*. This second volume, in the author's words, "is far in advance of the previous one, exhibiting a more careful finish, more art, and a higher degree of mentality." Included are such patriotic poems as "A Song for Canada," "The Plains of Abraham," "Wolfe" and "Brock." Then followed eighteen unproductive and frustrating years during which he worked in Ottawa as a civil servant in the Post Office Department, from which he retired in poor health in 1886. Returning to Kingston, he spent his remaining years laboriously arranging his literary work into four volumes of manuscript poems. Although *Our Norland* (1893) was printed in a limited edition, the last two volumes planned by Sangster, *Norland Echoes and Other Strains* and *The Angel Guest and Other Poems,* were never printed, and their manuscripts seem to have disappeared.

Although much of his poetry is heavy, solemn and even inept, Sangster in his best lyrics portrays with skill and charm the beauties of the Canadian landscape, the solace of love and the stirring note of national pride. Arthur S. Bourinot, *Five Canadian Poets* (Montreal, 1954); E. H. Dewart, "Charles Sangster, A Canadian Poet of the Last Generation," *Essays for the Times* (Toronto, 1898); Desmond Pacey, *Ten Canadian Poets* (Toronto, 1958).

MARSHALL SAUNDERS (1861-1947). **Born** in Milton, Nova Scotia, Margaret Marshall Saunders was educated privately at home, in France and Great Britain. On her return to Canada, she taught, wrote articles for various magazines and travelled extensively. The success of *Beautiful Joe: The Autobiography of a Dog* (1894) prompted Miss Saunders to make writing her serious occupation. This charming story, which won first prize in a contest designed to find a sequel to Anne Sewell's *Black Beauty,* was enthusiastically received and has found continuing popularity with translation into some twenty languages.

Although she wrote historical romances like *My Spanish Sailor* (1889) and *Rose of Acadia* (1898), which were set in her native Maritimes, her greatest literary achievement was her treatment of the animal kingdom. Among her subjects are *Princess Sukey* (1905), a pigeon; *Alpatok* (1906), an Eskimo dog; *Golden Dickie* (1919), a canary; *Bonnie Prince Fetlar* (1920), a pony; and *Jimmy Gold-Coast* (1923), a monkey. Writing from a lifetime of sympathetic, realistic and close observation of animals, and passionately interested in their welfare, she skilfully depicts humans as seen through the eyes of their pets. In 1946, *Beautiful Joe* proved its perennial appeal by being made into a movie.

FELIX-ANTOINE SAVARD (1896-   ). Né à Québec, Mgr Savard a étudié au Séminaire de Chicoutimi où, devenu prêtre, il a ensuite enseigné de 1919 à 1927. Il a fait du ministère dans le comté de Charlevoix, puis est devenu professeur à la faculté des Lettres de l'Université Laval dont il a été le doyen. Membre de la Société royale (1945-1953), il est membre de l'Académie canadienne-française. Lauréat de la médaille Lorne Pierce et du Prix Duvernay, il s'occupe surtout de folklore depuis quelques années.

Menaud, maître-draveur (1937), qui lui valut la célébrité, est une sorte de poème épique et lyrique en prose qui vaut beaucoup plus par la qualité de l'écriture poétique que par l'affabulation qui est trop sommaire et trop peu vraisemblable pour en faire un vrai roman. C'est une sorte d'épopée nationaliste qui chante l'attachement aveugle au pays et la haine de l'envahisseur anglo-américain qui vient s'emparer des forêts pour les monnayer.

La Minuit (1948) n'est guère plus un roman, mais une sorte de parabole socio-religieuse aussi invraisemblable que nébuleuse et artificielle. Bien meilleurs sont les textes courts— poèmes en prose, chroniques, méditations, reportages folkloriques—qui composent *L'Abatis* (1943) et *Le Barachois* (1959) et qui comptent quelques-unes des meilleurs pages de prose écrites au Canada français. On y retrouve les mêmes thèmes presque racistes inspirés par la vie des colons français, mais aussi des images d'une grande beauté inspirées par un vif et profond sentiment de la nature.

Dans *La-Dalle-des-Morts* (1965), drame poétique qui évoque l'appel du lointain auquel succombaient les anciens voyageurs et la douleur des femmes restées seules au foyer, on retrouve le lyrisme de *Menaud*.

Sur son oeuvre on pourra lire le discours de présentation de l'abbé Savard à la Société royale du Canada par Jean-Marie Gauvreau (*Présentation,* no 3, 1945/6); *La portée sociale de l'oeuvre de Monseigneur Savard* par Flavien Charbonneau (Lectures, vol. 9).

JOSEPH SCHULL (1910-   ). Born in South Dakota, John Joseph Schull moved in 1913 with his parents to Moose Jaw, Saskatchewan, where he attended school. After taking extramural courses from Queen's and the University of Saskatchewan, he moved to Montreal in 1935 to write advertising copy. He served as an Intelligence and

Information officer during World War II, and then returned to Quebec City to become a freelance writer.

Schull published his first volume of verse, *Legend of Ghost Lagoon,* in 1938. After another long poem, *I, Jones, Soldier* (1944), he turned to writing successful radio and television scripts and documentaries. His knowledge of the sea is reflected in *The Far Distant Ships* (1950, abridged as *Ships of the Great Days,* 1962) which relates in easy, informal language the official account of the operations of the R.C.N. during World War II, and *The Salt Water Men* (1958), a collection of true stories of the men and ships of Canada's golden age of sail. *Battle for the Rock* (1960), one of a series for children entitled "Great Stories of Canada," describes the background to the battle of Wolfe and Montcalm for Quebec. *Laurier: the First Canadian* (1965), is a sympathetic biography of Canada's first French-Canadian Prime Minister.

In these works Schull displays a talent for turning facts into imaginative and fascinating drama or documentary, and for presenting technical detail with clarity and precision developed by the conditions of radio and television production.

DUNCAN CAMPBELL SCOTT (1862-1947). Born in Ottawa, the son of a Methodist minister, Scott attended various Ontario and Quebec schools and Stanstead College before joining the federal Department of Indian Affairs. Although he was interested in music and art, it was not until he was encouraged by his friend Lampman that Scott began in his middle twenties to write and publish poems and short stories. From 1892 to 1893, he contributed to the weekly literary column "At the Mermaid Inn" which appeared in the Toronto *Globe.* His first book of poems, *The Magic House and Other Poems* (1893), revealed his ability not only to depict natural landscape with realistic detail but also to evoke atmosphere with subtlety and suggestiveness. Many of his lyrics have a Pre-Raphaelite richness of colour and air of enchantment. His narrative "At the Cedars," presents with stark simplicity a tragic incident exemplifying one of his favourite themes, the conflict of man with nature.

In 1896, Scott published his first volume of short stories, *In the Village of Viger,* a group of delightfully nostalgic sketches of the people in a little French-Canadian village outside Montreal. His next collection of verse, *Labour and the Angel* (1898), apart from "The Piper of Arll" and "Avis," was marred by a frequent note of didacticism. In *New World Lyrics and Ballads* (1905), however, Scott again produced lyrics with vitality of description and emotional intensity. He treated Indian life with tragic irony in ballads like "On the Way to the Mission" and "The Forsaken." The following year he published *Via Borealis* (1906), seven poems written during an official visit made into Northern Ontario, in which he portrays admirably both the landscape and the moods of the wilderness.

In 1907, Scott's travels in Europe with his wife were interrupted by his daughter's sudden death. The profound shock of this event is recorded in "The Closed Door." Promoted in 1909 to Superintendent of Indian Education in the Department of Indian Affairs, he did not publish a further volume of his verse until *Lundy's Lane and Other Poems* (1916) which, although it has good descriptive pieces, is marred by sentimentalism and moralizing.

In 1921 he published another volume of verse, *Beauty and Life.* In the best of these poems he succeeds in making his landscapes and atmospheres a vivid background to human aspiration and dilemma. In 1922, Scott became President of the R.S.C. to which he had been elected Fellow in 1899. A second volume of short stories, *The Witching of Elspie*, tales of violent physical and emotional struggle, appeared in 1923, as did his one-act domestic play *Pierre*. After producing a second edition of Lampman's poems, Scott turned to a collection of his own *Poems of Duncan Campbell Scott* (1926). His last two volumes of verse, *The Green Cloister* (1935), with its passionate and primitive "At Gull Lake, August, 1810," and *The Circle of Affection* (1947) which also included essays and short stories, indicate that his creative powers were still vital.

The last of the Confederation poets, Scott was a careful artist whose interpretive observation of nature and man, and sense of verbal colour and music, gave universal significance to the themes of contrast and conflict, especially as revealed in wild and Indian life. Desmond Pacey, *Ten Canadian Poets* (Toronto, 1958); A. J. M. Smith, "The Poetry of D. C. Scott," *Dalhousie Review*, 28 (April, 1948); A. J. M. Smith, "Duncan Campbell Scott" in *Our Living Tradition*, 2nd series (Toronto, 1959).

F. G. SCOTT (1861-1944). Born in Montreal, Frederick George Scott was educated there and at Bishop's College, Lennoxville. After taking his M.A. degree, he was ordained in the Church of England, in which he served in various positions in Canada and England prior to World War I. His first volume *The Soul's Quest and Other Poems* (1888) was followed by *My Lattice and Other Poems* (1894), *The Unnamed Lake and Other Poems* (1897) and similar books which are notable for his moods and impressions of the Laurentian hills.

In 1914, Scott joined the Canadian Army and became a Major and Senior Chaplain of the First Canadian Division. He served with distinction, winning the C.M.G. (1916) and D.S.O. (1918); he brought out a book of poems based on his experiences entitled *In the Battle Silences* (1916). On his return he was made Archdeacon at Quebec and wrote *The Great War as I Saw It* (1922) a skilful prose work of battle reminiscences. Poetry was his best medium of expression, and in his *In Sun and Shade* (1926) and *Lift Up Your Hearts* (1941) he wrote verses of inspiration and patriotism which reflect his philosophy of life in peace and war. He was elected F.R.S.C. (1900).

F. R. SCOTT (1899-   ). Born in Quebec, City, the son of the well-known poet Archdeacon F. G. Scott, Francis Reginald Scott was educated at Bishop's College, Lennoxville, where he graduated with honours in 1919. After some teaching experience, he went abroad in 1920 as a Rhodes Scholar for three years to Magdalen College, Oxford (B.A. 1922, B.Litt. 1923). On his return to Canada in 1924, he entered McGill University to study law. His earliest poems and essays began to appear in 1925 in the *McGill Fortnightly Review*, which was established as an outlet for the new Canadian poetic movement. He and A. J. M. Smith were the founders and editors. In 1927 he was called to the Quebec bar, and the following year was appointed to the Faculty of Law at McGill, of which he was later Dean for several years. A member of the "Montreal Group" of poets, he became one of the four editors of the newly formed *The Canadian Mercury*.

Scott's first book was one he jointly edited: a co-operative effort with Finch, Kennedy, Klein, Pratt and A. J. M. Smith entitled *New Provinces: Poems of Several Authors* (1936), in which twelve of his own poems appeared. His first independent collection, *Overture* (1945), contained sixty-one poems concerned with the depression, war, social issues, nature and love. In 1940 he was awarded a Guggenheim Fellowship to study at Harvard and subsequently published *Canada and the United States* (1941). On his return to Canada, he served from 1942 to 1950 as national chairman of the Canadian Cooperative Federation (CCF). He was elected F.R.S.C. in 1947. Another volume of verse, *Events and Signals,* appeared in 1954 and treated his familiar themes in a more mellow tone. *The Blasted Pine* (1957), edited by A. J. M. Smith and Scott, is "an anthology of Satire, Invective and Disrespectful Verse" by Canadian writers. *Eye of the Needle* (1957) presents a selection of Scott's best satire from 1925. *Poems by St. Denys Garneau and Anne Hébert* (1962) are Scott's verse translations of a selection of these French-Canadian poets. In 1964 he published *Signature,* a new collection of poems on a wide range of themes, which "explore the nature of being and becoming, of communication between individuals, of faith and death." *Selected Poems* appeared in 1966.

An ardent socialist, Scott has sought poetic form for his visions of a planned society; but it is in his satire that he sparkles. "Saturday Sundae," "The Canadian Authors Meet," "Financier" and "Professor" are delightful examples of his tough, sharp-edged imagery, keen wit and appreciation of the absurdly grotesque or pretentious. His lyrics of love and nature, brief and emotionally restrained in their clipped description, have an easy and spontaneous grace.

Scott has had an important influence in promoting the cause of poetry in Canada. He has encouraged young writers and new literary magazines. His poems, criticisms and articles on a wide variety of literary, legal and political subjects, have appeared regularly in Canadian and American periodicals. In all these, as in his poetry, there is an integrity of principle and an intelligent and intense concern for democratic freedom and social justice which Scott conveys with eloquence and wit. Scott was awarded the Lorne Pierce Medal in 1962.

As a member of the Royal Commission on Bilingualism and Biculturalism, he has contributed to an understanding of English-French relations in Canada by the publication in 1964, with Michael Oliver as co-editor, of *Quebec States Her Case.* W. E. Collin, "Pilgrim of the Absolute" in *The White Savannahs* (Toronto, 1936); Louis Dudek, "F. R. Scott and the Modern Poets," *Northern Review,* IV, 2 (December-January, 1950-1); Desmond Pacey, *Ten Canadian Poets* (Toronto, 1958).

ROBERT W. SERVICE (1874-1958). Born in Lancashire, England, Robert William Service was brought up in Glasgow where he attended high school. He came to Canada at the age of twenty-one, and after wandering up and down the Pacific Coast for some years working at an odd assortment of jobs became a clerk for a Canadian bank. He was posted to Victoria and Kamloops and later Whitehorse and Dawson in the Yukon District. From here he sent his first manuscript of rollicking, robust poems of the gold-rush days, *Songs of a Sourdough* (1907), to the publishing house of the Methodist Church in Toronto. Within weeks of the book's appearance, Service was famous and on his way to the financial independence which was his avowed aim as expressed in his autobiographical *Ploughman of the Moon* (1945) and *Harper of Heaven* (1948). From 1913 he had homes in Paris, Brittany and on the Riviera where he wrote continuously.

His verse resembles that of Kipling, whom he greatly admired. *Ballads of a Cheechako* (1909), *Rhymes of a*

Rolling Stone (1912) and *Rhymes of a Red Cross Man* (1916), based on his war experiences as an ambulance driver, maintained his tremendous popularity. In these he followed his own dictum, "I write of the things of today for the people of today," and took his themes from the inspiration of the moment.

Service's verse displays his facility with metre and rhyme. Yet such boisterous ballads as "The Shooting of Dan McGrew" and "The Cremation of Sam McGee," with their rapid and exciting action, emphatic rhythm, slangy diction and sly humour, will outlive many a more genteel work. Service's attempts at fiction in six different novels were less successful. His complete output in verse may be found in two recent volumes, *Collected Poems,* and *More Collected Verse.*

ERNEST THOMPSON SETON (1860-1946). Born in Durham, England, Seton emigrated to a farm near Toronto, Canada, with his parents when he was five. He received his education at the Ontario College of Art before going in 1879 to study at the Royal Academy in London, England. He returned to Manitoba as a naturalist for the provincial government, and during these five years he published *Mammals of Manitoba* (1886) and *Birds of Manitoba* (1891). Wishing to continue his art studies, he went to Paris until 1896, and then moved to the United States where he continued to write and lecture.

Of his many works, probably the best known was *Wild Animals I Have Known* (1898). These stories, beautifully illustrated by some two hundred of his own drawings, were based on facts and settings drawn from personal experience or from stories told to him. Seton's express purpose was to develop "the real personality of the individual [animal] and his view of life . . . rather than the ways of the race in general as viewed by a casual and hostile eye." In his other books like *The Trail of the Sandhill Stag* (1899), *The Biography of a Grizzly* (1900) and *Monarch, The Big Bear of Tallac* (1904), he continued to present realistic stories drawn from a scientific detailed observation of nature, translated with imagination, insight and colourful prose into the drama of wild animals and their inevitably tragic end.

Interested in the outdoor development of children, Seton founded in 1902 a youth organization, the Woodcraft League, and for a time was the Chief of the Boy Scouts of America (1910-1915). Much of the knowledge for his stories was gained during the many field trips in which he participated. *The Arctic Prairies* (1911) related his experiences on a canoe journey of two thousand miles in search of the caribou.

Practically all of his two score books, written with infinite patience and skill from his own observations and illustrated by his hand, were concerned with the animal kingdom. *Life-histories of Northern Animals* (1909) and *Lives of Game Animals* (1925-1928) won awards from scientific societies. In 1930 he established Seton Institute, a school in New Mexico for children interested in woodcraft and wildlife. He published his autobiography in 1940, *Trail of an Artist-Naturalist.* Alec Lucas, "Nature Writers" in *Literary History of Canada* (1965); S. E. Read, "Flight to the Primitive," *Can. Lit.,* 13 (Summer, 1962).

FRANCIS SHERMAN (1871-1926). Born in Fredericton, New Brunswick, Francis Joseph Sherman attended the University of New Brunswick and then entered banking. Sherman's book of verse, *Matins* (1896), and his works, like *In Memorabilis Mortis* (1896) and *A Prelude* (1897), exemplify his Pre-Raphaelite enthusiasm and his depth of expression. *The Complete Poems of Francis Sherman* (1935) was published with a memoir by Lorne Pierce.

JEAN SIMARD (1916-). Né à Québec, Simard a étudié au Séminaire de Québec et à l'Ecole des Beaux-Arts de Montréal dont il est diplômé et où il est aujourd'hui professeur. Membre de la Société royale du Canada, il a publié quatre romans, une pièce de théâtre et une sorte de journal intitulé *Répertoire* (1961) et *Nouveau Répertoire* (1965), dans lequel il livre ses réflexions sur la vie, les lettres et les arts.

Ses deux premiers livres, *Félix* (1947) et *Hôtel de la Reine* (1949) sont des récits satiriques, largement autobiographiques, où la verve de l'auteur s'exerce aux dépens des moeurs familiales, sociales et politiques de ses compatriotes. *Mon fils pourtant heureux* (1956) comporte une forte partie satirique de la même veine, mais il semble que l'auteur commence à se libérer de ses obsessions et découvrir des réalités spirituelles fécondes. Ce double registre de la satire sociale et de l'inquiétude religieuse se retrouve dans ce roman du ménage mal assorti qu'est *Les sentiers de la nuit* (1959). Mais sa pièce *L'Ange interdit* (1961) n'est qu'un divertissement frivole.

LISTER SINCLAIR (1921-). Born in Bombay, India, of English parents Lister Sheddon Sinclair was educated at Colet Court and at St. Paul's, London, England. Later he received his B.A. (1942) from the University of British Columbia. Following graduate studies in mathematics at the University of Toronto (M.A. 1945), he lectured there for three years. After resigning to devote full time to free-lance acting, play-writing and editorial work, he became a principal contributor of radio drama to the CBC. A published volume of collected plays appeared in 1948 under the title of *A Play on Words and Other Radio Plays*. In 1952 he produced for Jupiter Theatre in Toronto, and in the same year was appointed to the teaching staff of the Toronto Conservatory of Music. He was commissioned to write documentaries for the Ford Foundation in 1953.

Although most of Sinclair's work has not appeared in formal publications, plays such as *Socrates* (1947), *Encounter by Moonlight* (1948) and *The Empty Frame* (1955) are familiar to the Canadian public through the medium of CBC radio and television. His writing is characterized by a Shavian sparkle and playful irony. In addition to his distinction as a playwright, Sinclair has gained recognition as an actor, linguist and critic, and has contributed numerous articles to Canadian magazines and journals.

A. J. M. SMITH (1902-). Born in Montreal, Arthur James Marshall Smith was educated at McGill University (B.Sc. 1925, M.A. 1926) and the University of Edinburgh (Ph.D. 1931). As a student he edited a weekly literary page in the *McGill Daily* and was one of the founders of the *McGill Fortnightly Review* in which he published his early poems. Influenced by Yeats and Eliot, Smith revealed in these skilfully controlled lyrics with their fresh and philosophical approach his command of metaphysical imagery.

After returning from Edinburgh, he taught at various American colleges and was appointed in 1936 to the faculty of Michigan State University where he is now Professor of English. In 1936, along with F. R. Scott, he edited *New Provinces*, which contained many of his own poems as well as those of Pratt, Kennedy, Klein, Finch and Scott. He was awarded a Guggenheim Fellowship in 1940 to work on his critical and historical anthology *The Book of Canadian Poetry* which appeared in 1943. That same year he produced a selection of his own verse entitled *News of the Phoenix and Other Poems* which won a Governor General's Award. His language is precise, compact and, although intellectual, suggestive and even mystical; his metre and rhythm are disciplined and appropriate; his outlook, like his wit and humour, is sophisticated and cosmopolitan rather than regional. The title poem is typically contrapuntal in its association of the undying spirit of the phoenix with commonplace journalism and bureaucracy.

Seven Centuries of Verse (1947), an anthology of English and American poetry, and *The Worldly Muse* (1951), an anthology of serious light verse, were followed by two volumes of his lyrics—*A Sort of Ecstasy: Poems New and Selected* (1954) and *Collected Poems* (1962)—an anthology of satirical verse co-edited with F. R. Scott entitled *The Blasted Pine* (1959), and a further anthology, *The Oxford Book of Canadian Verse* (1960), surveying the poetry of both English and French Canada. *The Book of Canadian Prose: Volume 1* (1965) contains selections from "early beginnings to confederation." In the "New Canadian Library Series" he edited *Masks of Fiction* (1961) and *Masks of Poetry* (1962).

Smith has been a frequent contributor of scholarly articles to learned journals and has won international recognition as a distinguished Canadian poet and critic. In 1966 he was awarded an LL.D. by Queen's University and the Lorne Pierce Medal by the Royal Society of Canada. In 1966-67 he will be Professor and Poet-in-Residence at Dalhousie University. W. E. Collin, "Difficult Lonely Music" in *The White Savannahs* (Toronto, 1936); Desmond Pacey, *Ten Canadian Poets* (Toronto, 1958); W. P. Percival, *Leading Canadian Poets* (Toronto, 1948); "Salute to A. J. M. Smith," *Can. Lit.*, 15 (Winter, 1963); George Woodcock, "Turning New Leaves," *Can. Forum*, XLII (February, 1963).

GOLDWIN SMITH (1823-1910). Born in Reading, England, Smith was educated at Eton and Magdalen College, Oxford (B.A. 1845, M.A. 1848). Called to the bar at Lincoln's Inn in 1847, he became in 1858 Regius Professor of Modern History at Oxford. In 1864 he visited America briefly during the civil war and strongly sympathized with the North and its concept of the American democratic idea. In 1868 he returned to take an unsalaried position as professor of English Constitutional History at the newly established Cornell University, Ithaca, New York. After three years he came to Toronto where he spent the rest of his life.

In England, Smith had written articles for the *Saturday Review* and leaders for the *Pall Mall Gazette*. In Canada, he continued his journalistic interest and founded or was associated with *The Canadian Monthly*, *The Bystander*, *The Week* (the first editor of which was Charles G. D. Roberts), *The Weekly Sun*, the Toronto *Telegram* and Winnipeg *Tribune*. In these and other leading magazines and periodicals of Canada, England and the United States, he contributed articles on current topics, the best of which appeared in *Lectures and Essays* (1881) and *Essays on Questions of the Day, Political and Social* (1893). Perhaps his most provocative and controversial proposal was the political union of Canada and the United States, as a result of which he was called "the annexationist."

The range of Smith's publications indicates his restless and inquiring mind. He was a charter member of the Royal Society of Canada (1882), and for many years a member of the Senate of the University of Toronto. As a *litterateur,* he composed translations from Latin poets, *Bay Leaves* (1893), wrote biographies, *The Moral Crusader, William Lloyd Garrison* (1892) and *My Memory of Gladstone* (1904), produced studies of English, Irish and American modern history, essays on the nature of religion and scholarly examinations of such literary figures as Shakespeare and Jane Austen. Doctrinaire in his opinions, Smith may have been wrong in his prophecy of Canada's destiny, but he had a salutary influence in raising the standard of controversy, writing and journalism in Ontario. Malcolm Ross, "Goldwin Smith" in *Our Living Tradition,* 1st series (Toronto, 1957); F. H. Underhill, *In Search of Canadian Liberalism* (Toronto, 1960); Elisabeth Wallace, *Goldwin Smith, Victorian Liberal* (Toronto, 1957).

KAY SMITH (1911-   ). Born in Saint John, New Brunswick, Miss Smith teaches English and dramatics there. Several of her meditative and introspective poems have appeared from time to time in *First Statement, The Fiddlehead, Northern Review* and other such periodicals and in Gustafson's anthologies of *Canadian Poetry* (1942) and *Canadian Verse* (1958). She has published a book entitled *Footnote to the Lord's Prayer and Other Poems* (1951), a group of lyrics which blend religious, psychological and social themes. Her work is included in *Five New Brunswick Poets* (1962).

RAYMOND SOUSTER (1921-   ). Born in Toronto, Ontario, Souster was educated there. Upon graduation from high school, he worked for two years in a bank prior to joining the R.C.A.F. in 1941, and subsequently served in England. After discharge, he returned to Toronto where he continued writing poetry. In 1944 his poetry was included in *Unit of Five*, a book of poems by five Canadian authors, Dudek, Hambleton, Page, Souster and Wreford. Souster

produced *When We Are Young* (1946), *Go to Sleep World* (1947), *City Hall Street* (1951) and joined Dudek and Layton in bringing out *Cerberus* (1952). He has continued to publish verse in such volumes as *Shake Hands with the Hangman* (1953), *Selected Poems 1955-1958, A Local Pride* (1962) and *Place of Meeting* (1962). *The Colour of the Times* (1964), his collected poems from 1937 to 1963 won a Governor General's award. A more recent volume *Ten Elephants on Yonge Street* (1965), contains another eighty-six poems most of which are about Toronto scenes.

As the titles of some of his books suggest, Souster feels the disorder in civilization—first during the war and later in the inequalities of a capitalistic society where ugliness and individual heartache characterize urban life. As he describes vividly the actions of people on the streets of Toronto, his responses are personal, sardonic or ironic, rarely vindictive. He is worldly wise rather than philosophical; his language is straightforward, colloquial, increasingly lyrical and singularly uncomplicated.

His verse has appeared since the early forties in *First Statement.* As editor and publisher of the mimeographed magazines *Contact* and *Combustion,* and as a guiding light to the Contact Press, Souster has done much to encourage and nourish experimental poetry in Canada. Louis Dudek, "Groundhog Among the Stars: The Poetry of Raymond Souster," *Can. Lit.,* 22 (Autumn, 1964).

ROBERT STEAD (1880-1959). Born in Lanark County, Ontario, Robert James Campbell Stead moved West at the age of two with his family to homestead near Cartwright, Manitoba. After attending Winnipeg Business College, he worked at assorted jobs until 1898, when he established and published a newspaper *The Review* at Cartwright. In 1908, he became publisher of *The Courier* of Crystal City, Manitoba, and brought out his first book of poetry, *The Empire Builders* (1908). He published his second book of verse entitled *Songs of the Prairies* (1911). In 1913 he took a position as Assistant Director and later Director of Publicity for the Colonization Department of the Canadian Pacific Railway.

Stead's popularity as a novelist of hearty, swift-moving readable narratives of prairie life and of the foothills of the Rockies overshadowed his reputation as a poet. His first novel, *The Bail Jumper* (1914), was followed by another tale of the West, *The Homesteaders* (1916). He brought out a third book of verse, *Kitchener and Other Poems* (1917). In 1918 he published *The Cow Puncher,* his most popular book, and that same year moved to Ottawa to take a post as Director of Publicity for the Department of Immigration and Colonization of the Dominion Government. While there, he continued to produce such realistic novels of prairie life as *Grain* (1926), which deals with agrarian problems on the prairies, and many short stories and government publications. He was Superintendent of Parks and Resources Publicity in the federal Department of Mines and Resources from 1936 until his retirement in 1946. A. T. Elder, "Western Panorama: Settings and Themes in Robert J. Stead," *Can. Lit.*, 17 (Summer, 1963).

ARTHUR STRINGER (1874-1950) Born in Chatham, Ontario, Arthur John Arbuthnot Stringer was educated at the University of Toronto and Oxford. As a student, he published one of his poems in *The Week,* and early became a facile, prolific and successful writer of poetry, criticism and novels. In 1894, a collection of verse *Watchers of Twilight* appeared, and in 1897 his critical *Study in King Lear*. During 1897/98 he was a reporter for the Montreal *Herald*. He published *The Loom of Destiny* (1899), a story for boys, and, although he produced more verse and even drama, henceforth the writing of fiction became his major endeavour. His novels are of the "Jack London School," in which a strong hero wins through a series of adventures complicated by the antagonism both of nature and his fellow men, and the plots are usually relieved by a strong element of romantic love.

The trilogy, *The Prairie Wife* (1915), *The Prairie Mother* (1920) and *The Prairie Child* (1922), uses a Canadian setting as a colourful back-drop for the plots. *The Wine of Life* (1921) and his story of the early days of railroading, *Power* (1925), are perhaps the best of his forty novels. He also published a biography of Rupert Brooke, *Red Wine of Youth* (1948). For much of his adult life Stringer made his home in New Jersey, U.S.A. Victor Lauriston, *Arthur Stringer, Son of the North* (Toronto, 1941).

ALAN SULLIVAN (1868-1947). Born in Montreal, Edward Alan Sullivan was educated there, in Scotland, and at the University of Toronto from which he graduated as a mechanical-mining engineer. After employment with the Canadian Pacific Railway on construction jobs in the north and west, he worked in various mines in Northern Ontario. Experiences encountered during this period and information gained about the Canadian frontier of railroad men, prospectors and Eskimos formed the background of his later novels.

He began his literary career as a poet—*The White Canoe and Other Verse* (1891)—but he was primarily a writer of fiction. After his first collection of stories, *The Passing of Oul-I-But and Other Tales* (1913), he turned out more than forty novels. Among the best known are: *The Great Divide* (1935), a romantic novel dealing with the building of the Canadian Pacific Railway through the Rockies; *The Fur Masters* (1938), depicting the rivalry between the Hudson's Bay Company and the Nor' Westers; *Three Came to Ville Marie* (1941), a romance of Montreal during the French period which won a Governor General's Award; and *Cariboo Road* (1946), an exciting novel of the gold rush to Cariboo in the early eighteen-sixties. Many of these tales were published under the pseudonym "Sinclair Murray." In them, Sullivan depicted the spirit of physical courage and adventure which characterized the frontier days, and which he himself had demonstrated in the R.A.F. during World War I. John Stevenson, "Alan Sullivan, Poet and Engineer," *Saturday Night*, 62 (August 23, 1947).

BENJAMIN SULTE (1841-1923). Né à Trois-Rivières, il quitta l'école jeune et s'engagea dans la milice. Autodidacte, il fut successivement journaliste, puis traducteur à la Chambre des Communes et au ministère de la Défense. Il publia deux recueils de vers, mais s'intéressa surtout à notre histoire sur laquelle il publia de nombreux ouvrages que Gérard Malchelosse a réédités en vingt-et-un volumes sous le titre *Mélanges historiques* (1918-1934) Ses travaux de synthèse manquent d'ordre et de méthode, mais on trouve dans quantité de ses articles des aperçus sur des aspects peu étudiés de notre histoire. Il fut un des membres fondateurs de la Société royale du Canada, dont il fut président en 1904 .

JOHN SUTHERLAND (1919-1956). Born in Liverpool, Nova Scotia, John Sutherland attended at various times Queen's, McGill and the University of Toronto. In spite of ill-health, he made an impressive contribution to what Wynne Francis has called "the poetic renaissance of the Forties" in Montreal. In 1942 he founded the First Statement Press and *First Statement*, a controversial little magazine which was a rival of *Preview*. These two journals were merged in *Northern Review*, of which Sutherland was publisher and editor from 1945 until 1955.

His anthology, *Other Canadians* (1947) was compiled to present authors omitted from A. J. M. Smith's *The Book of Canadian Poetry*. In 1954 he became a Roman Catholic and moved to Toronto. Here, just before his death, he completed *The Poetry of E. J. Pratt* (1956), a religious interpretation of Pratt's works. Wynne Francis, "Montreal Poets of the Forties," *Can. Lit.*, 14 (Autumn, 1962); Robert Weaver, "John Sutherland and *Northern Review*, *Tamarack Review* 2 (Winter, 1957).

JOSEPH-CHARLES TACHE (1821-1894). Né à Kamouraska, Taché étudia au Séminaire de Québec et à l'Université Laval. Reçu médecin, il alla exercer sa profession à Rimouski et, en 1847, fut élu député à l'Assemblée législative. En 1855, il représenta le Canada à l'Exposition universelle de Paris et publia alors une *Esquisse sur le Canada*. Il a écrit des ouvrages sur la *Tenure seigneuriale* (1854) et sur le projet de confédération, *Des Provinces de l'Amérique du nord et d'une Union fédérale* (1858). En 1857, il fonda avec Hector Langevin un journal conservateur *Le Courrier du Canada* et il s'intéressa de plus en plus aux lettres et à l'histoire. Il enseigna la physiologie à la faculté de médecine de l'Université Laval. En 1864, il est nommé sous-ministre de l'Agriculture et de la Statistique et occupa ce poste jusqu'en 1888.

De 1861 à 1863, il publia dans les revues de Québec des légendes canadiennes qui sont parmi les meilleurs récits en prose de l'Ecole patriotique de

1860. Il les a réunis en volume: *Trois légendes de mon pays* (1861) et *Forestiers et voyageurs* (1863). Ces pages comptent parmi les plus belles qui aient été inspirées par la forêt canadienne et par les moeurs des bûcherons. Taché n'est pas un styliste raffiné, mais sa prose atteint à une force et à une sincérité émouvantes.

JULES-PAUL TARDIVEL (1851-1905). Né à Covington, Ky., aux Etats-Unis, il vint au Canada en 1868, y apprit le français en poursuivant ses études au Séminaire de Saint-Hyacinthe et s'engagea dans une carrière de journaliste. Après avoir collaboré au *Courrier de Saint-Hyacinthe* et à *La Minerve*, il fonda en 1881 à Québec l'hebdomadaire *La Vérité* qu'il publia jusqu'à sa mort. Disciple de Veuillot, il fut le plus farouche "defenseur du trône et de l'autel", un des chefs de file du parti ultramontain qui combattit avec acharnement toutes les formes de libéralisme. On trouvera un échantillonnage de ses idées et de sa prose dans trois volumes de *Mélanges* (1887-1903). Il a écrit un curieux roman d'anticipation, *Pour la Patrie* (1895) dans lequel il décrit ce que pourrait être un demi-siècle plus tard la province de Québec en proie à l'irréligion et dominée par les franc-maçons d'Ottawa, heureusement sauvée et libérée par un chevalier exalté et invincible. Nous lui devons aussi un ouvrage sur *La langue française au Canada* (1901), dans lequel cet Américain de naissance soulignait les dangers de l'anglicisation. Il prônait d'ailleurs l'indépendance du Québec.

TEKAHIONWAKE. *See* Johnson, Pauline.

YVES THERIAULT (1916-   ). Né à Québec, Thériault a fait ses études primaires à Montréal, a été employé à l'Office national du Film avant de gagner sa vie à écrire. Il a rédigé de nombreux programmes pour la radio et pour la télévision et a collaboré à plusieurs journaux. Membre de la Société royale du Canada, il a séjourné longuement en Europe et certains de ses romans ont été traduits en plusieurs langues. Il est le plus prolifique et le imprévisible des romanciers canadiens français: son oeuvre n'a aucune unité d'inspiration ou de style; chaque nouveau livre est une expérience nouvelle.

Après avoir débuté par des contes et un roman d'un naturalisme érotique qui rappelle le premier Giono (*Contes pour un homme seul*, 1944, et *La fille laide*, 1950), Thériault a abordé la satire sociale dans *Le dompteur d'ours* (1951) et surtout dans *Les vendeurs du temple* (1951) qui fait le procès de la politique et du clergé et a donné ensuite ses meilleurs romans: *Aaron* (1954), qui évoque les conflits qui opposent un juif fidèle à la tradition et son fils qui est marqué par son milieu canadien; *Agaguk* (1958, *Agaguk*, 1963), évocation presque épique de l'amour et de la paternité chez les Esquimaux du grand nord; et *Ashini* (1960), sorte de poème lyrique à la gloire des Montagnais où sont évoqués avec une grande beauté certains mythes indiens.

En 1961, il a publié trois romans, inférieurs aux précédents: *Les Commettants de Caridad*, roman espagnol; *Amour au goût de mer*, roman italien et un roman canadien, *Cul-de-sac*, histoire d'un alcoolique ruiné moralement et matériellement par son vice. Thériault a aussi écrit des romans d'aventures pour les jeunes, et une pièce, *Le Marcheur* (1950). La critique à commenté abondamment ses romans à leur parution, mais son oeuvre n'a encore fait l'objet d'aucune étude d'ensemble.

EDWARD WILLIAM THOMSON (1849-1924). Born in Peel County, Upper Canada, Thomson was educated at Trinity College School, Weston. After a period in the United States, during which he fought in 1865 for the Union Forces, he returned to Canada in 1866 and helped in suppressing the Fenian Raids. He worked as land surveyor and later civil engineer until 1878, when he joined the Toronto *Globe* as chief editorial writer. From 1891 to 1901, he was editor in Boston of *The Youth's Companion,* and later was correspondent for the *Boston Transcript* until just before his death. During this early period he published his first book, *Old Man Savarin and Other Stories* (1895), also known as *Old Man Savarin Stories* (1917). One of the tales, "The Privilege of the Limits," full of broad humour and rough local colour of Glengarry county on the Ottawa river, has won a place in anthologies.

Although primarily a short story writer, Thomson published in 1909 *The Many Mansioned House and Other Poems* which contained some creditable vernacular verse. In this same year he was elected F.R.S.L. and in 1910 F.R.S.C. Thomson's letters to Archibald Lampman, written from Boston during the 1890s, have considerable importance in throwing light upon that poet's friendship with a robust, realistic journalist. A. S. Bourinot, *Edward William Thomson (1849-1924), A* Bibliography With Notes (Ottawa, 1955); A. S. Bourinot, *The Letters of Edward William Thomson To Archibald Lampman (1891-1897)* (Ottawa, 1957).

PAUL TOUPIN (1918-   ). Né à Montréal, Toupin a étudié au Collège Jean de Brébeuf, à la Sorbonne et à Columbia University. Journaliste, il a été à l'emploi du Conseil des Arts du Canada, puis du ministère des Affaires culturelles du Québec. Il est professeur à l'Université de Sherbrooke depuis 1963. Membre de l'Académie canadienne-française, il a obtenu un prix du Gouverneur général pour la littérature en 1961.

Après un livre de réflexions sur l'art et l'âme espagnols (*Au delà des Pyrénées,* 1949) et un portrait de Berthelot Brunet (*Rencontre avec Berthelot Brunet,* 1950), Toupin a surtout écrit pour le théâtre, bien que son plus beau livre, *Souvenirs pour demain* (1960) soit un recueil de trois récits inspirés par ses souvenirs d'enfance, que domine la mort de son père, et écrits dans une des plus belles proses qui s'écrive au Canada français.

Son théâtre, réuni en un volume (1963), groupe *Brutus* (1951), *Chacun son amour* (1957) et *Le mensonge* (1960), mais Toupin n'y a pas retenu sa première pièce, *Le choix* (1951). Qu'elles soient inspirées par l'histoire ou par l'actualité, les pièces de Toupin sont serrées, le dialogue en est sobre et net et elles posent avec acuité des problèmes moraux qui sont de tous les temps. Il n'a peut-être pas donné encore le meilleur de lui-même, mais Toupin est déjà l'auteur d'une des rares oeuvres théâtrales canadiennes qui soient exportables. Il s'est expliqué sur sa conception du théâtre dans *l'Ecrivain et son théâtre* (1964).

CATHARINE PARR TRAILL (1802-1899). Born in London, England, a sister of Susanna Moodie, Catharine Parr Strickland Traill came to Canada as the wife of an emigrant officer in the early 1830s and settled on a farm in the Peterborough area. In England, she had published short stories for children. In Canada, Mrs. Traill wrote for the educated immigrant several documentary books on pioneer life which aimed to give a realistic picture of the bush life of Canada as well as to offset the extravagant accounts presented by the money-grabbing land companies. In her preface to *The Backwoods of Canada* (1836), a series of letters to her mother, she states this purpose, "The writer of the following pages has endeavoured to afford every possible information to the wives and daughters of emigrants of the higher class. . . .

Truth has been conscientiously her object in the work, for it were cruel to write in flattering terms calculated to deceive emigrants into belief that the land . . . is a land flowing with milk and honey, where comforts and affluence may be obtained with little exertion." Her presentation of this life is lively, and the prosaic facts are relieved by a quiet sense of humour.

Her novel *Canadian Crusoes* (1852), later republished as *Lost in the Backwoods,* was placed in a Canadian setting and depicted pioneer life in a realistic and interesting manner. She later pursued her objective of enlightening prospective settlers with *The Female Immigrant's Guide* (1854), published in several editions, and *Rambles in the Canadian Forest* (1859).

Although her accounts of early life in Canada are the most widely known of her works, Mrs. Traill was also a noted naturalist and published *Canadian Wild Flowers* (1869), *Studies of Plant Life in Canada* (1885) and *Pearls and Pebbles* (1894), dealing extensively with the botanical life of her adopted land. George H. Needler, *Otonabee Pioneers* (Toronto, 1953); Clara Thomas, Introduction to *The Back-Woods of Canada* (Toronto, 1966).

PIERRE TROTTIER (1925-   ). Né à Montréal, Trottier a étudié au Collège Jean de Brébeuf et à la faculté de droit de l'Université de Montréal. Avocat, il est entré au ministère des Affaires extérieures et a occupé des Postes à Ottawa, Moscou, Djakarta et Londres. Il a publié trois recueils de poèmes: *Le Combat contre Tristan* (1951), *Poèmes de Moscou* (1957) et *Les Belles au Bois dormant* (1960). Trottier est essentiellement un lyrique et il a créé une rhétorique personnelle où abondent les images typiquement canadiennes; sa poésie est claire, limpide et accessible à tous. Il a chanté successivement la recherche de la femme et des nourritures terrestres et l'insatisfaction

congénitale de l'homme qui aspire à la possession absolue; l'aspiration à éterniser l'instant et à dépasser le temps, mais aussi et enfin la conscience de la présence de la mort au coeur de tout ce qui vit. Il y a dans son dernier recueil une part excessive de littérature, mais les deux premiers renferment de nombreux poèmes d'une sincérité aussi grande que leur valeur symphonique. En 1963, il a publié un recueil d'essais *Mon Babel* où il situe certains aspects de la littérature canadienne dans les grands courants de la littérature universelle.

MARCEL TRUDEL (1917-   ). Né à Saint-Narcisse (Champlain), il a étudié aux universités Laval et Harvard et il a enseigné aux universités Laval, Carleton et d'Ottawa. Membre de l'Académie canadienne français, il est président du Conseil des Arts de Québec. Après un ouvrage sur *L'Influence de Voltaire au Canada* (1945), il a publié des ouvrages solides, bien documentés et très détaillés sur *Louis XVI, le Congrès américain et le Canada* (1949), *Le régime militaire dans le gouvernement des Trois-Rivières, 1760-1764* (1952), *Chiniquy* (1955), *L'Eglise canadienne sous le régime militaire* (2 v., 1956-1957), *L'Esclavage au Canada* (1960). Il a entrepris, avec son collègue Guy Frégault, une monumentale *Histoire de la Nouvelle-France*, dont il a publié le premier volume en 1965; *Les vaines tentatives, 1524-1603*. Il a aussi écrit un roman de moeurs rurales, *Vézine* (1946).

F. H. UNDERHILL (1889-   ). Born in Stouffville, Ontario, Frank Hawkins Underhill was educated at the Universities of Toronto and Oxford. From 1914 to 1927, he was Professor of Political Science at the University of Saskatchewan. During World War I, he served as an infantry officer in France. He wrote *The Canadian Forces in the*

War, a volume in Sir Charles Lucas' *The Empire at War* (1923).

In 1927, Underhill became Professor of History at the University of Toronto. He joined the editorial board of *The Canadian Forum* in 1929. One of the founders of the C.C.F., he was co-author of *Social Planning for Canada* (1935). He was elected F.R.S.C. in 1949. In 1956 he published *The British Commonwealth,* a series of lectures given at Duke University. After his retirement from the University of Toronto in 1955 he became Curator of Laurier House, Ottawa, until 1959. *In Search of Canadian Liberalism* (1960), which won a Governor General's Award, is a series of essays reflecting Underhill's incisive and challenging scrutiny of Canada and her political relationships. This book reveals Underhill's change from his earlier Fabian socialism to a less militant liberalism within the pattern and reality of a North American political environment. A master in the art of compression, he gives in his lucid and pungent prose a broad and highly personal interpretation of his subject.

BERTRAND VAC (1914-). Pseudonyme du docteur Aimé Pelletier, médecin et chirurgien de Montréal, célibataire et grand voyageur qui a consacré une partie de ses loisirs à écrire des romans et des nouvelles qui lui ont valu trois Prix du Cercle du Livre de France. Son premier roman, *Louise Genest* (1950) qui lui a valu son premier prix, est l'histoire d'une femme qui quitte son mari pour suivre un métis, mais le personnage le plus important du roman est la forêt où ils se réfugient et que l'auteur peint avec amour. Ce roman de chasse et de pêche renouvelle ici le mythe du bon sauvage. L'auteur a cherché à varier sa manière depuis et a publié, entre autres, une satire de nos moeurs politiques: *Saint Pépin* (1955), un gros roman historique inspiré par les aventures de Tamerlan: *La Favorite*

et le Conquérant (1963), et des nouvelles lestes et grivoises: *Histoires galantes* (1965).

MEDJE VEZINA (1896-). Née à Montréal, Ernestine Medjé Vézina a étudié au pensionnat Sainte-Anne de Lachine et à l'Université de Montréal. Publiciste au ministère de l'Agriculture de la province de Québec depuis 1930, elle n'a publié qu'un seul recueil, *Chaque heure a son visage* (1934) dont les poèmes sont des cris de révolte contre une vie monotone et des évocations rêvées de toutes les ivresses dont elle a été privée. Medjé Vézina est une des principales représentantes du romantisme féminin qui a fleuri au Canada français vers 1930.

GILLES VIGNEAULT (1928-). Né à Natashquan, il a étudié au Séminaire de Rimouski et à la faculté des Lettres de l'Université Laval. Professeur, il a lancé des cahiers de poésie, *Emourie* (où il a publié ses premiers poèmes) et les éditions du même nom, à Québec. Il est, depuis, devenu un des premiers chansonniers du Canada, son immense succès dépassant nos frontières. En 1965, il a remporté le Prix international de la chanson au Festival de Sopot, avec *Mon pays.* Ce chansonnier est aussi poète et conteur. Il chante l'amour, le pays et la mer en vers facilement accessibles à tous, qui restent près de la chanson populaire et valent plus par la sincérité et l'émotion que par l'écriture qui est souvent relâchée. On trouve également un charme un peu facile dans ses contes rapides et discrets.

MIRIAM WADDINGTON (1917-). Born in Winnipeg, Manitoba, Miss Waddington graduated from the University of Toronto, took her Master's degree at the University of Philadelphia in Sociology, was a social worker and is now in the Department of English at York University. As a child she began writing poems, many of which appeared in high school and college publications. Her first volume of poetry was *Green World* (1945). An accurate observer of nature and society, both urban and rural, Miss Waddington writes in a simple straightforward style colourful and melodic verse which is concerned with the theme that despite suffering the natural world is beautiful and essentially good.

Her next two publications, *The Second Silence* (1955) and *The Season's Lovers* (1958), more complicated in form, reflect the same attitudes, although there is an increased aware-ness of those social problems which the author has encountered in her work. In *The Glass Trumpet* (1966), Miss Waddington is concerned with the human desire for transparency in a world that is baffling and illusory, and with the process of personal resurrection and redemption. The poems of this collection reflect her particular interest in Joyce and the relation between sound and meaning.

DAVID WALKER (1911-). Born in Scotland, David Harry Walker received his early education at Sandhurst, England. Pursuing a military career, he served as an infantry officer in India and the Sudan (1932-1938), as an A.D.C. to the Governor General of Canada (1938/39) and as a prisoner of war in North West Europe (1940-1945). In the year following his release, he became Comptroller to the Viceroy of India, a position which he held for two years.

His life of activity and world-travel and spirited taste for adventure are reflected in his novels. He had already published *The Storm and the Silence* (1949) and *Geordie* (1950), when he received his first Governor General's Award for *The Pillar* in 1952. In 1953 he was similarly honoured for *Digby*, a humorous, escapist romance set in the Highlands.

Walker's familiarity with India serves him well in *Harry Black* (1956), a story of romance and big-game hunting in which he shifts from pure adventure-writing to a more highly developed treatment of character. It is in this novel that the Scottish expatriate first makes literary use, if only briefly, of Canada, his adopted country.

In 1957, Walker published *Sandy Was a Soldier's Boy* and was an advisor to the Canada Council. For his novel *Where the High Winds Blow* (1960), he chose an exclusively Canadian setting, confidently expressing his faith in the northern frontier as the keystone of "Canada's Century." *Dragon Hill* (1962) is a children's adventure story. *Storms of Our Journey* (1963) was made up of several short stories set in the Scottish Highlands, India and Canada. *Winter of Madness* (1964) is a spoof on literary fashions by way of a tale of characters brought together at a Scottish shooting lodge. *Mallabec* (1965) is a novel about some highly civilized people who resolve their problems violently at a fishing camp on the Mallabec. In *Come Back, Geordie* (1966) Walker produced a fine sequel to his earlier story of Scotland's shot-putting champion. Claude T. Bissell, "Letters in Canada: 1953," *UTQ*, XXIII (April, 1954); Claude T. Bissell, "Letters in Canada: 1956," *UTQ*, XXVI (April, 1957).

FREDERICK WILLIAM WALLACE (1886-1958). Born and educated in Glasgow, Scotland, Wallace settled in Quebec in 1904. After a period as a freelance journalist, he became editor in 1914 of *The Canadian Fisherman*. During the next year he helped organize the Canadian Fisheries Association.

His lifelong interest in fisheries and maritime history inspired and gave authenticity to his writings. *The Shack Locker* (1916) is the most significant of his collections of short stories.

In 1917 he was assigned to the Fish Section of the Canada Food Board.

The best of his novels *The Viking Blood* appeared in 1920. For six years following the war he edited an American publication, *Fishing Gazette*, and acted in an advisory capacity in the administration of U.S. Fisheries. During this period he turned to historical and descriptive writing, with *Wooden Ships and Iron Men* (1923) and *In the Wake of the Wind Ships* (1927). Returning to Canada in 1928, he became President of the Canadian Fisheries Association and Vice-President of National Business Publications. Wallace continued to write until 1936, when *Under Sail in the Last of the Clippers* appeared. He has maintained his popularity with maritime enthusiasts.

JAMES WREFORD WATSON. *See* Wreford, James.

JOHN WATSON (1847-1939). Born in Glasgow, Watson was educated at the University of Glasgow. He came to Canada in 1872 to join the faculty of Queen's University where he taught philosophy for over half a century. In numerous articles and books he defended philosophical idealism against the leading proponents of pragmatism and hedonism of his day. He was recognized as an international authority on Kant. His important works include: *Kant and His English Critics* (1881), *Schelling's Transcendental Idealism* (1882), *Hedonistic Theories from Aristippus to Spencer* (1895), *The Philosophical Basis of Religion* (1907), and *The Philosophy of Kant Explained* (1908). Watson's style is characterized by erudition and pungent wit. A member of the R.S.C. from its beginning in 1882, he was frequently honoured for his contribution to learning.

SHEILA WATSON (1909-   ). Born in New Westminster, British Columbia, Sheila Doherty Watson was a schoolteacher in the Western foothills during the depression. She moved with her husband, the poet and dramatist Wilfred Watson, to Ontario where she took graduate work at the University of Toronto. Some of her early short stories were published in *Queen's Quarterly*, "Brother Oedipus" (1954), "Black Farm" (1956), and in *The Tamarack Review*, "Antigone" (1959).

Her novel *The Double Hook* (1959), described by Philip Child as a "Canadian prose-poem," is set in a small, isolated ranch community in a narrow valley of the Rockies. Within this limited arena, and with a restricted cast of characters, the author presents a human drama which encompasses most of the basic passions and timeless situations of life. The title indicates the complex nature of even a rustic existence: "When you go fish for the glory you catch the darkness too." Strongly symbolical and allegorical, the tale is powerfully presented in a ballad-like prose style. Mrs. Watson is working on a biography of Wyndham Lewis, of whom she made a particular study during her graduate work.

WILFRED WATSON (1911-   ). Born in England, Watson was educated at Malden Grammar School before emigrating with his parents to British Columbia in 1926. After undergraduate work at the University of British Columbia, he took his doctorate at the University of Toronto. Following service with the R.C.N. during the war, he joined the faculty of the University of Alberta in 1951. He published in England a collection of poems *Friday's Child* (1955), a series of meditations on love and human will in modern life, which won a Governor General's Award as well as the Arts Council of Britain Award. Watson's sensitive awareness of the tragedy of existence and his warm humanity are evident in all his work. He has recently turned to dramatic production, and *Cockrow and The Gulls*, a religious drama in verse form, and *Mail for*

Two Pedestals are to be published. He is married to Sheila Watson, author of *The Double Hook*. John W. Bilsland, "Vision of Clarity. The Poetry of Wilfred Watson," *Can. Lit.,* 4 (Spring, 1960); John W. Bilsland, "First Night in Edmonton," *Can. Lit.,* 12 (Spring, 1962).

REGINALD E. WATTERS (1912-   ). Born in Toronto, Reginald Eyre Watters studied at Toronto (B.A., 1935; M.A. 1937), California, and Wisconsin (Ph.D., 1941). He has taught English at the universities of Washington (Seattle), Indiana, British Columbia (1946-1961), Toronto, and the Royal Military College of Canada at Kingston (where he is now Head of the Department).

Watters is the author of many articles in learned journals on literature of the United States and Canada. As a teacher and anthologist he has published *The Creative Reader*, with R. W. Stallman (1954, 1961), *Canadian Anthology*, with C. F. Klinck (1955, 1966), and *British Columbia: A Centennial Anthology* (1958, 1961). For English-Canadian literature he has also rendered valuable service as a bibliographer; his *Check List of Canadian Literature and Background Materials, 1628-1950* appeared in 1959, and *On Canadian Literature*, a check list of books, articles and theses on the subject, with Inglis Bell as co-compiler, in 1965.

PHYLLIS WEBB (1927-   ). Born in Victoria, British Columbia, Miss Webb was educated at the University of British Columbia under Earle Birney and at McGill University. After spending some time in England studying and travelling, she returned in 1956 to take a position as a secretary in Montreal. Her first group of poems, "Falling Glass," was published along with those of Eli Mandel and Gael Turnbull, in a collection entitled *Trio* (1954). In 1956 her first book *Even Your Right Eye* appeared, in 1962 *The Sea Is Also a Garden,* and in 1965 *Naked Poems.* Miss Webb's poems range in mood from intense seriousness to spontaneous rollicking. In evocative imagery and individual idiom, she responds with sensitive insight to experiences of love, art and religion.

FRANCES SHELLEY WEES (1902-   ). Born in Oregon, Frances Shelley Johnson Wees was educated there as well as in Saskatchewan and Alberta schools, and then taught briefly in Saskatchewan. She did public relations work in Toronto and Ottawa and for many years was Director of Canadian Chautauquas. Her home is near Stouffville, Ontario. She has contributed poems, stories and articles to various Canadian periodicals. *Maestro Murders* (1931) was the first of some dozen successful mystery novels, such as *Under the Quiet Water* (1948), *M'Lord, I Am Not Guilty* (1954), *The Country of the Strangers* (1959) and *Faceless Enemy* (1966).

GEORGE WHALLEY (1915-   ). Born in Kingston, Ontario, Whalley was educated at Bishop's University (B.A. 1935, M.A. 1948), Oxford (B.A. 1939, M.A. 1945), where he was a Rhodes Scholar, and the University of London (Ph.D. 1950). After World War II, in which he served as a Commander in the R.C.N. (1940-1945), he taught at Bishop's University for three years before joining the faculty of Queen's University where he is now Professor and Head of the Department of English.

In 1953 he published *The Poetic Process: An Essay in Poetics.* His own verse has appeared in *Poems 1939-1944* (1946) and *No Man an Island* (1948). These poems evoke with graceful restraint and wistful tenderness the intense experiences and associations of a humanist who quietly clings to artistic and intellectual realities in the midst of the strangely unreal events of war. Associated with Kathleen Coburn in her studies of Coleridge, he published *Coleridge and Sara Hutchinson and the Asra Poems* (1955). Whalley edited *Writing in Canada* (1955), the proceedings of the Canadian Writers' Conference held at Queen's University. He was elected F.R.S.C. in 1959. His biography *The Legend of John Hornby* (1962), tells of a colourful figure of the Canadian North in the early part of this century. He edited *A Place of Liberty: Essays on the Government of Canadian Universities* (1964), and is currently engaged in preparing part of a new complete edition of Coleridge's prose and verse.

ANNE WILKINSON (1910-1961). Born in Toronto, Anne Gibbons Wilkinson spent her early years in London, Ontario, and received a sporadic education mainly in American and European schools. She published two books of verse, *Counterpoint to Sleep* (1951) and *The Hangman Ties the Holly* (1955), and three lyric sequences which appeared in *The Tamarack Review*. In her poems, she celebrates the sensuous aspects of life with delicacy, irony and wit. As A. J. M. Smith remarks, she belongs with Emily Dickinson "among the small group of women poets who have written of love and death with a peculiarly feminine intuition, an accuracy, and an elegance that does not hide but enhance the intensity of the emotion."

In addition to her poetry, Mrs. Wilkinson published *Lions in the Way* (1956), a discursive history of the Osler family from which she was herself descended, and *Swann and Daphne* (1960), a rather melancholy modern fantasy for children. A. J. M. Smith, "A Reading of Anne Wilkinson," *Can. Lit.*, 10 (Autumn, 1961); Anne Wilkinson, "Four Corners of My World," *Tamarack Review*, 20 (Summer, 1961).

ETHEL WILSON (1888-   ). Born in Port Elizabeth, South Africa, the daughter of a Methodist Missionary, Ethel Bryant Wilson passed her early childhood in England. An orphan at the age of eight, she came to Canada to live with relatives in Vancouver. After several years at a British boarding school, she returned to Vancouver, where she completed her education and became a public school teacher. In 1921 she married Dr. Wallace Wilson, a physician.

Mrs. Wilson, who developed her narrative skill by creating extemporaneous stories for pupils, submitted her first published short story "I Just Love Dogs" to the *New Statesman and Nation* in 1937. Her first novel, *Hetty Dorval* (1947), did not appear for another ten years. In 1949 she produced a second novel, *The Innocent Traveller*, arranged as a series of sketches of a family which moved from England to Vancouver. The basic theme in both of these early works is innocence in conflict with experience. Events, people and situations are seen and presented with a fresh simplicity and a quiet humour. Although she places most of her stories in a British Columbia setting, her writing can not properly be called regional, for character takes precedence over locality.

Equations of Love (1952) consists of two novelettes "Tuesday and Wednesday" and "Lilly's Story." In these stories, as in *Swamp Angel* (1934), Mrs. Wilson expresses a characteristic interest in the irrational element in nature and human life, a constant awareness of the truth of Donne's "No man is an island, entire of itself," and a confidence in the ability of men, however imperfect, to live together in a spirit of compassion and charity.

In *Love and Salt Water* (1956), Mrs. Wilson created a world of universal emotions peopled with warm and human characters. The plot is developed chronologically within the narrowly defined scope typical of the author, in a style that has an urbanity free of conscious artifice, with an irony and unobtrusive symbolism.

Mrs. Wilson's short stories, which have appeared in many Canadian journals and magazines, have recently been published in collected form as *Mrs. Golightly and Other Stories* (1961). In this volume, her deft sketches, evocative imagery and social satire produce a set of engagingly human miniatures. Dorothy Livesay, "Ethel Wilson: West Coast Novelist," *Saturday Night,* LXVII (July, 1952); Desmond Pacey, "The Innocent Eye," *Queen's Quarterly,* LXI (Spring, 1954); R. E. Watters, "Ethel Wilson, The Experienced Traveller," *British Columbia Library Quarterly,* XXI, 4 (April, 1958); Ethel Wilson, "A Cat Among the Falcons," *Can. Lit.,* 2 (Autumn, 1959).

ADELE WISEMAN (1928-   ). Born in Winnipeg, Adele Wiseman graduated from the University of Manitoba in 1949 with a B.A. in Psychology and English. In 1955 she went to England, where she has become a voluntary worker at the Jewish Girls' Hospital in Stepney.

Her novel, *The Sacrifice* (1956), which received a Governor General's Award, is set in an unnamed city, presumably Winnipeg, and deals with a Jewish immigrant family's struggle to orientate itself in unfamiliar customs and surroundings. In her central character, Abraham, she creates a figure of almost heroic proportions, who is intensely individual, and yet representative of his race. The Jewish dilemma is forcefully brought out, both in the context of the story, and in the religious symbolism employed. A successful blend of character and background emphasizes the centrality of the human being and the strength of family relationships in a warm and appealing presentation. Ruth Mackenzie, "Life in a New Land," *Can.Lit.,* 7 (Winter, 1961).

GEORGE WOODCOCK (1912-   ). Born in Winnipeg, Woodcock as a child moved with his parents to England, where he was educated. He worked at various times as farmer, railroad clerk and journalist. Although his first publications were small volumes of verse— *The White Island* (1940), *The Centre Cannot Hold* (1943) and *Imagine the South* (1947)—he gained literary recognition by his scholarly treatment of *William Godwin* (1946), *The Incomparable Aphra* (1948) and *The Paradox of Oscar Wilde* (1949). He is the co-author of *The Anarchist Prince* (1950), a biographical study of Peter Kropotkin.

Woodcock returned to Canada in 1950. He travelled extensively in British Columbia, Alberta and Southern Alaska and recorded his experiences of this trip in *Ravens and Prophets* (1952). In 1956 he joined the faculty of the University of British Columbia, where he now teaches English, and is editor of the important literary quarterly *Canadian Literature.*

His early poetry, his scholarly books and articles, his reflections on his Mexican travels, *To a City of the Dead* (1957) and *Incas and Other Men* (1959) and *Anarchism: A History of Libertarian Ideas and Movements* (1962) all reveal Woodcock's keen interest in the realization by the individual of his own nature. A versatile writer, he is in sympathetic understanding with men as different in outlook as Godwin, Kropotkin, Lowry, Proudhom and Wilde, and as concerned for the peasant workers in Mexico and the refugee Tibetans in India as for the oppressed native Indians in British Columbia. Many recent articles, essays and poems in *Canadian Literature, Tamarack Review, History Today* and other journals show further expansion of similar themes. In

[156]

1963 he travelled eastward from Aden to Pakistan, India, Thailand, Cambodia, Malaysia, Hong Kong, and Tokyo. *Asia, Gods and Cities* (1966) is a running narrative of this trip. *Faces of India* (1964) deals more specifically with India. In 1966 Woodcock also published *The Greeks in India*. J. W. Bilsland, "George Woodcock: Man of Letters," *British Columbia Literary Quarterly*, XXIII (1959); "East of Suez" [a review of *Asia, Gods and Cities*], *The Times Literary Supplement*, May 12, 1966.

A. S. P. WOODHOUSE (1895-1964). Born in Port Hope, Ontario, Arthur Sutherland Pigott Woodhouse was educated at the University of Toronto (B.A. 1919) and Harvard (M.A. 1922). He returned to Canada to the University of Manitoba (1923-1928), and then to the University of Toronto as Professor and Head of the Department of English at University College. As a teacher he became famous for his Johnsonian wit and learning. Editor of "Letters in Canada" in the *University of Toronto Quarterly* from 1935 to 1945, he contributed numerous articles on Milton to learned journals in Canada and the U.S.A. His publications include *Puritanism and Liberty* (1938, 1950 and 1966), *The Humanities in Canada* (1947), produced in collaboration with Watson Kirkconnell, and studies of Collins and the creative imagination, of nature and grace in the *Fairie*

Queene, and of various nineteenth-century figures.

Elected F.R.S.C. in 1942, Woodhouse was honoured with fellowships and honorary degrees for his writings and distinguished foundation lectures, and he gained international fame as a brilliant scholar and influential humanist. A series of lectures given by him on "Religion and Poetry in England from Spenser to Eliot and Auden" was published under the title *The Poet and His Faith* in 1965. Millar MacLure and F. W. Watt, editors, *Essays in English Literature from the Renaissance to the Victorian Age: Presented to A. S. P. Woodhouse* (Toronto, 1964).

JAMES WREFORD (1915-   ). Born in North China, James Wreford Watson was educated there and at the University of Edinburgh. In 1939, he came to teach at McMaster University and later worked as a government geographer in Ottawa. He left Canada after World War II and lives in Edinburgh.

His poetry appeared in *Unit of Five* (1944) and in *Of Time and the Lover,* which won the Governor General's Award for 1950. His early verse of vigorous social comment has a directness and intensity which are less evident in his facile meditations on the problems of time and love. In 1959, with Ronald Miller, Wreford edited *Geographical Essays in Memory of Alan G. Ogilvie.*

BRANDON CONRON (1919-   ) is Professor of English at the University of Western Ontario. In addition to articles and reviews, his work as author and editor include collaboration as assistant Latin Editor of *The Literary Works of Matthew Prior* (1959), two chapters on "The Essay" in the *Literary History of Canada* (1965) and *Morley Callaghan* (1966), a critical exposition of Canada's foremost novelist, in the Twayne World Authors series.

CARL F. KLINCK (1908-   ) is a Senior Professor of English at the University of Western Ontario. He is the author of *Wilfred Campbell* (1942); co-author with Henry W.

Wells of *Edwin J. Pratt* (1947); editor of *William "Tiger" Dunlop* (1958), *Tecumseh* (1961), and of reprints of books by Frances Brooke, John Richardson and Susanna Moodie; co-editor with R. E. Watters of *Canadian Anthology* (1955, 1966); and General Editor of *Literary History of Canada* (1965). He was elected F.R.S.C. in 1961.

GUY SYLVESTRE (1918-   ) est bibliothécaire associé du Parlement à Ottawa. Il est l'auteur l'une *Anthologie de la poésie canadienne français,* d'un *Panorama des Lettres canadiennes-françaises* et de volumes d'essais littéraires. Il a été élu à la Société Royale du Canada en 1951 et à l'Académie canadienne-française en 1965.

BIBLIOGRAPHY/BIBLIOGRAPHIE

ANTHOLOGIES

Olivar Asselin et Jules Fournier, *Anthologie des poètes canadiens* (Montréal, 1933)

Earle Birney, *Twentieth Century Canadian Poetry* (Toronto, 1953)

Alain Bosquet, *La poésie canadienne* (Paris, 1962)

Louis Dudek and Irving Layton, *Canadian Poems 1850-1952* (Toronto, 1952)

Ralph Gustafson, *The Penguin Book of Canadian Verse* (Toronto, 1958)

C. F. Klinck and R. E. Watters, *Canadian Anthology* (Toronto, 1955, rev., 1966)

Desmond Pacey, *A Book of Canadian Stories* (Toronto, 1961)

Laure Rièse, *L'Ame de la poésie canadienne française* (Toronto, 1955)

Malcolm Ross, *Our Sense of Identity: A Book of Canadian Essays* (Toronto, 1954)

A. J. M. Smith, *The Book of Canadian Poetry* (Toronto, 1957)

A. J. M. Smith, *The Book of Canadian Prose,* Part I (Toronto, 1966)

A. J. M. Smith, *The Oxford Book of Canadian Verse* (Toronto, 1960)

Guy Sylvestre, *Anthologie de la poésie canadienne française* (Montréal, 1964)

Robert Weaver, *Canadian Short Stories* (Toronto, 1960)

Milton Wilson, *Poetry of Mid-Century, 1940-1960* (Toronto, 1964)

BIBLIOGRAPHIES

Canadian Index to Periodicals and Documentary Films (From 1948)

Canadian Periodical Index, 1928-1932; 1938-1947

Canadiana, Publications of Canadian interest noted by the National Library (From 1951)

Antonio Drolet, *Bibliographie du roman canadien français 1900-1950* (Québec, 1955)

Gérard Martin, *Bibliographie sommaire du Canada français* (Québec, 1954)

Répertoire bio-bibliographique de la Société des écrivains canadiens (Montréal, 1954)

R. E. Watters, *A Check List of Canadian Literature and Background Materials, 1628-1950* (Toronto, 1959)

R. E. Watters and Inglis Bell, *On Canadian Literature* (Toronto, 1966)

Archives des Lettres canadiennes (Ottawa, Depuis 1961)

Samuel Baillargeon, *Littérature canadienne française* (Montréal, 1960)

R. P. Baker, *A History of English-Canadian Literature to the Confederation* (Cambridge, 1920)

Gérard Bessette, *Les images en poésie canadienne française* (Montréal, 1960)

E. K. Brown, *On Canadian Poetry* (Toronto, 1943)

Berthelot Brunet, *Histoire de la littérature canadienne française* (Montréal, 1946)

W. E. Collin, *The White Savannahs* (Toronto, 1936)

Louis Dantin, *Gloses critiques* (Montréal, 1931 et 1935)

Louis Dantin, *Poètes de l'Amérique française* (Montréal, 1927 et 1934)

Dictionary of Canadian Biography, I (Toronto, 1966)

Wilfrid Eggleston, *The Frontier and Canadian Letters* (Toronto, 1957)

Encyclopedia Canadiana (Ottawa, 1957)

Pierre de Grandpré, *Dix ans de vie littéraire au Canada français* (Montréal, 1966)

English Poetry in Quebec (Montreal, 1965)

Carl F. Klinck et al., *Literary History of Canada* (Toronto, 1965)

Littérature et société canadiennes françaises (*Recherches sociographiques,* 1964)

J. D. Logan and D. G. French, *Highways of Canadian Literature* (Toronto, 1924)

Edward McCourt, *The Canadian West in Fiction* (Toronto, 1949)

Gilles Marcotte, *Une littérature qui se fait* (Montréal, 1962)

Séraphin Marion, *Les lettres canadiennes d'autrefois* (Ottawa, 1939-1958)

Our Living Tradition series (Ottawa, Carleton University, 1957, 1959, 1962, 1965)

Desmond Pacey, *Creative Writing in Canada* (Toronto, 1961)

Desmond Pacey, *Ten Canadian Poets* (Toronto, 1958)

Julian Park, editor, *The Culture of Contemporary Canada* (Ithaca, N.Y., 1957)

Albert Pelletier, *Carquois* (Montréal, 1931)

Albert Pelletier, *Egrappages* (Montréal, 1933)

Walter P. Percival, editor, *Leading Canadian Poets* (Toronto, 1948)

Lorne Pierce, *An Outline of Canadian Literature* (Toronto, 1927)

R. E. Rashley, *Poetry in Canada: The First Three Steps* (Toronto, 1958)

V. B. Rhodenizer, *A Handbook of Canadian Literature* (Ottawa, 1930)

Réjean Robidoux et André Renaud, *Le roman canadien français au* xxᵉ *siècle* (Ottawa, 1966)

David Rome, *Jews in Canadian Literature* (Montreal, 1964)

Malcolm Ross, editor, *The Arts in Canada* (Toronto, 1958)

Camille Roy, *Essais sur la littérature canadienne* (Québec, 1907)

J. Ross Roy, *Le sentiment de la nature dans la poésie canadienne anglaise* (Paris, 1961)

A. J. M. Smith, editor, *Masks of fiction: Canadian Critics on Canadian Prose* (Toronto, 1961)

A. J. M. Smith, editor, *Masks of Poetry: Canadian Critics on Canadian Verse* (Toronto, 1962)

Lionel Stevenson, *Appraisals of Canadian Literature* (Toronto, 1926)

Guy Sylvestre, *Panorama des lettres canadiennes françaises* (Québec, 1964)

Clara Thomas, *Canadian Novelists, 1920-1945* (Toronto, 1946)

Gérard Tougas, *Histoire de la littérature canadienne française* (Paris, 1960 et 1964). *History of French-Canadian Literature.* Translated by Alta Lind Cook (Toronto, 1966)

Auguste Viatte, *Histoire littéraire de l'Amérique française* Paris et Québec, 1954)

George Whalley, editor, *Writing in Canada* (Toronto, 1956)

[163]

[165]

Dans un gant de fer, Claire Martin
D'Arcy McGee: A Collection of Speeches
  and Addresses
Dark as the Grave Wherein My Friend
  Is Laid, Malcolm Lowry
Dark Huntsman, The, Charles Heavysege
Dark Weaver, The, Laura Salverson
Darkness and the Dawn, The, Thomas
  B. Costain
Darkness in the Earth, A, Alden A.
  Nowlan
David and Other Poems, Earle Birney
David Thompson, The Explorer, Charles
  Norris Cochrane
Day and Night, Dorothy Livesay
Day of Wrath, Philip Child
D'azur à trois lys d'or, Edouard
  Montpetit
De l'autre côté du mur, Marcel Dubé
De livres en livres, Maurice Hébert
Dear Enemies, Gwethalyn Graham
Death of King Buda, The, Watson
  Kirkconnell
Découverte du Canada, La, Lionel
  Groulx
Deeper into the Forest, Roy Daniells
Défaut des ruines est d'avoir des
  habitants, Le, Roland Giguère
Deficit Made Flesh, The, John Glassco
Deirdre of the Sorrows, John Coulter
Delight, Mazo de la Roche
Délivrez-nous du mal, Claude Jasmin
Demi-civilisés, Les, Jean-Charles Harvey
Dernier Souper, Le, Albert Laberge
Des Provinces de l'Amérique du nord et
  d'une Union fédérale, Joseph-Charles
  Taché
Descent from Eden, Fred Cogswell
Deserter, The, Douglas LePan
Déserteur, Le, Claude-Henri Grignon
Désirs et les jours, Les, Robert
  Charbonneau
Desperate People, The, Farley Mowat
Despite the Distance, Will R. Bird
Destin des hommes, Le, Albert Laberge
Deux ans au Mexique, Faucher de Saint-
  Maurice
Deux copains, Louis Fréchette
Deux copains, William Chapman
Deux femmes terribles, André
  Laurendeau
Deux solitudes, Les, Hugh MacLennan
Devil's Picture Book, The, Daryl Hine
Diary, Anna Jameson
Diary of Samuel Marchbanks, The,
  Robertson Davies

Dictionnaire canadien, Pierre Daviault
Dictionnaire militaire, Pierre Daviault
Digby, David Walker
Dimanches naïfs, Eloi de Grandmont
Directives, Lionel Groulx
Discours et conférences, Thomas Chapais
Dix Ans au Canada, 1840-1850, Antoine
  Gérin-Lajoie
Doctor Luke of the Labrador, Norman
  Duncan
Documents Illustrative of Canadian
  Economic History, A. R. M. Lower
Dodge Club, The, James De Mille
Dodu, Le, Jacques Ferron
Dog Who Wouldn't Be, The, Farley
  Mowat
Dolorès, Harry Bernard
Dolphin Days, Patrick Anderson
Dominantes, René Chopin
Dominion of the North, Donald
  Creighton
Dompteur d'ours, Le, Yves Thériault
Double Hook, The, Sheila Watson
Doux-amer, Claire Martin
Dove of El-Djezaire, The, Laura
  Salverson
Dover Beach Revisited, Robert Finch
Down North, Norman Duncan
Down the Long Table, Earle Birney
Dragon Hill, David Walker
Drama of the Forests, The, A. Heming
Dread Voyage, The, Wilfred Campbell
Dreamland and Other Poems, Charles
  Mair
Drift of Pinions, The, Marjorie Pickthall
Drunken Clock, The, Gwendolyn
  MacEwen
Dryad in Nanaimo, A, Audrey Alexandra
  Brown
Dumbfounding, The, Margaret Avison
D'un livre à l'autre, Maurice Hébert
D'un océan à l'autre, Robert de
  Roquebrune
Dunkirk, E. J. Pratt
Dynamic Democracy, Philip Child

E

Each Man's Son, Hugh MacLennan
Earth and High Heaven, Gwethalyn
  Graham
Earth's Enigmas, Charles G. D. Roberts
East Coast, Elizabeth Brewster
East of the City, Louis Dudek
Eau est profonde, L', Diane Giguère
Eaux-fortes et tailles-douces, Henri
  d'Arles

Ecarté, or The Salons of Paris, John Richardson
Ecole littéraire de Montréal, L', Jean Charbonneau
Ecoute Notre Voix, O Seigneur, Malcolm Lowry
Ecrivain et son théâtre, L', Paul Toupin
Educated Imagination, The, Northrop Frye
Education in a Democracy, Lorne Pierce
Eglise canadienne . . . , L., Marcel Trudel
Egrappages, Albert Pelletier
Eight Years in Canada, John Richardson
Elements of Political Science, Stephen Leacock
Elise Velder, Robert Choquette
Elizabeth, Richard Diespecker
Elus que vous êtes, Les, Clément Lockquell
Embers, Gilbert Parker
Emigrant and Other Poems, The, Alexander McLachlan
Emily Carr: Her Paintings and Sketches, Emily Carr
Emily Climbs, L. M. Montgomery
Emily of New Moon, L. M. Montgomery
Emily's Quest, L. M. Montgomery
Emperor of Ice Cream, The, Brian Moore
Empire and Communications, H. A. Innis
Empire Builders, The, Robert Stead
Empty Frame, The, Lister Sinclair
Emu, Remember, Alfred W. Purdy
En haut lieu, Arthur Hailey
En México, Louis Dudek
En pleine terre, Germaine Guèvremont
Enchanted Echo, The, Alfred W. Purdy
Encircling Mist, The, Evelyn Eaton
Encounter by Moonlight, Lister Sinclair
Enfances de Fanny, Les, Louis Dantin
Engagés du Grand Portage, Les, Léo-Paul Desrosiers
English Governess, The, John Glassco
English Literature in the Earlier Seventeenth Century, Douglas Bush
English Poetry in Quebec, John Glassco
English Poetry: The Main Currents from Chaucer to the Present, Douglas Bush
Enseignement français au Canada, L', Lionel Groulx
Entail, The, John Galt
Entre ciel et terre, Gwethalyn Graham
Epaves poétiques, Louis Fréchette
Epithalamion in Time of War, Ralph Gustafson

Epîtres, Satires, Chansons, Epigrammes et Autres pièces de vers, Michel Bibaud
Equations of Love, Ethel Wilson
Erables en fleurs, Camille Roy
Eros at Breakfast and Other Plays, Robertson Davies
Escales, Rina Lasnier
Esclavage au Canada, L', Marcel Trudel
Esquisse sur le Canada, Joseph-Charles Taché
Essais critiques, Harry Bernard
Essais et conférences, Henri d'Arles
Essais sur la littérature canadienne, Camille Roy
Essays in Fallacy, Sir Andrew MacPhail
Essays in Politics, Sir Andrew MacPhail
Essays in Puritanism, Sir Andrew MacPhail
Essays on Questions of the Day, Political and Social, Goldwin Smith
Estampes, Henri d'Arles
Et le cheval vert, Cécile Chabot
Ethel et le terroriste, Claude Jasmin
Etoile pourpre, L', Alain Grandbois
Etrangère, L', Robert Elie
Ettinger Affair, The, Edward McCourt
Etudes et croquis, Camille Roy
Etudes sur les parlers de France au Canada, Adjutor Rivard
Europe, Louis Dudek
European Elegies, Watson Kirkconnell
European Heritage, The, Watson Kirkconnell
Evadé de la nuit, André Langevin
Even Your Right Eye, Phyllis Webb
Events and Signals, F. R. Scott
Every Man Is an Island, Ronald Hambleton
Every Month Was May, Evelyn Eaton
Evolution of the Idea of God, The, Grant Allen
Evolutionary Ethics in Samuel Butler, Claude T. Bissell
Evolutionist at Large, The, Grant Allen
Experiment 1923-29, W. W. E. Ross
Explorers of the Dawn, Mazo de la Roche
Eye of the Needle, F. R. Scott

F

Fable of the Goats and Other Poems, The, E. J. Pratt
Fables, George Thomas Lanigan
Fables of Identity, Studies in Poetic Mythology, Northrop Frye

Faceless Enemy, Frances Shelley Wees
Faces of India, George Woodcock
False Chevalier, The, W. D. Lighthall
Family Portrait, The, John Coulter
Fantaisies sur les péchés capitaux, Roger Lemelin
Far Distant Ships, The, Joseph Schull
Farewell My Dreams, Robert Elie
Fast, Fast, Fast Relief, Pierre Berton
Fasting Friar, Edward McCourt
Father Abraham, W. G. Hardy
Faussaires et faussetés en histoire canadienne, Gustave Lanctôt
Fausse Monnaie, Ringuet
Faust aux enfers, Roger Brien
Favorite et le conquérant, La, Bertrand Vac
Favourite Game, The, Leonard Cohen
Fearful Symmetry, Northrop Frye
Feast of Lupercal, The, Brian Moore
Féerie indienne, Rina Lasnier
Félix, Jean Simard
Female Immigrant's Guide, The, Catharine Parr Traill
Ferme des pins, La, Harry Bernard
Feu dans l'amiante, Le, Jean-Jules Richard
Feuilles d'érable, Les, William Chapman
Feuilles volantes, Louis Fréchette
Feux de Bengale à Verlaine glorieux, Marcel Dugas
Fiançailles d'Anne de Nouë, Rina Lasnier
Fiancée du matin, La, Jean-Guy Pilon
Fille du silence, La, Jean-Charles Harvey
Fille laide, La, Yves Thériault
Filles de joie ou filles du Roi, Gustave Lanctôt
Fils à tuer, Un, Eloi de Grandmont
Fin de roman, Albert Laberge
Fin des songes, La, Robert Elie
Fin du voyage, La, Albert Laberge
Final Diagnosis, The, Arthur Hailey
Finch's Fortune, Mazo de la Roche
First Statement, John Sutherland
Fisherman's Creed, A, W. H. Blake
Fisherman's Fall, Roderick Haig-Brown
Fisherman's Spring, Roderick Haig-Brown
Fisherman's Summer, Roderick Haig-Brown
Fisherman's Winter, Roderick Haig-Brown
Five Canadian Poets, A. S. Bourinot
Five New Brunswick Poets, Fred Cogswell, Kay Smith, Alden A. Nowlan

Five Poems, Daryl Hine
Flagon of Beauty, A, Wilson MacDonald
Flaming Hour, The, Edward McCourt
Flamme ardente, La, Jean Charbonneau
Fleurs boréales, Louis Fréchette
Fleurs de givre, Les, William Chapman
Flight Into Danger, Arthur Hailey
Flight Into Darkness, Ralph Gustafson
Flint and Feather, Pauline Johnson
Flora Lindsay, Susanna Moodie
Floraisons matutinales, Les, Nérée Beauchemin
Flore laurentienne, Marie-Victorin
Florence, Marcel Dubé
Flowers for Hitler, Leonard Cohen
Flowing Summer, The, Charles Bruce
Flying a Red Kite, Hugh Hood
Flying Bull and Other Tales, The, Watson Kirkconnell
Flying Years, The, Frederick Niven
Fontaine de Paris, La, Eloi de Grandmont
Fontile, Robert Charbonneau
Footnote to the Lord's Prayer and Other Poems, Kay Smith
For My Great Folly, Thomas B. Costain
Forestiers et voyageurs, Joseph-Charles Taché
Forêt, La, Georges Bugnet
Forges of Freedom, Franklin McDowell
Fortune My Foe, Robertson Davies
Four Ages of Man, Jay Macpherson
Four Jameses, The, William Arthur Deacon
Français, Le, Damase Potvin
France et nous, La, Robert Charbonneau
François Bigot, administrateur français, Guy Frégault
François de Bienville, Joseph Marmette
Fraser, The, Bruce Hutchison
Frederick Philip Grove, Desmond Pacey
Fresh Wind Blowing, Grace Campbell
Friction of Lights, A, Eldon Grier
Friday's Child, Wilfred Watson
Friendly Acres, Peter McArthur
Friendship of Art, The, Bliss Carman
From the Book of The Myths, Bliss Carman
From the Green Book of the Bards, Bliss Carman
Frost on the Sun, D. G. Jones
Fruits of the Earth, Frederick Philip Grove
Fur Masters, The, Alan Sullivan
Fur Trade in Canada, The, Harold A. Innis

[170]

Incomparable Aphra, The, George
  Woodcock
Incomparable Atuk, The, Mordecai
  Richler
Incomplete Anglers, The, John D. Robins
Incredible Canadian, The, Bruce
  Hutchison
Incubation, L', Gerard Bessett
Indépendance économique du Canada
  français, L', Errol Bouchette
Influence de Voltaire au Canada, L',
  Marcel Trudel
Influence d'un livre, L', Philippe Aubert
  de Gaspé
Influences françaises au Canada, Les,
  Jean Charbonneau
Infusoires, Les, Monique Bosco
Initiation à l'humain, Victor Barbeau
Inner Shrine, The, Basil King
Innocent Traveller, The, Ethel Wilson
Insolites, Les, Jacques Languirand
Instruction publique au Canada, L',
  P. J. O. Chauveau
Inutiles, Les, Eugène Cloutier
Invisible Gate, The, Constance Beresford-
  Howe
Iron Door, The, E. J. Pratt
Iroquoisie, Léo-Paul Desrosiers
Isolement dans le roman canadien-
  français, L', Monique Bosco
It's Never Over, Morley Callaghan

J

Jalna, Mazo de la Roche
Jancis, Leslie Gordon Barnard
Janey Canuck in the West, Emily
  Gowan Murphy
Jawbreakers, Milton Acorn
Jean Narrache chez le diable, Emile
  Coderre
Jean Rivard économiste, Antoine
  Gérin-Lajoie
Jean Rivard le défricheur, Antoine
  Gérin-Lajoie
Jean Talon, Thomas Chapais
Jephthah's Daughter, Charles Heavysege
Jest of God, A, Margaret Laurence
Jeu de la voyagère, Le, Rina Lasnier
Jeune Latour, Le, Antoine Gérin-Lajoie
Jezebel, Charles Heavysege
Jimmy Gold-Coast, Marshall Saunders
John Keats, Douglas Bush
John Milton, Douglas Bush
Johnny Courteau and Other Poems,
  William Henry Drummond
Jonathas, Gustave Lamarche

Jour malaisé, Gatien Lapointe
Journal, Saint-Denys-Garneau
Journal d'Anatole Laplante, François
  Hertel
Journal d'un hobo, Jean-Jules Richard
Journal du siège de Paris, Octave
  Crémazie
Journal of Saint-Denys-Garneau, The,
  John Glassco
Journal of The Movements of the British
  Legion, John Richardson
Journalistes, écrivains et artistes, Albert
  Laberge
Jours sont longs, Les, Harry Bernard
J'parl' tout seul quand Jean Narrache,
  Emile Coderre
Juana, mon aimée, Harry Bernard
Judgement House, The, Gilbert Parker
Judgment Glen, Will R. Bird
Julian, the Magician, Gwendolyn
  MacEwen
Just Add Water and Stir, Pierre Berton
Just Ask for George, Morley Callaghan

K

Kant and His English Critics, John
  Watson
Kildeer and Other Plays, The, James
  Reaney
Kindred of the Wild, The, Charles
  G. D. Roberts
Kinship of Nature, The, Bliss Carman
Kitchener and Other Poems, Robert
  Stead
Kite, The, W. O. Mitchell
Klee Wyck, Emily Carr
Klondike, Pierre Berton
Klondike Mike, Merrill Denison
Kootenay Highlander, The, Earle
  Birney
Kristli's Trees, Mabel Dunham

L

Labour and the Angel, Duncan Campbell
  Scott
Laconics, W. W. E. Ross
Lake Lyrics and Other Poems, Wilfred
  Campbell
Lamp of Poor Souls and Other Poems,
  Marjorie Pickthall
Langage et traduction, Pierre Daviault
Langue française au Canada, La,
  Louvigny de Montigny
Langue française au Canada, La, Jules-
  Paul Tardivel
Lanterne, La, Arthur Buies
Lark Ascending, Mazo de la Roche

Loved and the Lost, The, Morley Callaghan
Lover's Diary, A, Gilbert Parker
Lowlands Low, Kenneth Leslie
Low Life, Mazo de la Roche
Low Tide on Grand Pré, Bliss Carman
Loyal Verses of Joseph Stansbury and Doctor Jonathan Odell, Jonathan Odell
Luck of Ginger Coffey, The, Brian Moore
Luke Baldwin's Vow, Morley Callaghan
Lunar Caustic, Malcolm Lowry
Lundy's Lane and Other Poems, Duncan Campbell Scott
Lyra Sacra, Watson Kirkconnell
Lyric Year, The, Wilson MacDonald
Lyrics, Alexander McLachlan
Lyrics from the Hills, A. S. Bourinot
Lyrics of Earth, Archibald Lampman
Lyrics on Freedom, Love and Death, George Frederick Cameron
Lyrics Unromantic, Ralph Gustafson

M

Ma Gaspésie, Blanche Lamontagne
Madame Homère, Pierre Baillargeon
Madones canadiennes, Rina Lasnier
Mad Shadows, Marie-Claire Blais
Maestro Murders, Frances Shelley Wees
Magic House and Other Poems, The, Duncan Campbell Scott
Magnificent Century, The, Thomas B. Costain
Magyar Muse, The, Watson Kirkconnell
Maid of the Marshes, Will R. Bird
Mail for Two Pedestals, Wilfred Watson
Maison vide, La, Harry Bernard
Major, The, Charles William Gordon
Major British Writers, Northrop Frye
Making of Personality, The, Bliss Carman
Malebête, La, Suzanne Paradis
Malgré tout, la joie, André Giroux
Mallabec, David Walker
Mammals of Manitoba, Ernest Thompson Seton
Man and His World, Malcolm Ross
Man from Glengarry, The, Charles William Gordon
Manor House of de Villerai, The, Rosanna Eleanor Leprohon
Man's Moral Nature, Richard Maurice Bucke
Manuel de la parole, Adjutor Rivard
Many Minds, Maurice Hutton
Many Colored Coat, The, Morley Callaghan

Many Mansioned House and Other Poems, The, Edward William Thomson
Many Moods, E. J. Pratt
Manzanillo and Other Poems, Eldon Grier
Marcel Faure, Jean-Charles Harvey
Marcheur, Le, Yves Thériault
Maria Chapdelaine, Sir Andrew MacPhail, W. H. Blake
Mariage blanc d'Armandine, Le, Berthelot Brunet
Marie-Didace, Germaine Guèvremont
Marjorie Pickthall: A Book of Remembrance, Lorne Pierce
Mark, The, Charles Israel
Mark Hurdlestone, Susanna Moodie
Mark Twain, Stephen Leacock
Marquis de Montcalm, Le, Thomas Chapais
Martyr of the Catacombs, James De Mille
Mask for Mr. Punch, A, Robertson Davies
Masks of Fiction, A. J. M. Smith
Masks of Poetry, A. J. M. Smith
Masques déchirés, Les, Jovette Bernier
Master of Jalna, The, Mazo de la Roche
Master of Life, The, William Douw Lighthall
Master of the Mill, The, Frederick Philip Grove
Matins, Francis Sherman
Matrimonial Speculations, Susanna Moodie
Matthew Arnold: A Study in Conflict, E. K. Brown
Mauvais Passant, Le, Albert Dreux
Measure of the Year, Roderick Haig-Brown
Mechanical Bride, The, Marshall McLuhan
Médisances de Claude Perrin, Les, Pierre Baillargeon
Mélanges, Jules-Paul Tardivel
Mélanges, Thomas Chapais
Mélanges historiques, Benjamin Sulte
Mémoire sans jours, Rina Lasnier
Mémoires Chapais, Julienne Barnard
Mémoires, Philippe Aubert de Gaspé
Mémoires intimes, Louis Fréchette
Memoirs of Celebrated Female Sovereigns, Anna Jameson
Memoirs of the Loves of the Poets, Anna Jameson
Men and Women, Hugh Garner

[177]

[179]

[185]

White Island, The, George Woodcock
White Narcissus, Raymond Knister
White Rajah, The, Nicholas Monsarrat
White Savannahs, The, W. E. Collin
White Wampum, The, Pauline Johnson
Whiteoak Harvest, Mazo de la Roche
Whiteoak Heritage, Mazo de la Roche
Whiteoaks of Jalna, Mazo de la Roche
Who Has Seen the Wind, W. O. Mitchell
Who Knows One?, Phyllis Gotlieb
Who Was Then The Gentleman?, Charles Israel
Wild Animals I Have Known, Ernest Thompson Seton
Wild Apples, Charles Bruce
Wild Geese, Martha Ostenso
Willa Cather: A Critical Biography, E. K. Brown
William Godwin, George Woodcock
Wind in a Rocky Country, Alden A. Nowlan
Wind Our Enemy, The, Anne Marriott
Window on the North, A, R. A. D. Ford
Windward Rock, Kenneth Leslie
Wine of Life, The, Arthur Stringer
Wings of Night, The, Thomas H. Raddall
Winter of Madness, David Walker
Winter Road, Leslie Gordon Barnard
Winter Studies and Summer Rambles in Canada, Anna Jameson
Winter Sun, Margaret Avison
Witches' Brew, The, E. J. Pratt
Witching of Elspie, The, Duncan Campbell Scott

Within the Zodiac, Phyllis Gotlieb
Woman Who Did, The, Grant Allen
Wood of the Nightingale, The, Philip Child
Woodcarver's Wife and Other Poems, The, Marjorie Pickthall
Wooden Horse, The, Daryl Hine
Wooden Ships and Iron Men, Frederick William Wallace
Wooden Sword, The, Edward McCourt
Worldly Muse, The, A. J. M. Smith
Wound Dresser, The, (Whitman), Richard Maurice Bucke
Wounded Prince and Other Poems, The, Douglas LePan
Wrath of Homer, The, L. A. MacKay
Wrestle with an Angel, R. G. Everson
Writing in Canada, George Whalley

Y

Yellow Sweater and Other Stories, The, Hugh Garner
Yeux fixes, Roland Giguère
Yeux sur nos temps, Les, Roger Brien
Young Politician, The, Donald Creighton
Young Renny, Mazo de la Roche
Young Seigneur, The, William Douw Lighthall
Yvon Tremblay, Louis Arthur Cunningham

Z

Zone, Marcel Dubé

The
DUSTY ROAD
FROM PERTH
James Morton